A SOCIAL PORTRAIT OF EUROPE

At the time of writing these few lines to introduce this new Eurostat publication, the world—and Europe in particular—is confronted by events whose scope and impact are both uncertain and difficult to gauge.

The far-reaching changes and improvements in living and working conditions which the European Community hopes to see achieved by the end of the century are not immune to outside events capable of disrupting the anticipated course of progress. It is therefore all the more important that we have at our disposal instruments allowing us to measure accurately the various social and economic factors on which the future of Europe depends.

One such basic instrument is this new Eurostat publication, which—through an array of statistical indicators—deepens our mutual understanding and paints in bold yet accurate brush-strokes a social portrait of Europe.

Henning CHRISTOPHERSEN

Vasso PAPANDREOU

TABLE OF CONTENTS

POPULATION — 5

Population dynamics	6
Movements	7
Structure	8
Density	11
Fertility	12
Life expectancy	14
General mortality	16
Infant mortality	17
Foreign population	18

HOUSEHOLDS — 21

Structure	22
Marriages and divorces	24
Births	26
Children	28

EDUCATION — 31

Numbers in full-time education	32
Equal opportunities	34
Languages and computer studies	35
Expenditure	36
Opinions	37

EMPLOYMENT AND UNEMPLOYMENT — 39

Labour market	40
Active population	42
Activity: regional distribution	44
Activity and marital status	46
Employment	48
Unemployment rate	50
Structure of unemployment	52
Long-term unemployment	54
Unemployment and households	55
Foreign workers	56

WORKING CONDITIONS — 59

Working hours	60
Part-time work	62
Temporary contract	64
Hours lost	65

STANDARD OF LIVING — 67

GDP	68
Income	70
Compensation of employees	71
Earnings of employees	72
Use of income	74
Pattern of consumption	76
loverty	78

SOCIAL PROTECTION		81
	Social benefits and GDP	82
	Per capita social benefits	83
	Social benefits by function	84
	Receipts	85
HEALTH		87
	Infrastructure	88
	Expenditure	89
	Life expectancy	90
	Risk factors	91
	Causes of death	92
	Cancers	94
	AIDS	96
	Suicide	98
	Accidents	100
THE ENVIRONMENT		103
	Land use	104
	Climate	105
	Opinions	106
	Energy	108
	Transport	110
	Pollution	112
	Nature conservation	114
HOUSING		117
	Dwelling stock	118
	Age of dwellings	120
	Amenities	121
	Consumer durables	122
	Consumption and expenditure	123
LEISURE		125
	Holidays	126
	Expenditure	128
	Sports	129
	Media	130
EUROPARTICIPATION		133
	Elections	134
	Participation	135
	Euro-opinions	136
	Court of Justice	138
	Structural Funds	139

SIGNS AND ABBREVIATIONS

:   data not available
*   Eurostat estimate
–   not applicable
<   less than
>   greater than

CFC	Chlorofluorocarbon
CMA	Chemical Manufacturers Association
Corine	Information system on the state of the environment in Europe
CO_2	Carbon dioxide
EAGGF	European Agricultural Guidance and Guarantee Fund
ECSC	European Coal and Steel Community
Ehlass	European home and leisure accident surveillance system
EIB	European Investment Bank
ERDF	European Regional Development Fund
ESF	European Social Fund
Esspros	European system of social protection statistics
Euratom	European Atomic Energy Community
Eurobarometer	*Eurobarometer* European public opinion surveys, which have been conducted on behalf of the European Commission's Directorate-General for Information, Communication and Culture each spring and autumn since 1973
Eurydice	Education information network in the European Community
GDP	Gross domestic product
ICRC	International Agency for research on cancer
kg-oe	Kilogram oil equivalent
LFS	Labour force survey
NCI	New Community instrument
NO_x	Nitrogen oxide
OECD	Organization for Economic Cooperation and Development
PPS	Purchasing power standard
SME	Small (and medium-sized) enterprises(s)
t	tonne
toe	tonne(s) oil equivalent
Unesco	United Nations Educational, Scientific and Cultural Organization
WHO	World Health Organization

For technical reasons, territories and islands not located on the European continent are not reproduced on any map in this publication.

The data concerning the Federal Republic of Germany refer to the borders which were in existence before 3 October 1990.

POPULATION

As at 1 January 1990, the European Community, with 327 million inhabitants, had the third highest population in the world after China (1 135 million) and India (853 million). Currently, 6% of the world's population live in the Community. In 1950, 10% lived in the Europe of the Twelve, but by 2020, only 4% of the world's population will live there (1.1).

The population of the European Community is growing older: in 1988, 62.8 million (or 19.4%) of its 324 million inhabitants were over 60, while 85 million—26.3%—were under 20. The 'oldest' countries are Denmark and the Federal Republic of Germany. Ireland is the only country that is still 'young' (1.9).

The average population density of the European Community is 143 inhabitants per km^2, but in the most densely populated regions—the most industrialized areas, from north-west England to northern Italy and the main capital cities or regional capitals—there are more than 350 inhabitants per km^2 (1.15).

Since the 1960s, fertility in the European Community countries has fallen to below generation-replacement level. The total fertility rate for the Community as a whole fell from 2.63 children per woman in 1960 to 1.58 in 1989 (1.18) (1.19).

For Europeans, life expectancy at birth is one of the highest in the world, with women living longer than men: 78.6 years as against 72.0 (1.22).

Since 1960, there has been a spectacular drop in infant mortality, from 34.8‰ in 1960 to 8.2‰ in 1989 (1.29) (1.30).

Eight million foreigners out of a total of 13 million come from countries that are not Member States of the Community (1.32).

More than three-quarters of foreigners in the Community live in the Federal Republic of Germany, France and the United Kingdom (1.32).

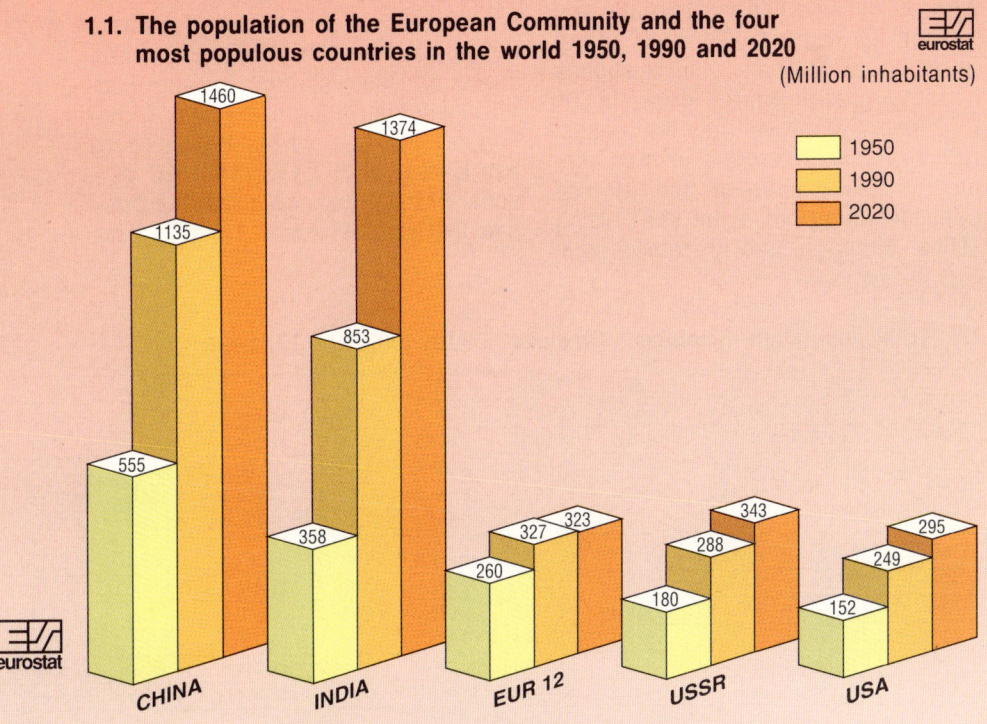

1.1. The population of the European Community and the four most populous countries in the world 1950, 1990 and 2020
(Million inhabitants)

POPULATION
POPULATION DYNAMICS

1.2. Total population dynamics — EUR 12 (1 000)

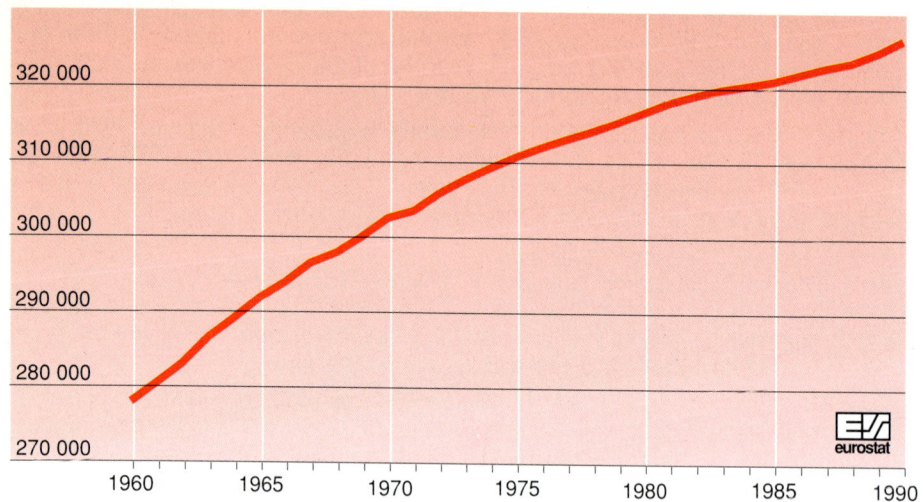

Between 1960 and 1990, there was a 48 million increase in the population of the European Community, from 279 million to 327 million. Over that period, the population of all the Community countries grew, at rates varying from 9% in Belgium to 31% in the Netherlands. Since 1960, the population increase has gradually slowed down.

Rates of natural increase vary considerably from country to country. With its old population structure and low fertility rate, in 1989 the Federal Republic of Germany had a slightly negative growth figure—down 16 000 (−0.3‰). Ireland still has the highest rate of natural increase in the Community (5.8‰), although this rate has been declining since the start of the 1980s. Although its birth rate is comparable with that of France, the United Kingdom has seen a lower natural increase owing to its older age structure: 120 000 as against 237 000 in France.

In 1989, the only two countries with a negative net migration figure were Ireland and Spain, with the figure for Spain being only slightly negative (an estimated −0.3‰) but for Ireland very high at −12.1‰.

Two countries have a high positive net migration figure: owing to recent upheavals in the East European countries, the estimate for the Federal Republic of Germany was 1 million (+16.1‰), while Luxembourg has a rate of +7.4‰, or 2 800 persons. In the other countries, the positive increase is lower, ranging from +2.6‰ in the Netherlands to +0.6‰ in Italy.

In the Federal Republic of Germany and in Luxembourg, the impact of immigration is higher than the impact of natural population movements, to give a substantial total increase of 15.8‰ in the Federal Republic of Germany and 9.2‰ in Luxembourg.

1.3. Total population dynamics — Member States and EUR 12 (1 000)

	EUR 12	B	DK	D	GR	E	F	IRL	I	L	NL	P	UK
1960	278 626,6	9 095,4	4 565,5	55 123,4	8 300,4	30 327,0	45 464,8	2 835,3	50 023,4	313,0	11 417,3	8 996,7	52 164,4
1965	292 259,3	9 414,8	4 741,0	58 587,5	8 528,5	31 889,0	48 561,8	2 873,0	51 815,5	330,0	12 212,3	9 135,7	54 170,2
1970	302 989,2	9 624,6	4 906,9	61 194,6	8 780,4	33 603,0	50 528,2	2 944,0	53 490,4	338,5	12 957,6	9 074,7	55 546,4
1975	311 276,3	9 783,0	5 054,4	61 991,5	8 986,2	35 338,0	52 600,0	3 164,0	55 293,0	357,4	13 599,1	8 879,1	56 230,7
1980	317 200,8	9 843,3	5 122,1	61 439,3	9 587,5	37 242,0	53 731,4	3 392,8	56 388,5	363,5	14 091,0	9 713,6	56 285,9
1985	321 528,5	9 857,7	5 111,1	61 049,3	9 919,5	38 423,0	55 062,5	3 537,3	57 080,5	366,2	14 453,8	10 128,9	56 538,8
1986	322 324,2	9 858,9	5 116,3	61 020,5	9 949,1	38 586,0	55 278,4	3 540,4	57 202,3	367,2	14 529,4	10 185,1	56 690,6
1987	323 167,4	9 864,8	5 124,8	61 140,5	9 978,1	38 655,0	55 510,0	3 542,4	57 290,5	369,5	14 615,1	10 230,0	56 846,7
1988	324 010,7	9 875,7	5 129,3	61 238,1	9 988,9	38 736,1	55 750,4	3 539,3	57 399,1	371,7	14 714,9	10 269,5	56 997,7
1989	325 314,6	9 927,6	5 129,7	61 715,1	10 020,0	38 851,9	56 016,9	3 520,9	57 504,6	374,9	14 805,2	10 304,7	57 143,1
1990	327 065,0	9 947,8	5 135,4	62 700,0	10 046,0	38 924,5	56 304,0	3 498,8	57 576,4	378,4	14 891,9	10 335,2	57 326,6

POPULATION
MOVEMENTS

1.4. Natural increase — 1989
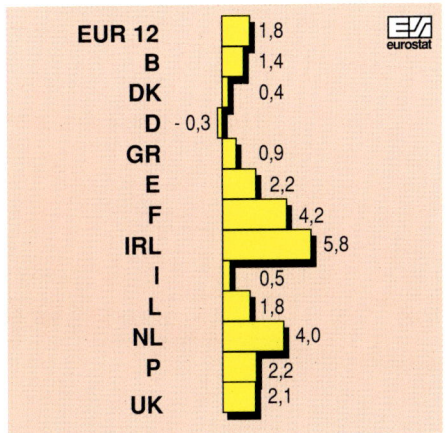
Per 1 000 inhabitants (average population).

1.5. Net migration — 1989
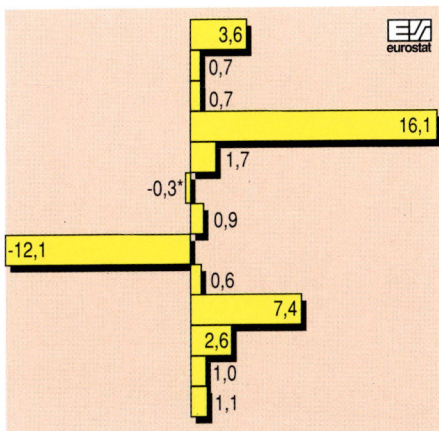
Per 1 000 inhabitants (average population).

1.6. Total increase — 1989
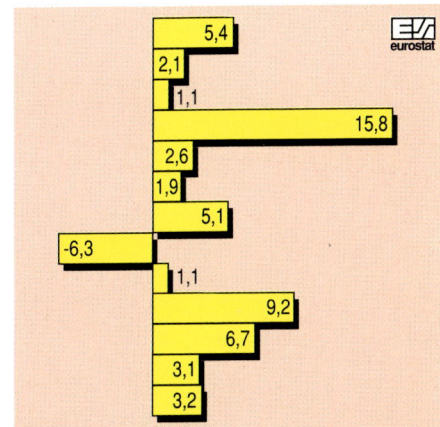
Per 1 000 inhabitants (average population).

In the Community in 1989, the natural increase resulting from births minus deaths was 584 000 persons but, in view of the plus figure for net migration—1 173 000—the total increase was 1 758 000.

Since 1960, the annual change in the Community population has been on a generally downward trend (1 758 000 in 1989 as against 2 284 000 in 1960) but with peaks (3 254 000 in 1962) and troughs (790 000 in 1985).

1.7. Components of population movements — EUR 12
(1 000)

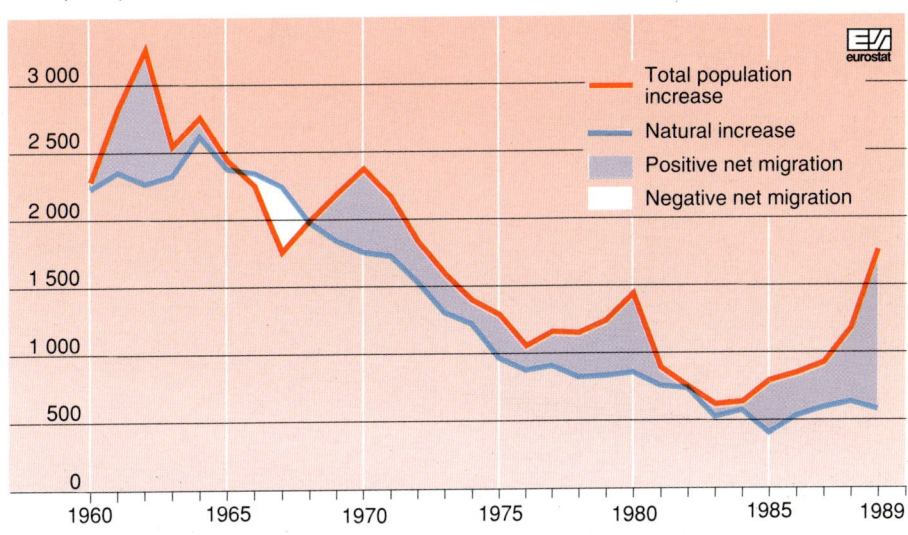

1.8. Population movements — EUR 12

Year	Population 1 January (1 000)	Births (1 000)	Deaths (1 000)	Natural increase (1 000)	Net migration (1 000)	Total increase (1 000)	Birth	Mortality	Natural increase	Net migration	Total increase
1960	278 627	5 184	2 947	2 237	47	2 284	18.5	10.5	8.0	0.2	8.2
1965	292 259	5 488	3 095	2 393	39	2 432	18.7	10.6	8.1	0.1	8.2
1970	302 989	4 974	3 215	1 759	613	2 372	16.4	10.6	5.8	2.0	7.8
1975	311 276	4 303	3 325	978	308	1 286	13.8	10.7	3.1	1.0	4.1
1980	317 201	4 134	3 270	864	567	1 431	13.0	10.3	2.7	1.8	4.5
1985	321 529	3 798	3 307	491	299	790	11.8	10.3	1.5	0.9	2.4
1986	322 324	3 812	3 280	532	312	844	11.8	10.2	1.6	1.0	2.7
1987	323 167	3 811	3 214	597	326	923	11.8	9.9	1.9	1.0	2.9
1988	324 011	3 873	3 231	642	540	1 182	11.9	10.1	1.8	1.7	3.5
1989 [1]	325 315	3 832	3 247	584	1 173	1 758	11.8	10.0	1.8	3.6	5.4

Rates (per 1 000 inhabitants) of:

[1] Provisional results.

POPULATION STRUCTURE

1.9. Population structure — 1.1.1988 (1 000)

Age	EUR 12	B	DK	D	GR	E	F	IRL	I	L	NL	P	UK
0 - 19	85 299.2	2 499.6	1 270.6	13 147.0	2 727.8	11 592.2	15 726.1	1 337.7	14 790.4	87.1	3 922.3	3 130.8	15 067.5
20 - 39	98 003.6	3 048.5	1 551.5	18 970.3	2 804.7	11 475.6	17 071.0	1 005.9	17 093.8	120.7	4 862.3	3 042.3	16 957.0
40 - 59	77 861.3	2 347.2	1 260.6	16 381.0	2 567.1	8 809.9	12 513.2	668.8	14 357.6	94.8	3 418.6	2 279.2	13 163.3
60 years and over	62 846.6	1 980.5	1 046.5	12 739.8	1 889.3	6 858.4	10 440.1	526.9	11 157.3	69.1	2 511.7	1 817.2	11 809.9
of which 80 years and over	10 250.9	328.4	177.8	2 209.0	288.9	999.1	1 959.4	70.2	1 607.0	10.4	405.8	235.6	1 959.9
Total	324 010.7	9 875.7	5 129.3	61 238.1	9 988.9	38 736.1	55 750.4	3 539.3	57 399.1	371.7	14 714.9	10 269.5	56 997.1

1.10. Age pyramid — Estimate as at 1 January 1989 — EUR 12 (%)

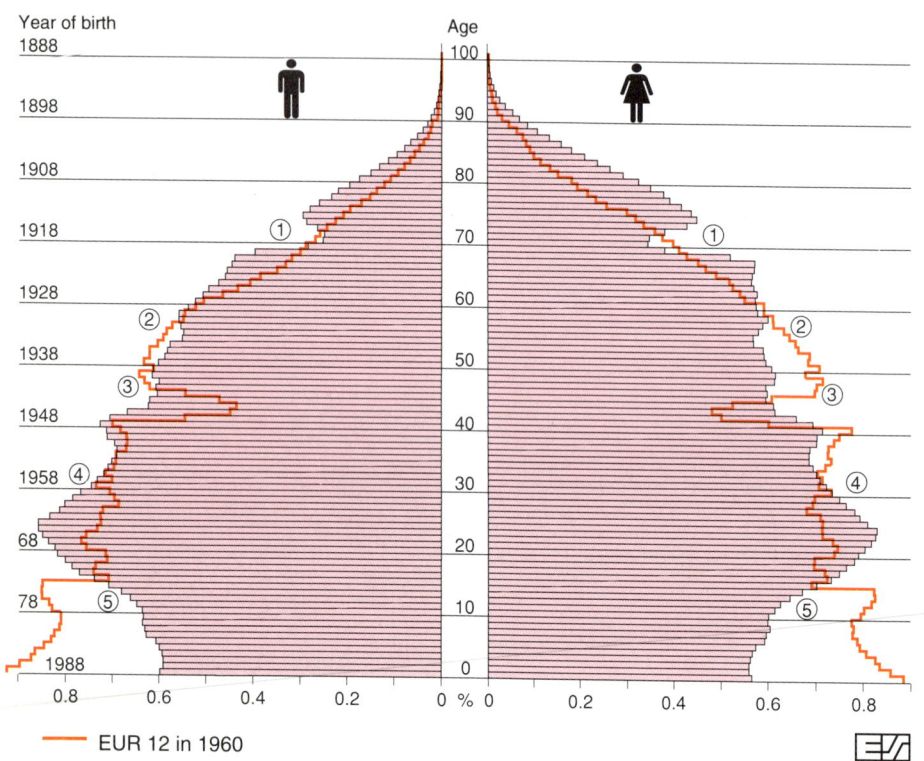

— EUR 12 in 1960

1. Birth deficit due to the First World War.
2. Low birth-rate generations reach the age of fertility.
3. Birth deficit due to the Second World War.
4. Baby boom.
5. Non-replacement of generations.

The most noticeable feature of population dynamics in the Community is its ageing population. This ageing is generalized, but varies from country to country. It affected the Federal Republic of Germany and the United Kingdom earlier and more markedly, and the southern European countries (Spain, Portugal and Greece) and Ireland later.

The European Community's age pyramid is characteristic of an ageing population: its base is shrinking from the effect of the lower birth-rate and its apex expanding because the population is living longer. A comparison of the 1989 and 1960 pyramids shows very clearly how the birth rate has plummeted since the mid-1960s (following the baby boom after the Second World War) and declined even faster after the mid-1970s when the southern European countries (Italy, Spain, Portugal and Greece) joined the low birth-rate club.

The 'oldest' regions of the Community are in the Federal Republic of Germany and northern Italy. These are the only two countries which have regions where fewer than 23 % of the population are aged under 20.

POPULATION
STRUCTURE

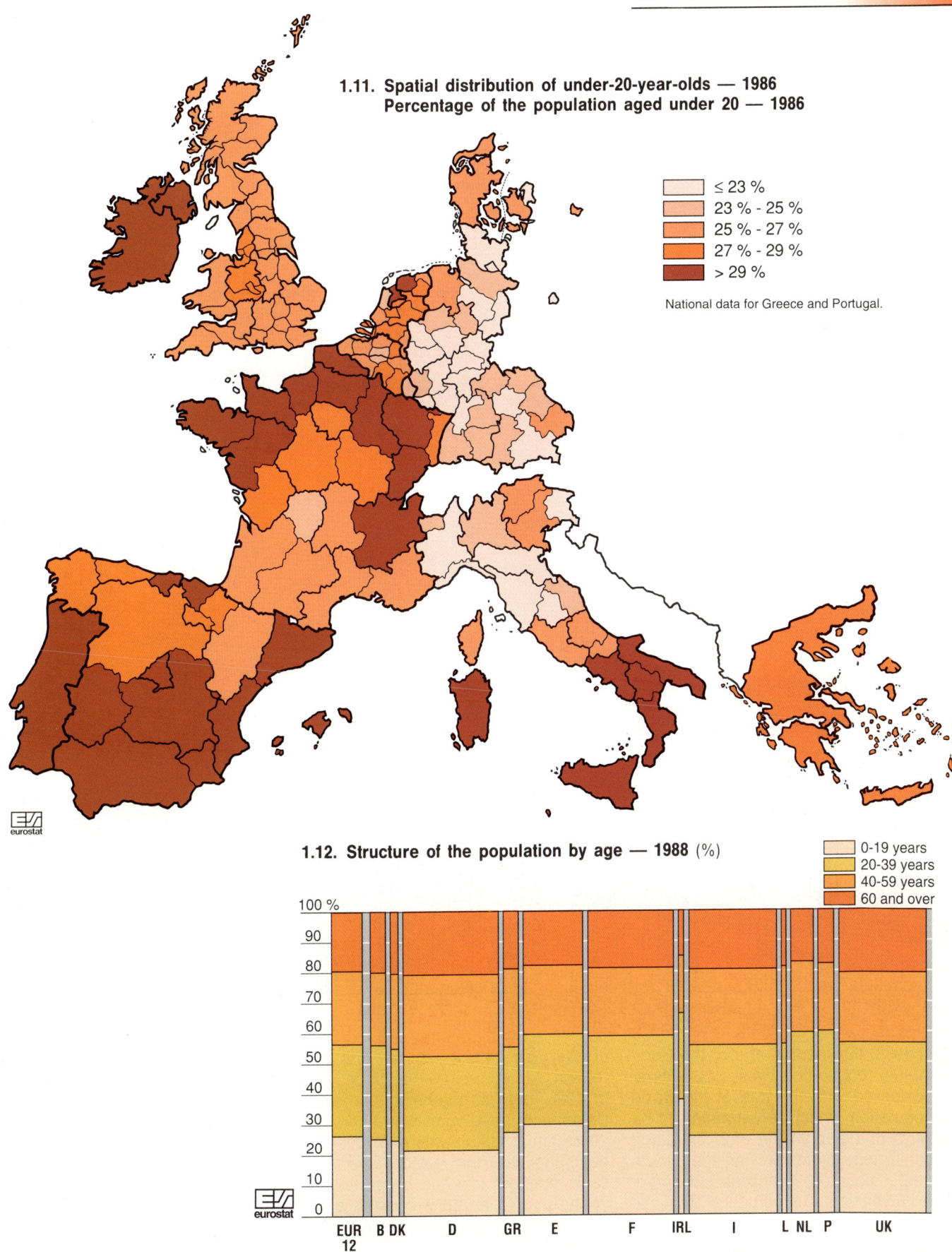

1.11. Spatial distribution of under-20-year-olds — 1986
Percentage of the population aged under 20 — 1986

≤ 23 %
23 % - 25 %
25 % - 27 %
27 % - 29 %
> 29 %

National data for Greece and Portugal.

1.12. Structure of the population by age — 1988 (%)

0-19 years
20-39 years
40-59 years
60 and over

POPULATION
STRUCTURE

1.13. Median age of the population — 1988 (in years)

	EUR 12	B	DK	D	GR	E	F	IRL	I	L	NL	P	UK
1988	34,3	34,7	35,6	37,2	34,9	31,6	33,3	27,7	35,0	35,2	32,8	31,3	34,5

1.14. Percentages of under-20-year-olds and persons aged 60 and over

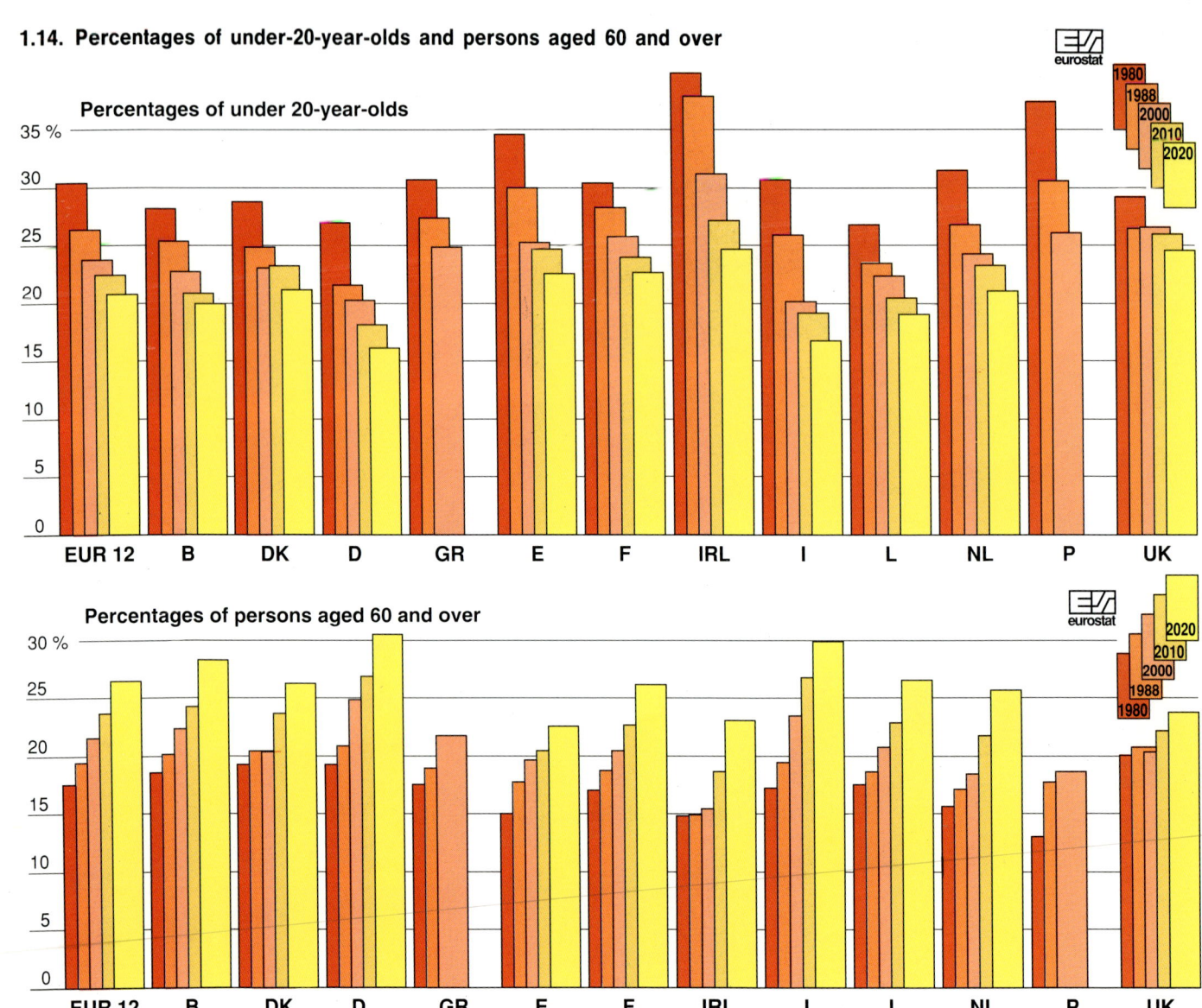

In 1988, the median age of the Community population was 34.3 years, compared with the age of the world population, which is estimated to be 24. With a median age of 27.7, Ireland confirmed its position as the 'youngest' country, whereas Denmark (35.6 years) and the Federal Republic of Germany (37.2 years) are the 'oldest'.

In 1988, only a quarter of the total Community population was under 20 years and one-fifth was over 60. The population is growing older and forecasts suggest that the proportion of young people to old will reach equilibrium around the year 2010, after which the balance will be tipped in favour of old people from the year 2020 onwards.

POPULATION
DENSITY

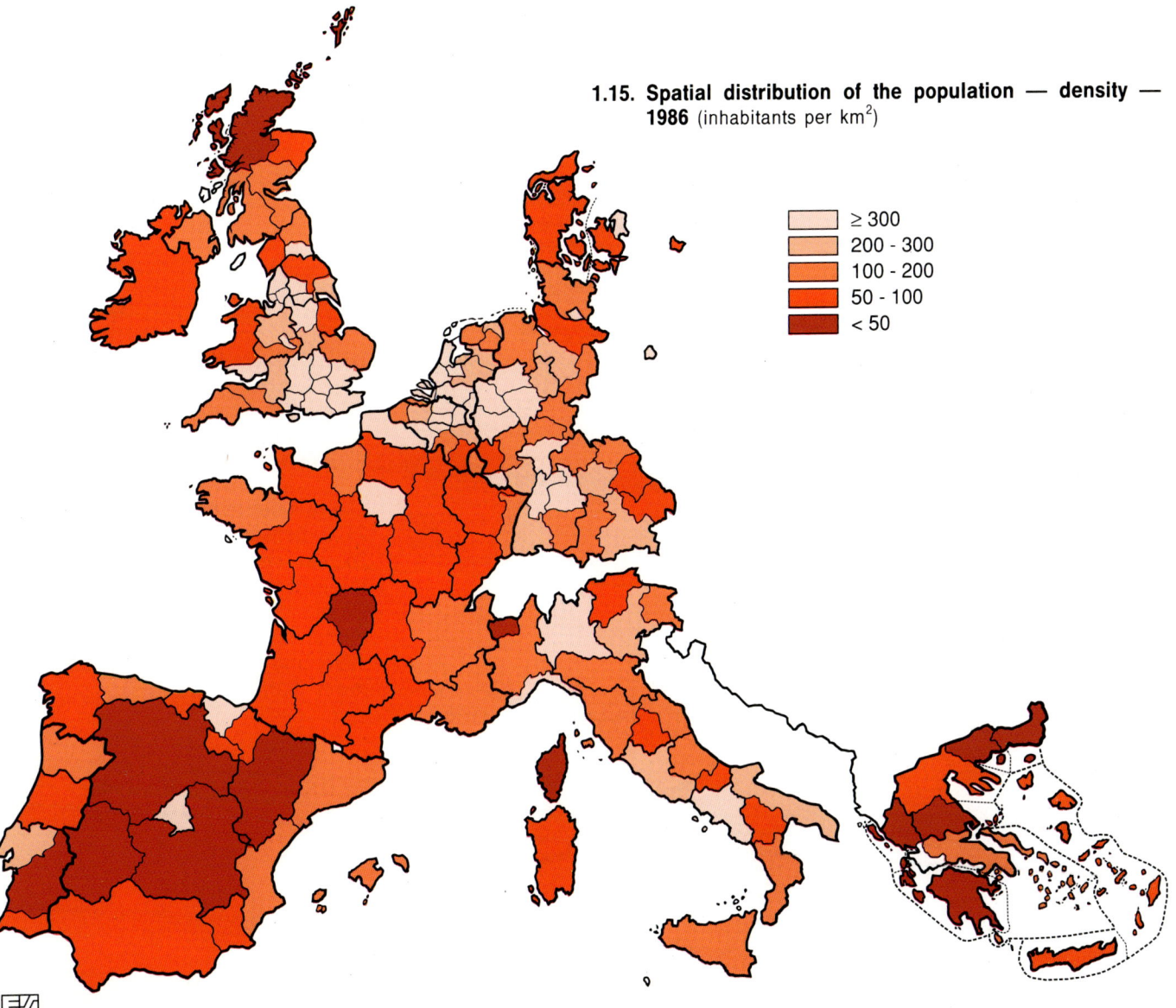

1.15. Spatial distribution of the population — density — 1986 (inhabitants per km^2)

- ≥ 300
- 200 - 300
- 100 - 200
- 50 - 100
- < 50

1.16. Evolution of the density of the population (inhabitants per km^2)

	EUR 12	B	DK	D	GR	E	F	IRL	I	L	NL	P	UK
1960	124	298	106	222	63	60	84	41	166	120	277	98	214
1970	134	316	114	246	67	67	93	43	178	130	315	99	228
1980	141	323	119	247	73	74	99	49	187	140	342	105	231
1989	144	325	119	248	76	77	103	51	191	144	359	112	234

The high-population-density zones are concentrated along a diagonal line from north-west England to the north of Italy through north Belgium, south Netherlands and the industrial regions of the Ruhr. Outside this band are the conurbations of Paris, Rome, Madrid, Barcelona and Lisbon, surrounded by regions with a lower population density. Areas with a high population density are industrialized regions or administrative centres (capital cities). In Spain, the population has tended to cluster round the coastal areas owing to the development of tourism since the end of the 1960s and the resulting job-creation. The sea and sun of the Mediterranean coasts of the Italian and French Rivieras have had a similarly magnetic effect.

POPULATION
FERTILITY

1.17. Numbers of births (1 000)

	EUR 12	B	DK	D	GR	E	F	IRL	I	L	NL	P	UK
1960	5 184	155	76	969	157	660	820	61	910	5	239	214	918
1970	4 974	142	71	811	145	661	850	64	901	4	239	181	904
1980	4 134	124	57	621	148	571	800	74	640	4	181	158	754
1988	3 874	119	59	677	108	416	771	54	568	5	187	122	788
1989 (¹)	3 832	121	62	677	101	410	764	51	556	5	189	119	777

(¹) Provisional results.

1.18. Total fertility rate — EUR 12
(average number of children per woman)

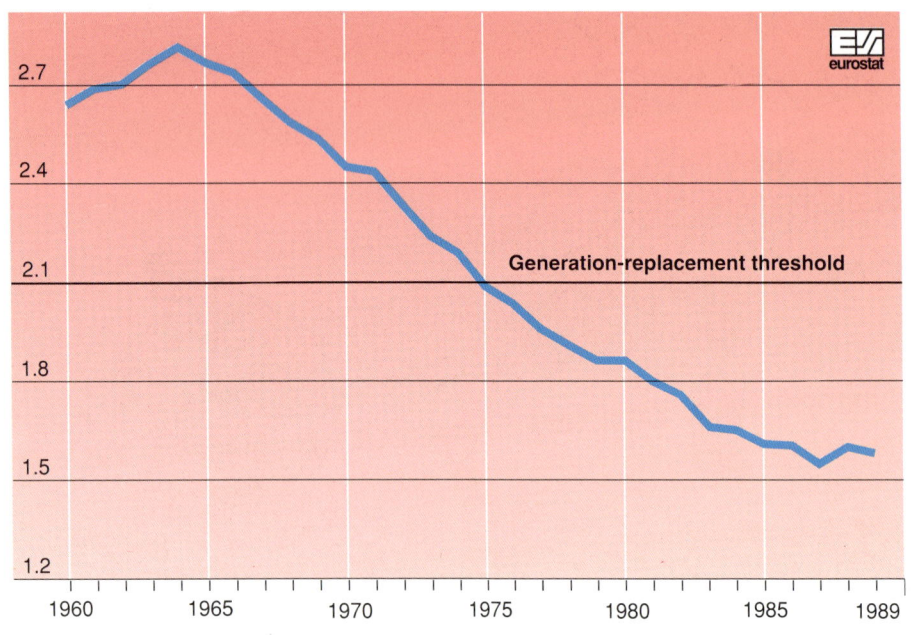

The number of births in the EC fell by 25 % between 1960 and 1989. The 25-year continuous decline appears to have stabilized since 1986, with a slight increase in the number of births in 1988 (1.7 % higher than in 1987) and a slight fall in 1989 (1.1 % lower than in 1988).

1.19. Total fertility rate (average number of children per woman)

	EUR 12*	B	DK	D	GR	E	F	IRL	I	L	NL	P	UK (²)
1960	2,63	2,58	2,54	2,37	2,28	2,86	2,73	3,76	2,41	2,28	3,12	3,01	2,69
1965	2,77	2,61	2,61	2,51	2,30	2,94	2,83	4,03	2,67	2,38	3,04	3,08	2,86
1970	2,45	2,20	1,95	2,02	2,34	2,84	2,48	3,87	2,43	1,97	2,57	2,76	2,44
1975	2,08	1,74	1,92	1,45	2,37	2,79	1,93	3,40	2,21	1,52	1,66	2,52	1,81
1980	1,87	1,67	1,55	1,45	2,23	2,22	1,95	3,23	1,69	1,50	1,60	2,19	1,89
1985	1,82	1,51	1,45	1,28	1,68	1,63	1,82	2,50	1,41	1,38	1,51	1,70	1,80
1988	1,60	1,56	1,56	1,42	1,52	1,38 (¹)	1,82	2,17 (¹)	1,34 (¹)	1,51	1,55	1,53	1,84
1989 (¹)	1,58	1,58	1,62	1,39	1,50	1,30	1,81	2,11	1,29	1,52	1,55	1,50	1,85

(¹) Provisional results.
(²) Before 1975, Great Britain data only.

POPULATION
FERTILITY

1.20. Total fertility rate
(average number of children per woman)

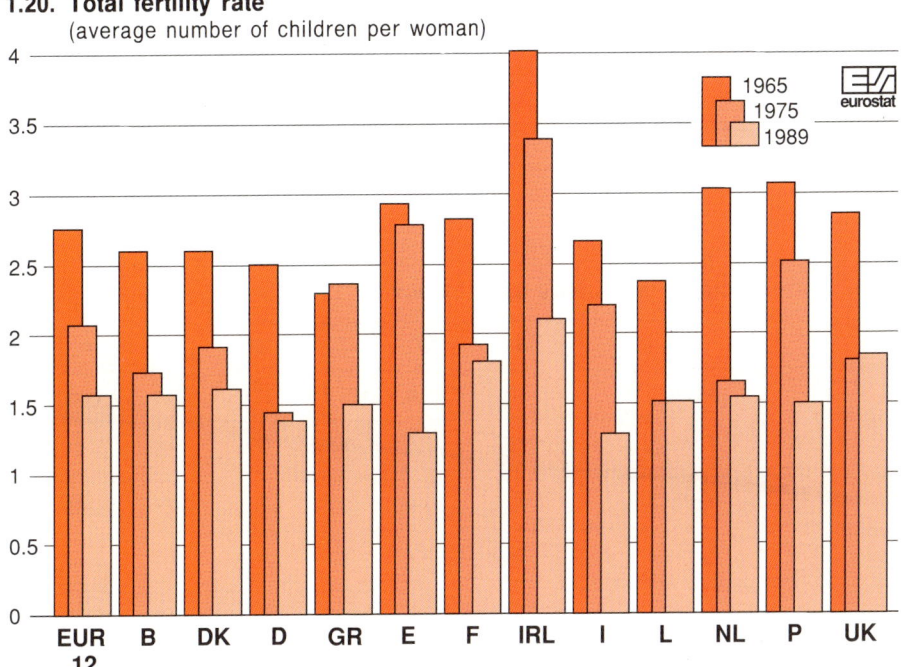

The fall in the birth-rate affected the northern Community countries (apart from Ireland) first of all, between 1965 and 1975. In the following decade, the decline slowed down or stopped in those countries (Belgium, Denmark, Federal Republic of Germany, France, Luxembourg, the Netherlands and the United Kingdom). The fall in the birth-rate began in the southern Community countries (Italy, Greece, Spain and Portugal) in the 1970s, and was even more rapid because of its later start. These countries, in particular Italy and Spain, have caught up with or even overtaken the fertility levels of the northern European countries.

In 1989, Ireland was the only EC country which kept its total fertility rate (2.11 children per women) at a level close to the replacement threshold (2.10 children per woman). But the late start appears to have made the Irish fertility rate fall even more sharply.

Despite slight fluctuations in numbers of births (the total fertility rate was 1.55 children per woman in 1987, with estimates of 1.60 for 1988 and 1.58 for 1989), the total fertility rate remains very much below the generation-replacement threshold, and this has been the case since the mid-1970s. Only three-quarters of the number of children needed to replace the present generation are actually being born.

1.21. Fertility rate by age group, 1988
(births per 1 000 women in each age group)

	15-19	20-24	25-29	30-34	35-39	40-44	45-49
B [86]	12,2	88,7	129,9	58,9	16,6	2,9	0,3
DK	9,1	71,3	128,1	76,7	23,4	3,2	0,2
D [87]	9,6	56,6	107,2	78,0	24,5	4,1	0,2
GR	26,3	100,1	99,8	54,6	19,5	4,1	0,4
E [85]	18,3	72,5	116,4	74,6	33,5	9,9	0,9
F	9,5	83,0	143,0	89,0	33,3	6,9	0,4
IRL	14,9	70,8	141,6	125,1	62,6	17,3	1,3
I	10,0	59,8	97,1	68,9	27,2	5,4	0,3
L	13,2	70,0	117,6	77,5	25,2	3,7	0,2
NL	5,6	44,3	122,4	103,5	29,7	4,3	0,5
P	26,4	90,6	98,9	59,0	24,5	6,9	0,6
UK	32,3	94,9	124,4	82,6	28,0	4,8	0,3

POPULATION
LIFE EXPECTANCY

1.22. Life expectancy at birth — EUR 12 (in years)

	1950	1960	1970	1980	1988
Male	64,0	67,3	68,5	70,7	72,0
Female	68,2	72,7	74,8	77,4	78,6

Since 1950, i.e. over the past 40 years, life expectancy at birth for the European Community as a whole has gone up by about 10 years, more for women (10.4 years) than for men (8 years).

1.23. Life expectancy at various ages by sex — 1985-88 (in years)

		B (¹)	DK	D	GR	E	F	IRL	I	L	NL	P	UK
Birth	Male	70,0	71,8	71,8	72,6	73,1	71,8	71,0	72,6	70,6	72,2	70,6	71,7
	Female	76,8	77,6	78,4	77,6	79,6	80,0	76,7	79,1	77,9	78,9	77,7	77,5
30 years	Male	42,3	43,4	43,5	45,1	45,2	43,8	42,7	44,3	42,6	43,8	43,4	43,4
	Female	48,4	48,7	49,5	49,4	51,0	51,2	47,8	50,3	49,0	80,0	49,4	48,7
60 years	Male	16,3	17,3	17,3	18,2	18,7	18,2	16,0	17,7	16,4	17,0	17,7	16,7
	Female	20,9	21,7	21,7	21,1	22,9	23,4	20,1	22,2	21,3	22,2	21,7	21,1
75 years	Male	7,6	8,5	8,1	8,4	9,0	8,8	7,3	8,6	7,5	8,0	8,3	7,9
	Female	9,8	11,0	10,3	9,4	11,0	11,5	9,5	10,7	9,8	11,5	10,1	10,1

(¹) 1980 for Belgium.

1.24. Life expectancy at birth by sex — 1985-88 (in years)

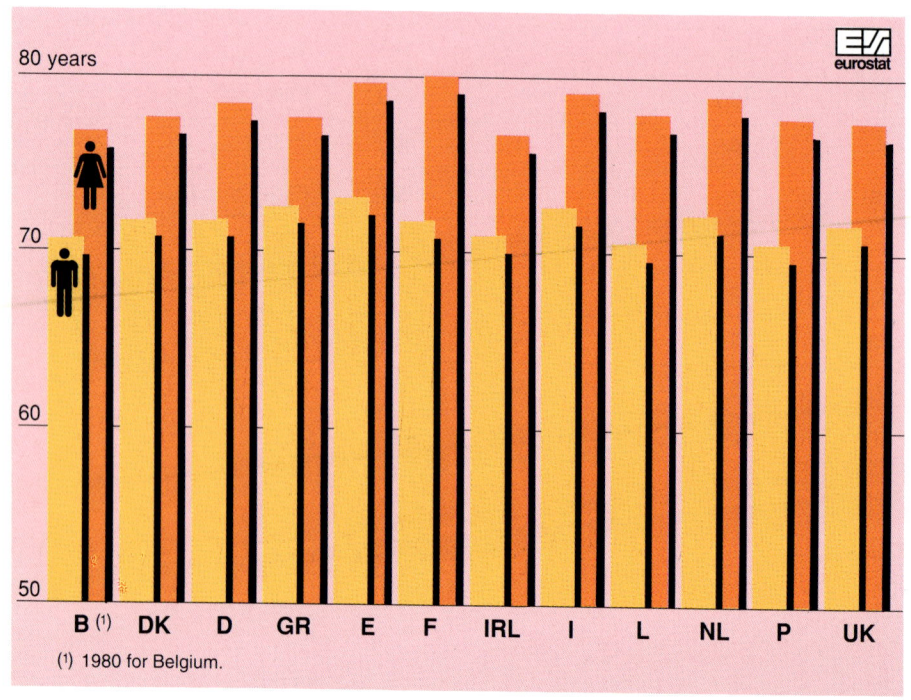

(¹) 1980 for Belgium.

POPULATION
LIFE EXPECTANCY

All the Community countries have made progress during this period. Between 1985 and 1988, life expectancy at birth was more than 70 years in all countries for men and 78 years for women. Spanish men (73.1 years) and French women (80.0 years) had the highest life expectancy at birth. At 30, 60 and 75 years, life expectancy is also higher for women than for men in all countries.

Excess male mortality has been one of the characteristic features of population dynamics in the EC: the difference between the figures for the two sexes at birth was 4.2 years in 1950 and is now 6.6 years, with the highest figure in France: 8.2 years.

The male death rate has led to a 'surplus of women' among older people: on average, for every two 90-year-old women, there is only one man.

1.25. Excess female life expectancy at birth (in years)

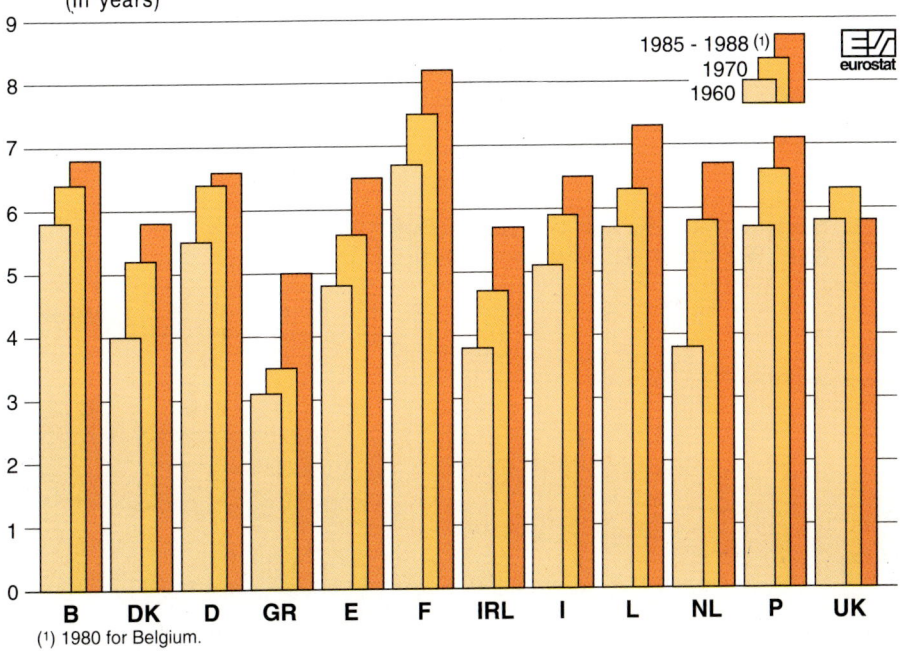

(1) 1980 for Belgium.

1.26. Proportion of women among elderly people — 1988 (%)

	EUR 12	B	DK	D	GR	E	F	IRL	I	L	NL	P	UK
60 - 69	54,9	53,6	53,0	59,3	53,4	53,7	54,1	52,5	54,6	57,1	53,8	54,8	53,2
70 - 79	60,7	60,5	57,7	65,5	56,0	59,5	60,4	55,6	59,2	61,2	59,7	58,8	59,4
80 - 89	68,9 (1)	69,2	66,2	70,6	59,4	64,8	68,3	64,7 (1)	66,6	70,1 (1)	67,8	67,1 (1)	69,5
90 and over		75,3	72,0	79,3	58,8	70,7	79,9		74,5		71,7		79,7

(1) 80 and over.

POPULATION
GENERAL MORTALITY

1.27. Standardized mortality rates by sex — 1987
(per 1 000 inhabitants of the standard population)

	Total	Male	Female
B (3)	8,9	11,7	6,9
DK (3)	8,8	11,1	7,0
D	8,2	11,1	6,4
GR (3)	7,8	9,3	6,6
E (1)	7,6	9,8	5,6
F (3)	8,0	11,0	5,8
IRL	9,6	12,1	7,6
I (2)	8,5	11,2	6,6
L	9,6	12,4	7,5
NL (3)	7,9	10,6	5,9
P	9,0	11,5	7,1
UK	8,6	11,0	6,9

Source: WHO.
Standard population: Europe region (WHO).
[1] 1984.   [2] 1985.   [3] 1986.

The standardized mortality rate table shows a clear difference between the sexes and between countries. Thus Spain and Greece would appear to be in pole position, with rates of 7.6‰ and 7.8‰, whilst Ireland has the highest rates (9.6‰ overall) for both men (12.1‰ as against 9.3‰ in Greece) and women (7.6‰ as against 5.6‰ in Spain). In general, female mortality rates are lower than male ones — another illustration of excess male mortality.

1.28. Mortality rates by age and sex — EUR 12 — 1986
(per 1 000 inhabitants in each age group)

	15 - 24	25 - 34	35 - 44	45 - 54	55 - 64	65 - 74	75 and over
Male	0.95	1.17	2.13	5.82	16.58	38.32	110.37
Female	0.35	0.51	1.14	3.00	7.10	19.45	82.82

POPULATION
INFANT MORTALITY

1.29. Infant mortality rate (per 1 000 live births)

	EUR 12	B	DK	D	GR	E	F	IRL	I	L	NL	P	UK
1960	34,8	31,2	21,5	33,8	40,1	43,7	27,4	29,3	43,9	31,5	17,9	77,5	22,5
1970	24,0	21,1	14,2	23,6	29,6	28,1	18,2	19,5	29,6	24,9	12,7	55,5	18,5
1980	12,6	12,1	8,4	12,6	17,9	12,3	10,0	11,1	14,6	11,5	8,6	24,3	12,1
1988	8,5	9,1	7,6	7,5	11,0	8,1	7,8	9,2	9,5	8,7	6,8	13,1	9,0
1989 (¹)	8,2	8,6	7,5*	7,5	9,9	8,3	7,4	7,6	8,8	9,9	6,8	12,2	8,4

¹ Provisional results.

The infant mortality rate has dropped spectacularly since 1960: in 29 years, it has fallen more than fourfold, from 34.8‰ to 8.2‰. In 1989, the European Community was in the forefront of world rankings, behind Japan and Sweden. In 1989, the Netherlands (6.8‰), France (7.4‰), Denmark (7.5‰), the Federal Republic of Germany (7.5‰) and Ireland (7.6‰) had rates below the Community figure of 8.2‰, whilst Portugal (12.2‰) and Greece (9.9‰) had higher levels.

The similar fall in the perinatal mortality rate in the Community—35.9‰ in 1960 and 9.6‰ in 1988—contributed to the fall in the infant mortality rate. The perinatal rate was lowest in the Federal Republic of Germany (6.5‰) and highest in Portugal (16.6‰).

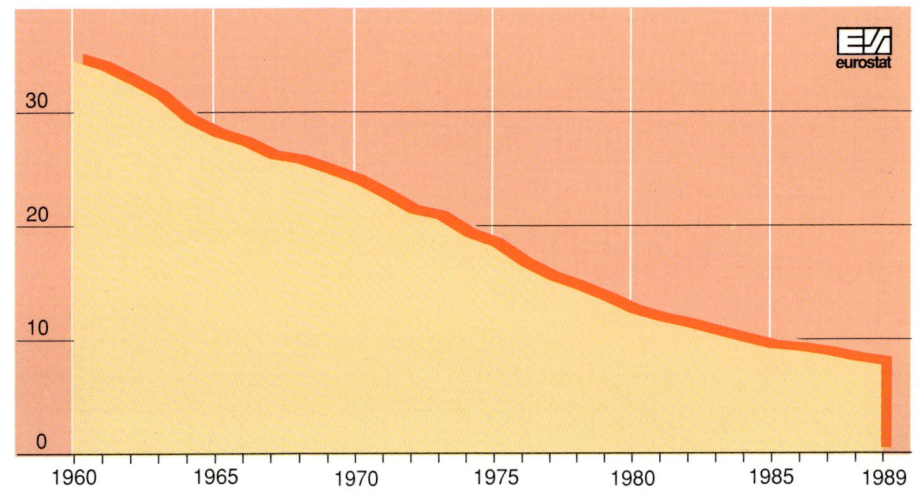

1.30. Infant mortality — EUR 12 (per 1 000 live births)

1.31. Perinatal mortality rate (deaths between 180th day of gestation and seventh day of life per 1 000 live births)

	EUR 12*	B	DK	D	GR	E	F	IRL	I	L	NL	P	UK
1960	35,9	31,9	26,2	35,8	26,4	—	31,3	37,7	41,9	32,2	26,6	41,1	33,5
1970	26,7	23,3	17,9	26,4	27,4	—	23,3	24,3	31,2	24,7	18,6	37,0	23,7
1980	14,5	14,1	8,9	11,6	20,3	14,4	12,9	14,8	17,8	9,8	11,1	26,1	13,4
1988	9,6	10,4 (¹)	8,7	6,5	12,9	10,9 (²)	9,2	10,4 (³)	12,3	7,1	9,1	16,6	8,7

(¹) 1986.   (²) 1985.   (³) 1987.

POPULATION
FOREIGN POPULATION

1.32. Composition of the resident population — 1988 (1 000)

	Extra-EC foreigners	EC foreigners	Nationals	Total population
EUR 12	7 858	4 912	311 240	324 010
B	321	537	9 018	9 876
DK	109	27	4 993	5 129
D	3 213	1 276	56 749	61 238
GR	109	108	9 772	9 989
E	140	193	38 403	38 736
F	2 102	1 578	52 070	55 750
IRL	17	66	3 456	3 539
I	317	90	56 992	57 399
L	7	89	276	372
NL	435	157	14 123	14 715
P	69	25	10 175	10 269
UK	1 019	766	55 213	56 998

In 1988, 7.9 million of the 324 million inhabitants of the European Community, or 2.5% of the total population, were nationals of non-Community countries. A further 4.9 million were Community nationals living in a country other than their country of origin.

Almost four-fifths of the extra-Community foreigners were living in three countries: the Federal Republic of Germany (3.2 million), France (2.1 million) and the United Kingdom (1.0 million). 74% of 'Community foreigners' were living in those three countries.

Luxembourg had the greatest concentration of foreigners overall: 25.8% of the population, mainly of Community origin. In the Federal Republic of Germany and France, foreigners accounted for 7.3% and 6.6% of the total population respectively, with most foreigners in the Federal Republic of Germany coming from non-Community countries.

43% of 'extra-Community' foreigners came from European countries not members of the EC, in particular Turkey and Yugoslavia. 28% came from Africa, mainly from the Maghreb countries, Algeria, Morocco and Tunisia.

1.33. Composition of the resident population — 1988 (%)

	Extra-EC foreigners	EC foreigners	Nationals	Total population
EUR 12	2,5	1,5	96,1	100
B	3,3	5,4	91,3	100
DK	2,1	0,5	97,3	100
D	5,2	2,1	92,7	100
GR	1,1	1,1	97,8	100
E	0,4	0,5	99,1	100
F	3,8	2,8	93,4	100
IRL	0,5	1,9	97,3	100
I	0,6	0,2	99,3	100
L	1,9	23,9	74,2	100
NL	3,0	1,1	96,0	100
P	0,7	0,2	99,1	100
UK	1,8	1,3	96,9	100

1.34. Distribution of extra-EC foreigners — EUR 12 — 1988

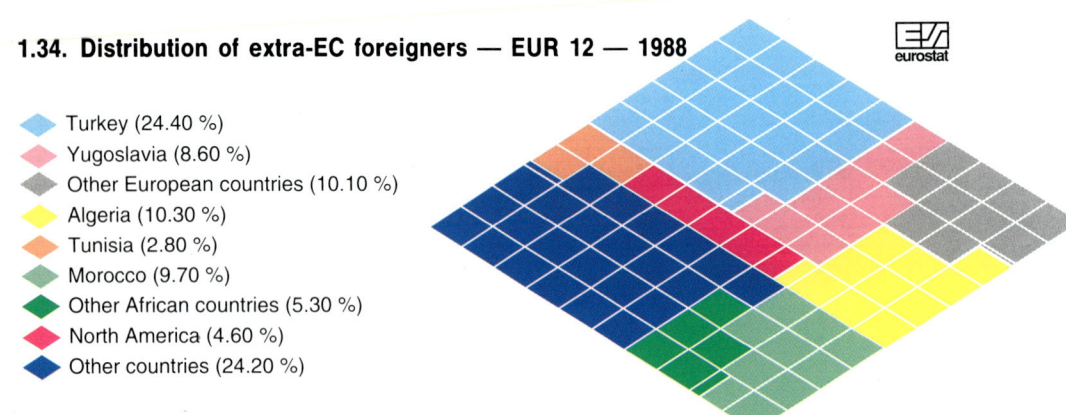

- Turkey (24.40 %)
- Yugoslavia (8.60 %)
- Other European countries (10.10 %)
- Algeria (10.30 %)
- Tunisia (2.80 %)
- Morocco (9.70 %)
- Other African countries (5.30 %)
- North America (4.60 %)
- Other countries (24.20 %)

POPULATION
FOREIGN POPULATION

A comparison of age pyramides shows that foreigners make up a younger population than the total population of the EC, and this is particularly noticeable in the case of 'extra-Community' foreigners, where the age pyramid has a very broad base and a very narrow apex.

The age pyramid of 'Community' foreigners shows a concentration of people of adult, i.e. working, age. The narrow base indicates different patterns of family make-up in comparison with the age pyramid for people living in their native countries.

1.35. Age pyramid, extra-EC foreigners — EUR 12 — 1988 (%)

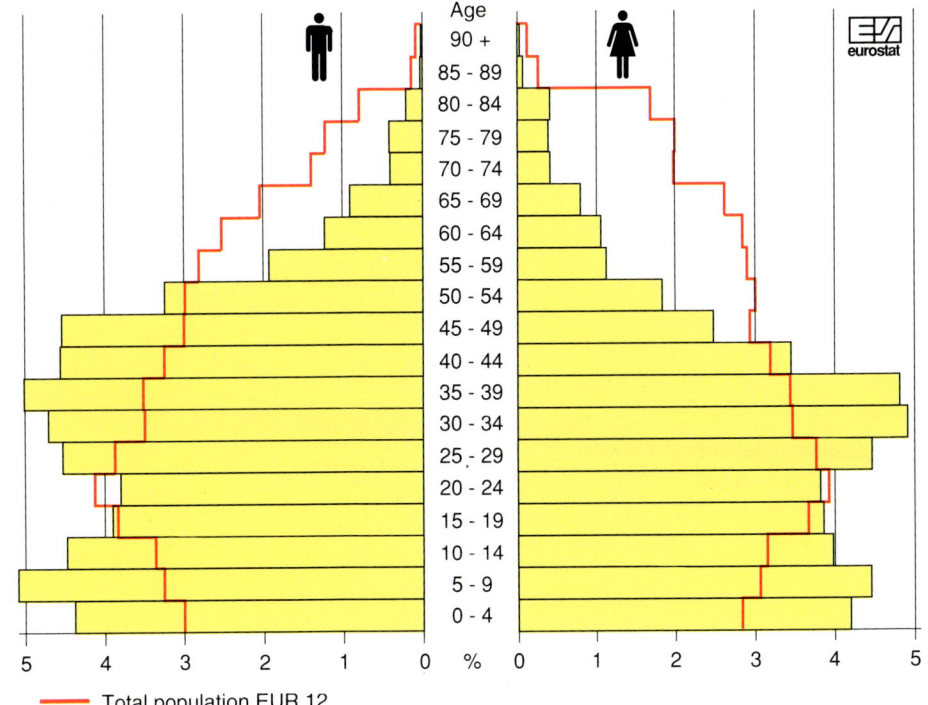

1.36. Age pyramid, EC foreigners — EUR 12 — 1988 (%)

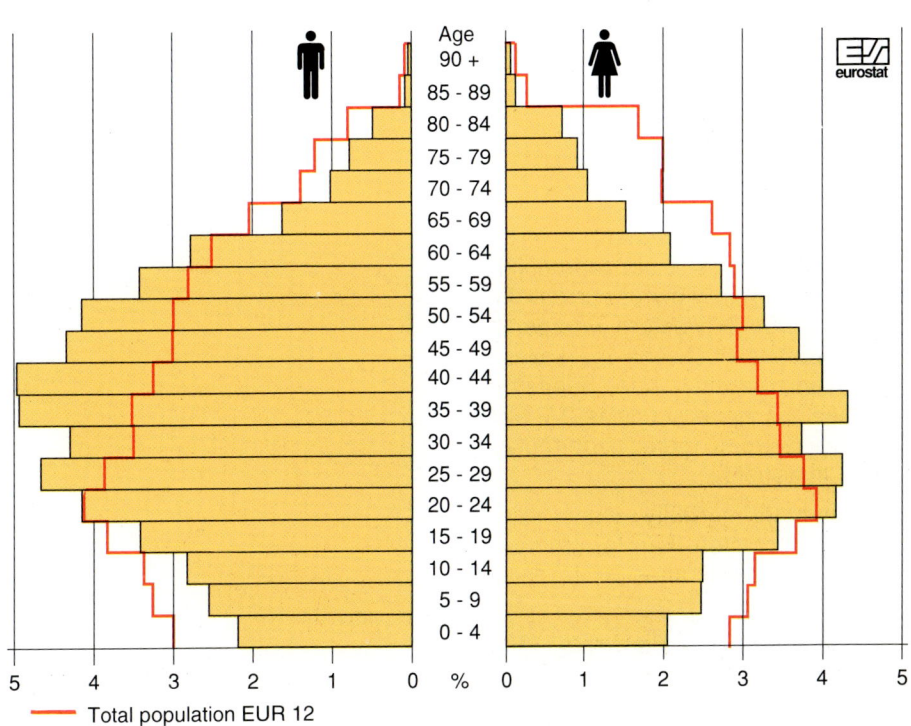

POPULATION
FOR FURTHER INFORMATION

Definitions

Natural increase: difference between the number of births and the number of deaths over a given period.

Median age: the age which divides the individuals who make up a population into two groups of equal numbers.

Life expectancy: average number of years of life remaining to people of a given age, under the mortality conditions to which a given population is subject at successive ages.

Short-term fertility indicator: the short-term fertility indicator for a given period is obtained by adding together fertility rates by age for a given year. It represents the number of children a woman would have if, at each age, she followed the reproductive behaviour observed in that year.

Migrant: a person who makes a move as a result of a change of residence. Migrants are people who have left their own country to settle in another one.

Infant mortality: mortality of children under one year.

Perinatal mortality: mortality of children who are stillborn or who die during the first week.

Generation replacement: fertility level which gives a net reproduction figure of 100. In view of current mortality figures in western Europe and the imbalance between the sexes at birth, the fertility rate needed to replace the generations is 2.1 children per woman (generation-replacement threshold).

Excess male mortality: higher rate of mortality for men than for women. It may refer to all ages or to certain ages only.

Standardized mortality rate (direct method of standardization): in order to compare the varying mortality rates in the Community, the mortality by age series relating to the populations of each of the countries whose mortality rates are to be compared have been compared with a common reference structure by age which, in our case, is the structure by age of the 'Europe region' population as defined by the WHO.

References

Eurostat
— Demographic statistics, 1989, 1990
— Rapid reports: Population and social conditions, 1990-4
— Labour force survey results, 1988

UN
— World population prospects, 1988

WHO
— World health statistics annual, 1988

Eurostat – databank
— Cronos
— Regio

HOUSEHOLDS

Almost half the households in the EC are one- or two-person households: households of five persons or more represent only 13.3% of the total (2.3).

Private households have an average of 2.3 persons and a large majority of them comprise a single family, which is sometimes a one-parent family (9.5% of them in Ireland and 4.3% in France) (2.4) (2.5) (2.6).

After reaching a peak in 1972, the number of marriages fell until 1986, since when it has slightly increased, standing at 1 941 000 in 1989 for the EC as a whole (2.1).

The average age at which people marry for the first time went down until 1975 and has been increasing since. In 1987 it was 27.1 years for men and 24.6 for women (2.10).

Between 1960 and 1988 the number of divorces more than quadrupled in the Europe of the Twelve, reaching 534 000 (2.1) (2.11).

In 1989 births out of wedlock represented almost half of live births in Denmark, over a quarter in France and the United Kingdom but only 1 in 50 in Greece (2.13).

The size of families has decreased throughout the EC. The number of third or subsequent births fell by more than 60% in all the EC countries between 1960 and 1988, except in Ireland, where it fell by only 40% (2.15).

62.4% of EC households do not include children under 15 years; 6.5% include three or more children, and only 0.5% include five or more children (2.17).

2.1. Number of marriages, divorces and births — EUR 12 (1 000)

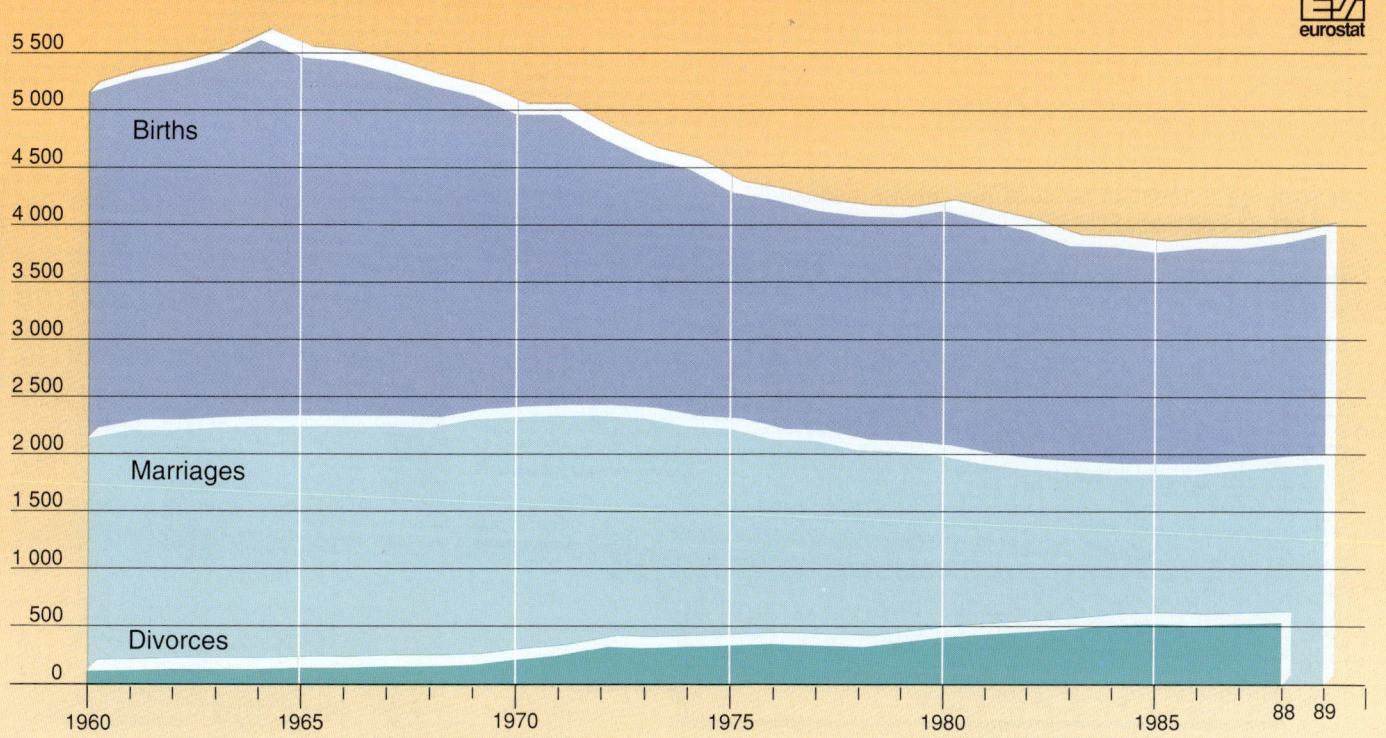

HOUSEHOLDS
STRUCTURE

2.2. Population distribution by type of household (%)
1981-82 censuses

	EUR 12	B	DK	D	GR	E	F	IRL	I	L	NL	P	UK
Private households	98,5	98,9	98,1	98,7	97,1	99,3	97,6	96,8	99,2	98,2	97,9	99,4	98,5
Collective households	1,5	1,1	1,9	1,3	2,9	0,7	2,4	3,2	0,8	1,8	2,1	0,6	1,5

2.3. Distribution of private households by size — EUR 12 (%)

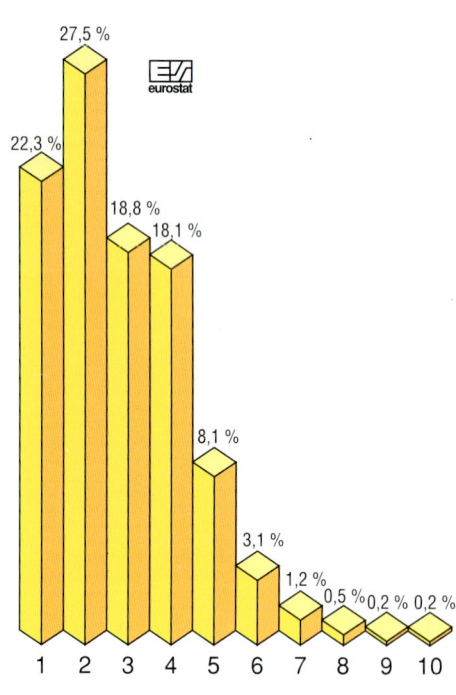

The population censuses carried out in the countries of the European Community in 1981-82 recorded 111 485 000 private households. These represent 98.5% of the total population. The percentage of the population recorded as belonging to collective households is very low but varies considerably between Member States: in Ireland (3.2%) it is five times higher than in Portugal (0.6%).

One- or two-person households make up almost half the total number of households, while households of five persons or more represent only 13.3% of the total.

The average number of persons in a private household is 2.8. The highest average per household (from 3 to 3.6 persons) is found in the countries in the south of the EC (Greece, Spain and Portugal) and in Ireland.

The vast majority of private households comprise a single family (83% in Spain and 61% in Denmark). Except in Portugal and Spain, where they represent 7% and 3.4% respectively of the total number of private households, households made up of two or more families are rare.

The percentage of non-family households, i.e. those made up of single persons, is highest in Denmark (38.4%) and in the Federal Republic of Germany (33.8%).

2.4. Average number of persons per private household
1981-82 censuses

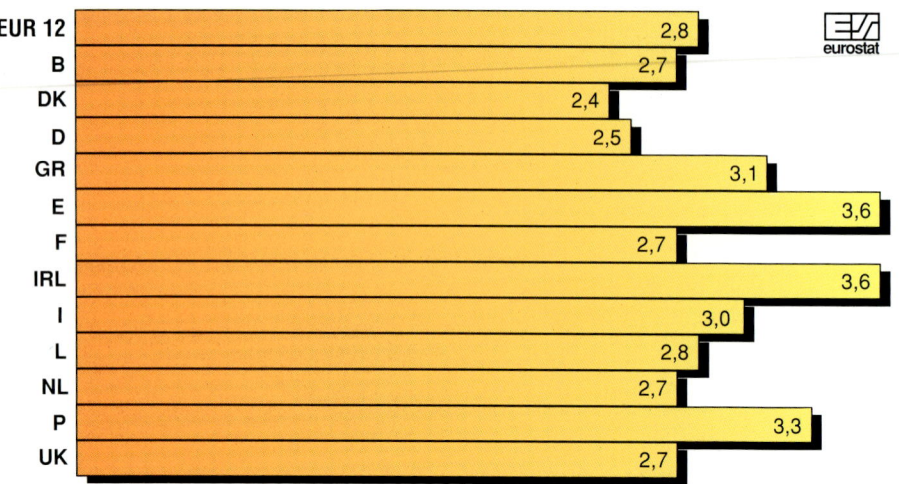

HOUSEHOLDS
STRUCTURE

2.5. Distribution of private households (%)
1981-82 censuses

	B	DK	D	GR	E	F	IRL	I	L	NL	P	UK
Single-family households	73.3	61.0	65.6	:	83.1	70.5	73.2	78.2	72.4	72.5	77.3	72.7
Households of two or more families	0.4	0.6	0.6	:	3.4	0.8	2.2	0	2.2	0.2	7.0	0.9
Non-family households	26.3	38.4	33.8	:	13.5	28.7	24.6	21.8	25.4	27.3	15.7	26.4

The term 'one-parent family' is a neologism to describe families in which only one of the parents lives with the children. Their number is relatively high in Ireland (9.5%), the United Kingdom (8.4%) and Italy (8.1%). Most one-parent families are made up of the mother and the children.

One-person households represent more than one-fifth of the total number of households in the EC. The figure is far higher in the Federal Republic of Germany (30.8%) and Denmark (29.5%) but is a good deal lower in Spain (10.2%), Portugal (12.8%) and Greece (14.6%). In all the EC countries women make up the largest number of one-person households, especially after the age of 65. In the Federal Republic of Germany 12.4% of households are made up of single women over 65, this being the highest percentage in the EC.

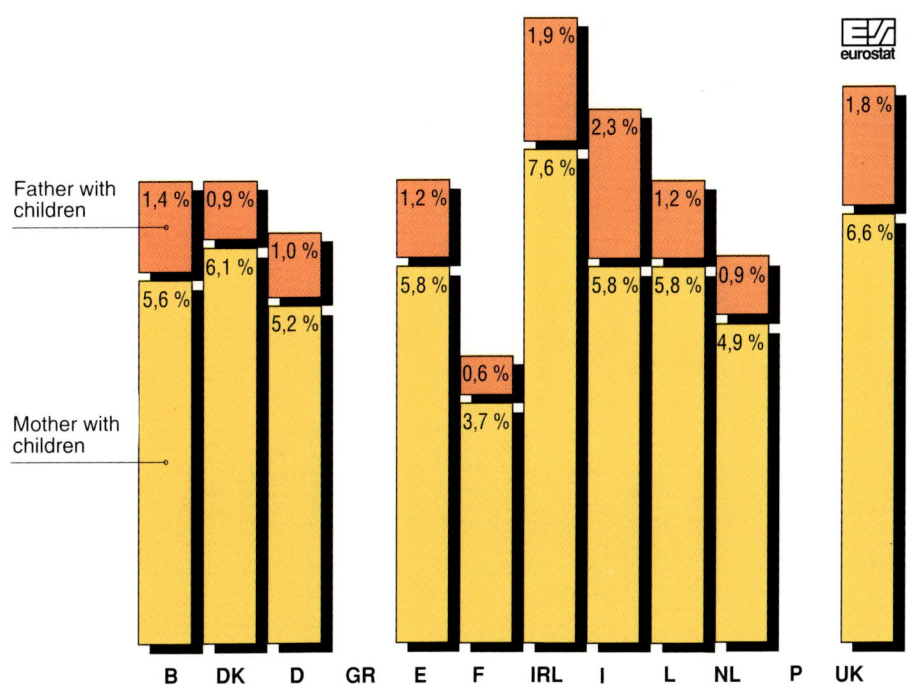

2.6. One-parent families (as % of total households)
1981-82 censuses

2.7. One-person households (as % of total households)
1981-82 censuses

	EUR 12	B	DK	D	GR	E	F	IRL	I	L	NL	P	UK
Adult male between 15 and 64	5,2	5,8	8,8	7,4	4,2	1,9	6,2	5,6	3,6	5,3	6,7	2,5	4,4
Adult female between 15 and 64	6,0	5,6	7,9	8,9	4,6	2,7	6,9	4,0	4,5	6,2	7,0	3,6	4,7
Adult male over 65	2,1	2,7	3,0	2,1	1,5	1,1	2,3	2,6	2,1	1,7	1,8	1,5	2,6
Adult female over 65	9,0	9,2	9,8	12,4	4,3	4,5	9,2	4,8	7,7	7,5	7,3	5,2	10,0
Total one-person households	22,3	23,3	29,5	30,8	14,6	10,2	24,6	17,0	17,9	20,7	22,8	12,8	21,7

23

HOUSEHOLDS
MARRIAGES AND DIVORCES

2.8. Number of marriages (1 000)

	EUR 12	B	DK	D	GR	E	F	IRL	I	L	NL	P	UK
1960	2 194,1	65,2	35,8	521,4	58,1	235,9	319,9	15,4	387,6	2,2	89,1	69,4	393,6
1970	2 357,2	73,2	36,3	444,5	67,4	247,4	393,6	20,7	395,5	2,1	123,6	81,4	471,0
1980	2 000,2	66,3	26,4	362,4	62,3	220,6	334,3	21,7	322,9	2,1	90,1	72,1	418,4
1988	1 911,7	59,0	32,0	397,7	47,8	214,8	271,1	17,9	315,4	2,0	87,8	71,0	394,5
1989	1 941,3	63,5	30,8	397,0	61,4	218,0*	280,8	17,6	311,6	2,2	90,2	73,2	395,0

2.9. Number of marriages — EUR 12 (1 000)

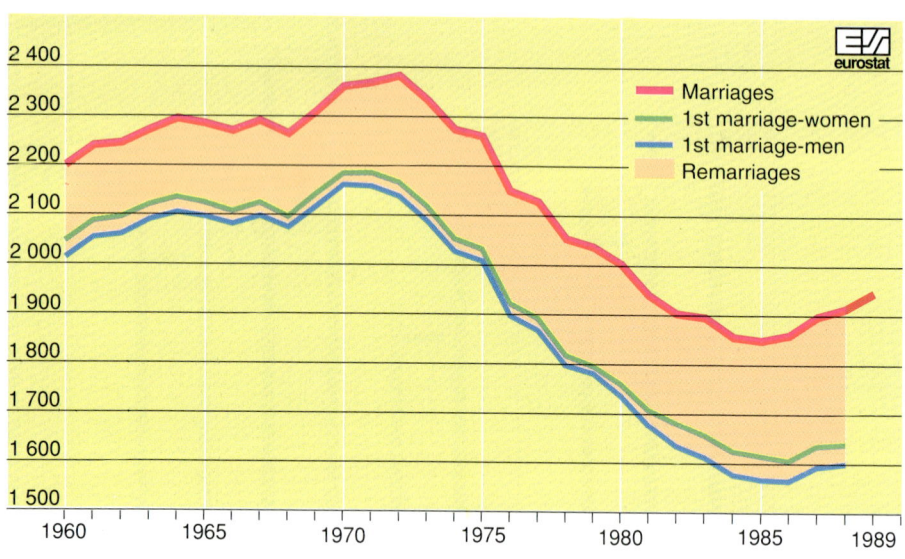

2.10. Average age at first marriage — EUR 12

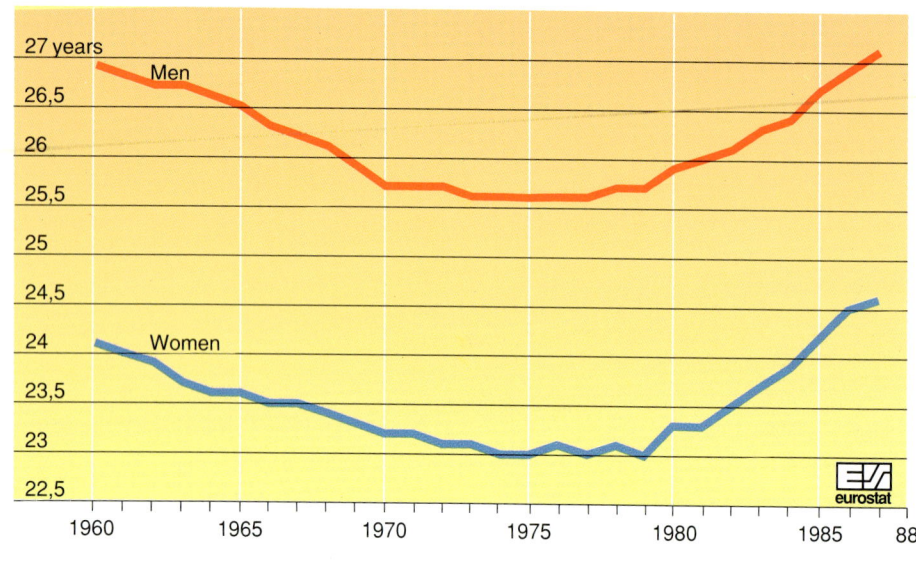

The number of marriages in the Community fell from 2 194 000 in 1960 to 1 941 000 in 1989. It actually rose during the 1960s and then fell during the next two decades. This trend is common to almost all the EC countries, although with slight differences, especially in Denmark, Luxembourg and the Federal Republic of Germany, where the number of marriages remained constant or even fell in the 1960s.

The curve of the graph shows that the number of marriages reached its peak in 1972, after which it fell steadily until 1986, since when there has been a slight upturn. At the same time the number of remarriages increased so that in 1987 it was almost double the 1960 figure: 303 000 men and 278 000 women remarried in 1987 as against 183 000 and 146 000 in 1960.

The average age at first marriage also reflects the new behaviour patterns of the EC populations with regard to marriage: between the 1950s and the mid-1970s the average age was lower (25.6 for men and 23.0 for women in 1975), after which it rose, the 1987 figures being 27.1 and 24.6 respectively.

HOUSEHOLDS
MARRIAGES AND DIVORCES

2.11. Number of divorces (1 000)

	EUR 12	B	DK	D	GR	E	F	IRL	I	L	NL	P	UK
1960	125,3	4,6	6,7	48,9	2,5	— (³)	30,2	— (²)	— (³)	0,2	5,7	0,7	25,9
1970	207,8	5,2	9,5	76,5	3,5	— (³)	38,9	— (²)	— (³)	0,2	10,3	0,5	63,2
1980	415,8	14,5	13,6	96,2	6,7	:	81,1	— (²)	11,8	0,6	25,8	5,9	159,7
1988	534,2	20,8	14,7	128,7	8,6	21,1 (¹)	106,1	— (²)	30,8	0,8	27,9	9,0	165,7

¹ 1987.
² There is no divorce in Ireland.
³ Divorce is illegal.

Young people's interest in marriage has declined, and at the same time the fragility of existing marriages has increased. The number of divorces has increased, relatively slowly at first in the 1960s and then very rapidly in the following decades, from 125 000 in 1960 to 534 000 in 1988 for the EC as a whole. During the 1970s there were reforms in the divorce laws in most countries, with Spain and Italy legalizing divorce for the first time. At present, Ireland is the only country where there is no legal provision for divorce. Compared with 1960, the 1988 figure was 3.5 times higher in France, 4.5 times higher in Belgium and almost five times higher in the Netherlands.

In the age pyramid by marital status, the waning interest in marriage is reflected by a large proportion of young people remaining single. There are far more widows than widowers over the age of 60, which reflects women's longer life expectancy.

2.12. Age pyramid by marital status in the 1981-82 census — EUR 12
(% of total population)

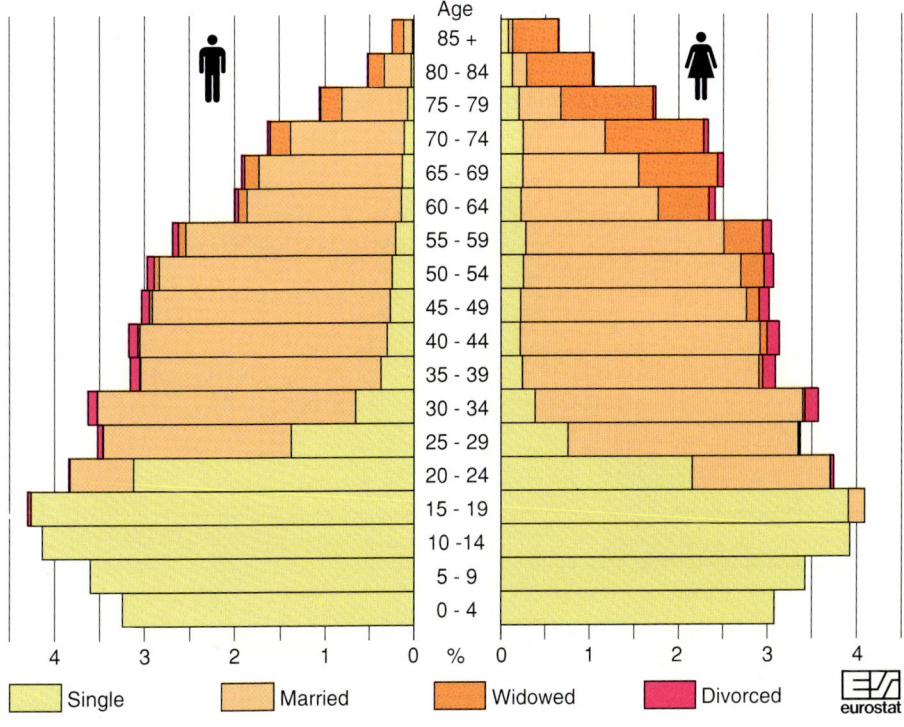

HOUSEHOLDS
BIRTHS

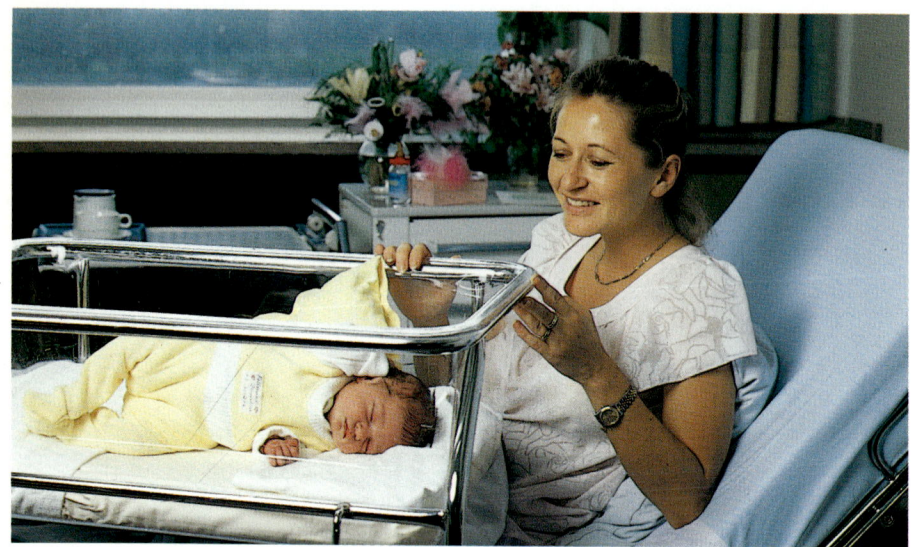

Since marriage has to face increasing competition from various types of more informal union, the number of births out of wedlock has increased considerably, from 4.5% of live births in 1960 to 17.1% in 1989 in the EC. All the Community countries recorded an increase during this period, although the starting situations and rates of increase vary considerably. In 1989 births out of wedlock represented almost half of live births in Denmark and more than a quarter in France and the United Kingdom, but only one out of 50 in Greece, one out of 17 in Italy and one out of 10 in the Federal Republic of Germany and the Netherlands.

2.13. Percentage of children born out of wedlock

	EUR 12	B	DK	D	GR	E	F	IRL	I	L	NL	P	UK
1960	4,5	2,1	7,8	6,3	1,2	2,3	6,1	1,6	2,4	3,2	1,4	9,5	5,2
1970	4,8	2,8	11,0	5,5	1,1	1,4	6,8	2,7	2,2	4,0	2,1	7,3	8,0
1980	7,9	4,1	33,2	7,6	1,5	3,9	11,3	5,0	4,3	6,0	4,1	9,2	11,5
1988	16,1	7,9 (¹)	44,7	10	2,1	8,0 (²)	26,3	11,7	5,8	12,1	10,2	13,1	25,1
1989 (³)	17,1	11*	45*	10,3	2,1	10*	28,4	12,6	6,1	11,8	10,7	14,5	26,6

(¹) 1987.
(²) 1986.
(³) Provisional results.

2.14. Number of births out of wedlock — EUR 12 (1 000)

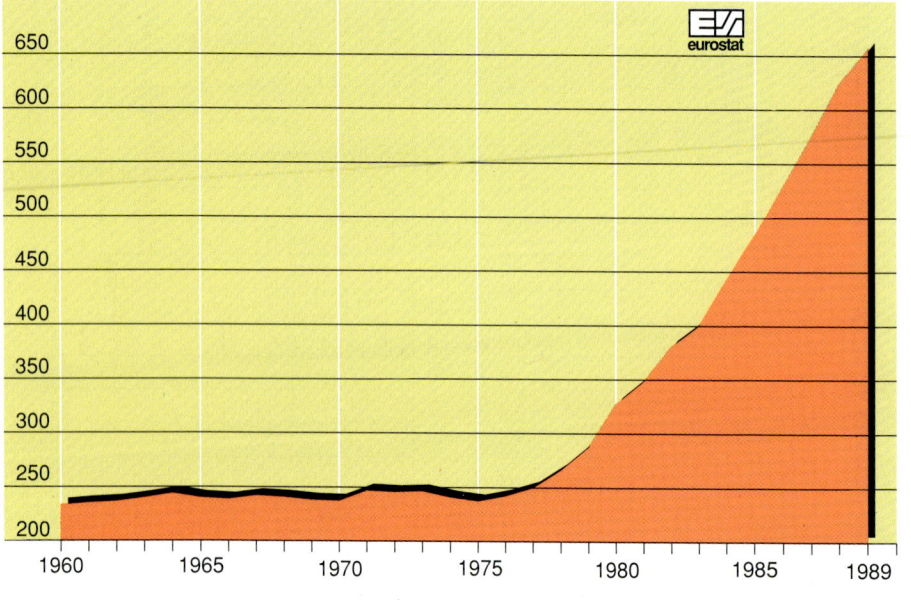

Since the mid-1960s there has been a trend towards smaller families. In all the EC countries the total number of births has fallen considerably; but if births are analysed according to their order, the picture which emerges is that it is mainly the higher-order births, especially from the third child on, which have been affected by the fall in the birth-rate since 1964: between 1960 and 1988 there was a 77% drop in the number of third or subsequent births in Portugal, 72% in Italy, but only 40% in Ireland. It is impossible to supply a total for the Community as a whole since the definitions of order vary from one country to another: in some it is calculated on the basis of children born both in and out of wedlock, in others

HOUSEHOLDS
BIRTHS

2.15. Number of live births by chronological order (1 000)

First

	B	DK	D	GR	E	F	IRL	I	L	NL	P	UK
1960	55,0	25,9	380,0	64,5	:	275,9	12,8	330,6	2,0	74,5	71,9	305,9
1970	59,0	29,7	321,4	60,1	:	335,1	17,5	340,7	1,8	74,5	63,8	307,7
1980	57,1	26,2	279,3	66,5	244,4	313,4	21,7	279,4	1,9	93,2	71,9	275,3
1988	49,9 (¹)	27,6	231,5	48,8	211,7 (¹)	231,5	17,3	245,7 (²)	1,9	83,2	61,1	238,0

(¹) 1985. (²) 1987.

Second

	B	DK	D	GR	E	F	IRL	I	L	NL	P	UK
1960	40,0	22,9	271,0	64,5	:	193,5	11,1	247,0	1,5	64,8	44,6	254,8
1970	38,9	25,4	243,8	60,1	:	219,0	13,8	274,8	1,3	80,1	43,3	263,4
1980	39,3	21,2	196,9	66,5	178,5	245,4	18,0	215,4	1,4	67,2	50,0	239,6
1988	35,9 (¹)	21,6	215,0	48,8	146,2 (²)	195,0	14,7	187,6 (³)	1,5	65,2	38,5	211,2

(¹) 1986. (²) 1985. (³) 1987.

Third

	B	DK	D	GR	E	F	IRL	I	L	NL	P	UK
1960	56,5	27,4	256,2	43,1	:	297,5	36,9	308,3	1,4	99,9	96,3	278,5
1970	40,4	15,7	201,3	29,6	:	235,8	33,0	266,0	1,1	65,7	73,5	229,3
1980	22,9	9,8	97,6	26,2	149,1	150,5	67,4	118,2	0,6	36,0	36,8	151,8
1988	22,2 (¹)	9,6	102,8	17,4	98,4 (¹)	141,6	22,3	86,1 (²)	0,7	38,2	22,5	140,4

(¹) 1985. (²) 1987.

it applies only to children born in wedlock, and in others it applies only to the current marriage.

Alongside this trend towards smaller families there has been a rise in the age of childbirth. The average age of the mother at the birth of her first child follows the same pattern as the average age at first marriage: a decrease up to the beginning of the 1970s (24.2 years in 1970 as against 25.2 in 1960), then an increase, with the 1987 figure at 25.9 years for Europe of the Twelve.

Thus the main features of the family in the European Community are later childbirth, smaller families and more children born out of wedlock.

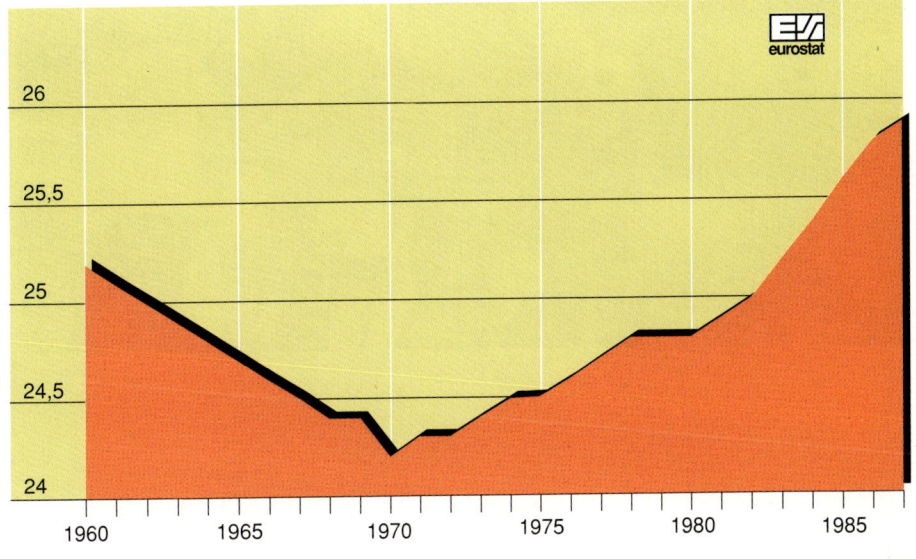

2.16. Average age of women at birth of first child — EUR 12

HOUSEHOLDS
CHILDREN

2.17. Percentage of private households by number of children under 15 1981-82 censuses

	0	1	2	3	4	5 +
EUR 12	62,4	16,9	14,2	4,6	1,3	0,6
B	67,8	16,5	11,1	3,3	0,9	0,7
DK	69,5	14,5	12,4	3,0	0,5	0,1
D	72,4	15,6	9,1	2,2	0,5	0,2
GR	57,6	17,6	18,9	4,7	0,9	0,3
E	50,5	19,3	18,0	7,9	2,8	1,4
F	65,9	16,1	12,0	4,3	1,1	0,6
IRL	54,3	13,0	13,6	9,8	5,4	3,9
I	61,1	19,8	14,1	3,9	0,8	0,3
L	65,7	17,9	12,2	3,3	0,7	0,2
NL	66,0	13,8	15,2	4,0	0,8	0,2
P	53,1	22,8	15,6	5,0	1,9	1,5
UK	66,2	14,0	13,9	4,4	1,1	0,4

The 1981-82 census revealed that in the EC as a whole almost four out of 10 private households included children under 15. The proportion of childless households is highest in the Federal Republic of Germany (72.4%); in Greece (57.6%), Ireland (54.3%), Portugal (53.1%) and Spain (50.5%), the proportion is well below the Community average (62.4%). Few households have three or more children: 6.5% in the EC, with 3.6% in Denmark and 2.9% in the Federal Republic of Germany, but higher than the average for Europe of the Twelve in Ireland (19.1%), Spain (12.1%) and Portugal (8.4%). Only 0.6% of EC households have five or more children: the figure for Ireland is 3.9%.

HOUSEHOLDS
CHILDREN

Childless married couples make up a fairly high proportion of the total number of family units: between one-fifth and one-third, except in Ireland (18.3%) and France (38.3%) (children of any age).

Children do not all live in a family unit composed of a married or unmarried couple. Between 5.8% (in Germany) and 13.6% (in Ireland) of family units are one-parent families in which the adult is most often the mother; the number of such families in which the adult is the father remains very small (0.9% in Germany and France), except in the United Kingdom (2.6%), Ireland (2.8%) and Italy (3.0%).

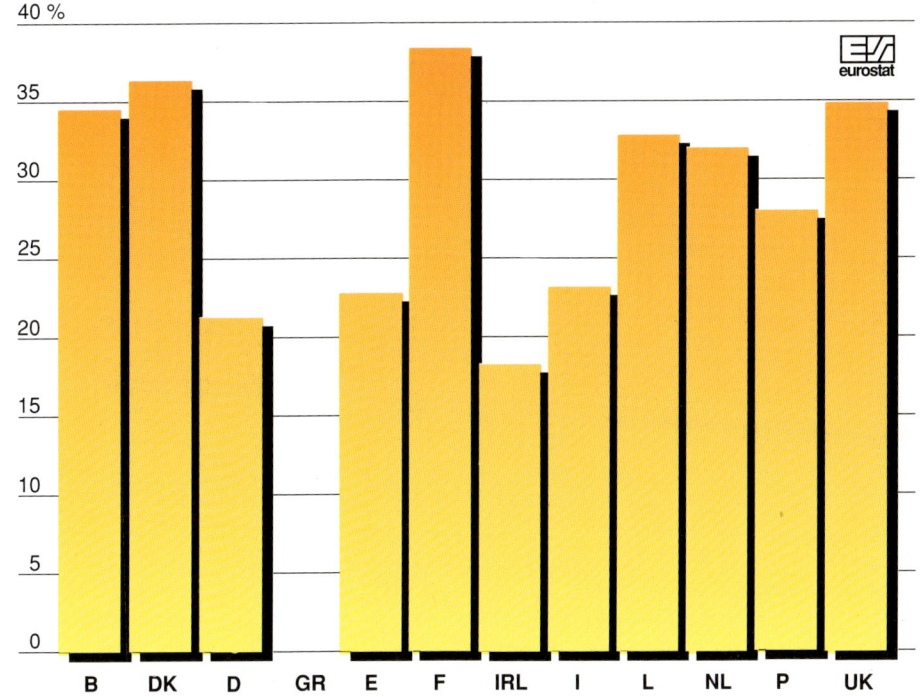

2.18. Childless married couples as a percentage of total family units
1981-82 censuses

2.19. Percentage of family units composed of fathers living alone with one or more children
1981-82 censuses

	B	DK	D	GR	E	F	IRL	I	L	NL	P	UK
Children under 15	0,5	0,8	0,2	:	0,3	0,3	0,5	0,8	0,5	0,3	:	0,9
Children under 15 and children over 15	0,2	0,2	0,1	:	0,2	0,1	0,4	0,5	0,2	0,2	:	0,3
Children over 15	1,1	0,8	0,6	:	1,1	0,5	1,9	1,7	1,1	0,9	:	1,4
Total	1,8	1,8	0,9	:	1,6	0,9	2,8	3,0	1,8	1,4	1,1	2,6

2.20. Percentage of family units composed of mothers living alone with one or more children
1981-82 censuses

	B	DK	D	GR	E	F	IRL	I	L	NL	P	UK
Children under 15	2,5	6,7	1,5	:	1,5	2,6	2,0	1,4	2,4	2,2	:	3,3
Children under 15 and children over 15	0,8	1,2	0,6	:	0,9	0,8	1,3	0,8	0,8	1,0	:	1,3
Children over 15	4,5	2,5	2,8	:	5,0	1,9	7,5	5,3	5,0	3,6	:	4,8
Total	7,8	10,4	4,9	:	7,4	5,3	10,8	7,5	8,2	6,8	7,6	9,4

HOUSEHOLDS
FOR FURTHER INFORMATION

Definitions

Family: for demographic purposes, the family refers to a group of persons made up of parents and children, including cases in which there are no children and cases in which the parental couple has been reduced to a single person as a result of the breakdown of the union, death or divorce.

One-parent family: a family composed of either parent, whether the father or the mother, living with his/her child or children.

Private household: a group of persons, irrespective of the type of union, living under the same roof (main residence) and taking their meals together. Private households may be made up of a person living alone (one-person household) or of two or more persons who may constitute one or more family units (multiple households).

Collective household: a group of persons living in collective accommodation for social, economic or administrative reasons and generally not related to each other (old people in homes, members of religious communities, soldiers in barracks, hospital patients and staff, prison inmates, students in hostels, etc.).

Non-family household: a household made up of persons not related to each other as a nuclear family (parents and children).

Family unit: a nuclear family made up of parents and their children, of a childless couple or of one of the parents with his/her children.

Order of birth: the chronological order of birth, depending on the number of children already born, either to the mother or within the current marriage.

Census: the purpose of population censuses is to collect information on the state of the population at a given time according to a varying range of demographic, social and economic criteria.

References

Eurostat
- Demographic statistics, 1990 1981-82 censuses
- Rapid Reports: Population and social conditions, 1990-4

Eurostat databank
- Cronos

EDUCATION

In 1986-87 there were 59 357 000 pupils and students in the European Community, spread across three levels of education: 22 733 000 at first level, 29 995 000 at second level and 6 629 000 at third level (3.1) (3.2).

Numbers of primary-school (first-level) pupils are steadily falling with the drop in the birth-rate, while numbers at the third level (in higher education) are rising all the time (3.3):

First level   1970/71: 29 093 000   Third level   1970/71: 3 510 000
              1980/81: 26 098 000   1980/81: 5 350 000
              1986/87: 22 733 000   1986/87: 6 629 000 (3.3).

Equality of opportunity between men and women has not yet been achieved at third level: in 1986-87, 46% of the Community total were women (3.7).

47% of young Europeans aged 15 to 24 claim to know how to use a computer (3.10).

3.1. Numbers of pupils and students at all three levels of education throughout the European Community (1 000)

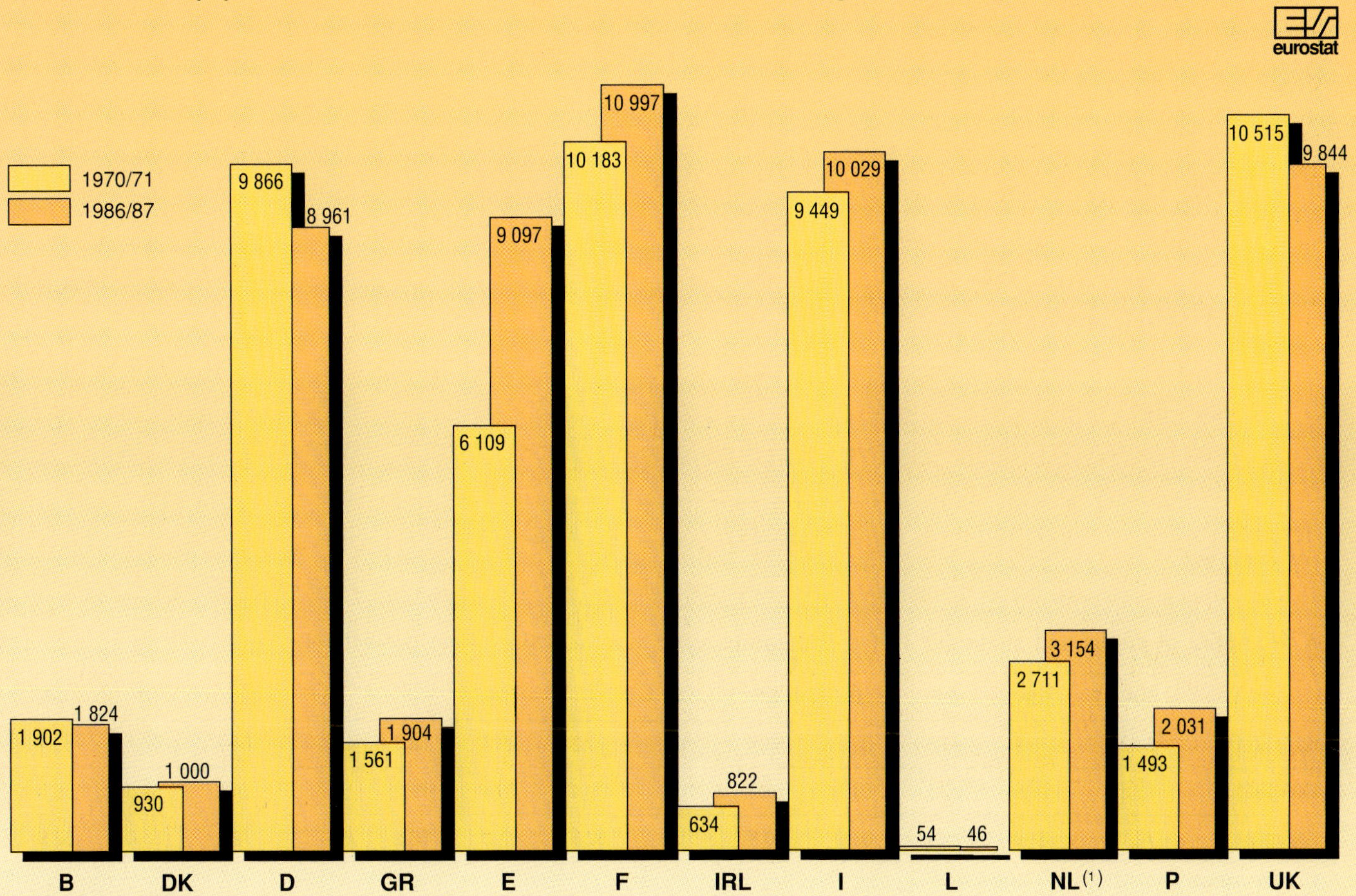

eurostat

	1970/71	1986/87
B	1 902	1 824
DK	930	1 000
D	9 866	8 961
GR	1 561	1 904
E	6 109	9 097
F	10 183	10 997
IRL	634	822
I	9 449	10 029
L	54	46
NL(1)	2 711	3 154
P	1 493	2 031
UK	10 515	9 844

1 Including pre-school.

EDUCATION

NUMBERS IN FULL-TIME EDUCATION

3.2. Numbers of pupils and students at each level of education — 1986/87 (1 000)

Member State	EUR 12	B	DK	D	GR	E	F	IRL	I	L	NL	P	UK
First level	22 733 ([1])	755	392	2 376	868	3 428	4 148	423	3 526	22	1 448 ([2])	1 234	4 462
Second level	29 995	843	489	5 026	838	4 684	5 559	342	5 362	24	1 394	668	4 769
Third level	6 629	226	119	1 559	198	985	1 290	57	1 141	:	312	129	613

[1] Estimate does not include pre-school in the Netherlands.
[2] Including pre-school.

3.3. Trends in numbers of pupils and students at each level of education EUR 12 (1 000)

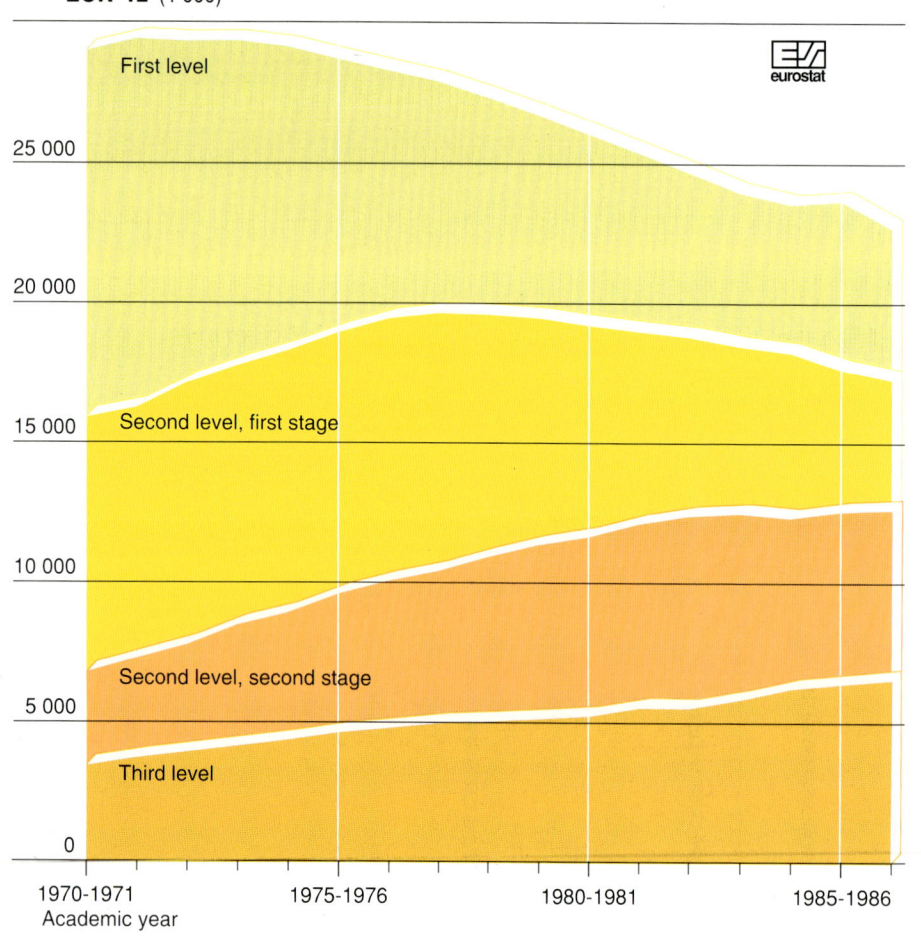

From 1970/71 to 1986/87 the number of pupils and students in the Community as a whole rose from 55 407 000 to 59 357 000 — an increase of 7.1 %.

In 1986/87, 72 % of Europeans aged five to 24 years were in full-time education, with as many as 82.8 % in France.

3.4. Numbers of pupils and students [1] in the population aged five to 24 (including pre-school) (%)

	EUR 12	B	DK	D	GR	E	F	IRL	I	L	NL	P	UK
1970/1971	65,3	78,4	61,3	63,3	59,7	60,2	73,2	69,7	66,1	62,1	68,2	47,7	63,4
1980/1981	71,5	77,6	72,5	68,9	65,6	74,6	79,4	70,4	72,2	59,0	74,5	54,6	65,8
1986/1987	72,1	81,0	73,1	66,9	70,8	79,6	82,8	73,3	68,9	61,7 (*)	72,3	63,0	62,5

[1] Full-time education only.   * Estimate.

EDUCATION

NUMBERS IN FULL-TIME EDUCATION

The biggest increase was at the third level: +89% in 16 years (from 3.5 million in 1970/71 to 6.6 million in 1986/87). This was due chiefly to the growth in numbers of female students (from 1.3 million to 3.1 million, i.e. +138%), while male students increased by 60%, from 2.2 million to 3.5 million. Pupils at the second stage of the second level showed an equally large increase (from 6.8 million to 12.7 million, or 85%). Numbers of primary-school pupils fell from 29.1 million to 22.7 million — a drop of 22%. This spectacular fall-off in numbers is due to the general decline in the birth-rate throughout the European Community since the mid-1960s, which inevitably affects numbers of pupils in primary education, since schooling at this level is compulsory.

The choice of subjects for study at third level changed over this 16-year period to the detriment in particular of literary subjects and teacher training; meanwhile there was a surge in the social sciences, with a sharp increase in new subjects (the 'Other' category, which accounted for only 4% in 1970/71, rose to 16% in 1986/87).

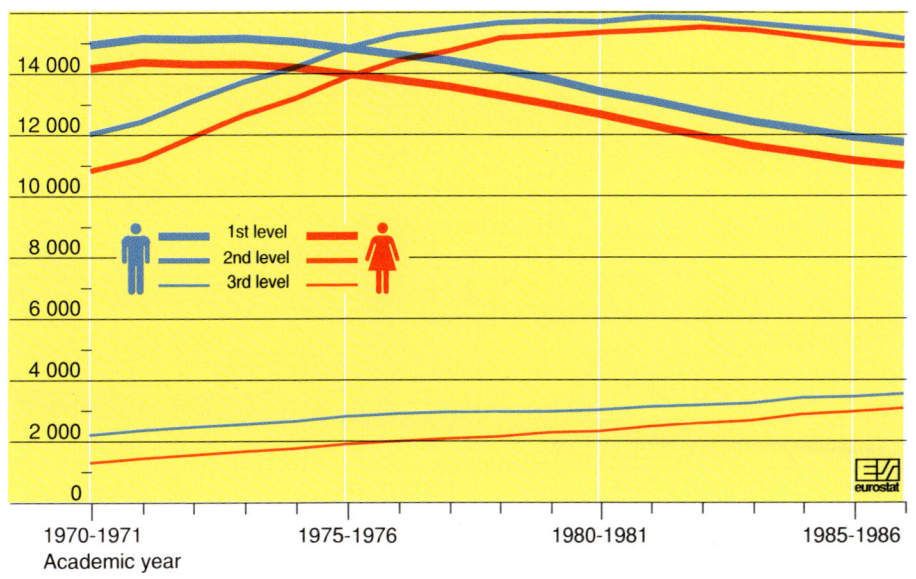

3.5. **Trends in numbers of pupils and students by level of education and by sex — EUR 12** (1 000)

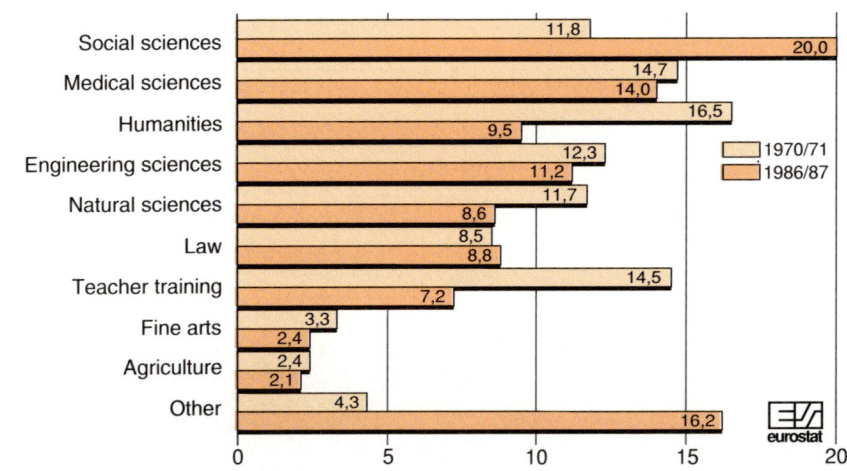

3.6. **Trends in numbers of students by field of study at third level — EUR 12** (%)

Field	1970/71	1986/87
Social sciences	11,8	20,0
Medical sciences	14,7	14,0
Humanities	16,5	9,5
Engineering sciences	12,3	11,2
Natural sciences	11,7	8,6
Law	8,5	8,8
Teacher training	14,5	7,2
Fine arts	3,3	2,4
Agriculture	2,4	2,1
Other	4,3	16,2

EDUCATION
EQUAL OPPORTUNITIES

3.7. Trends in percentages of females by level of education

	EUR 12	B	DK	D	GR	E	F	IRL	I	L	NL	P	UK
First level													
1976-77	49	48	49	49	48	49	48	47	49	49	48	48	49
1986-87	48	49	49	49	48	49	48	49	49	49	49	48	48
Second level													
1976-77	48	48	46	49	42	48	51	51	46	48	47	48	49
1986-87	50	49	49	50	47	51	50	51	49	50	48	53	49
Third level													
1976-77	40	42	47	38	37	36	46	39	39	33	32	46	42
1986-87	46	48	50	41	49	50	51	46	47	:	41	52	44

3.8. Trends in numbers of females per 100 males of second level, second stage and at third level — EUR 12

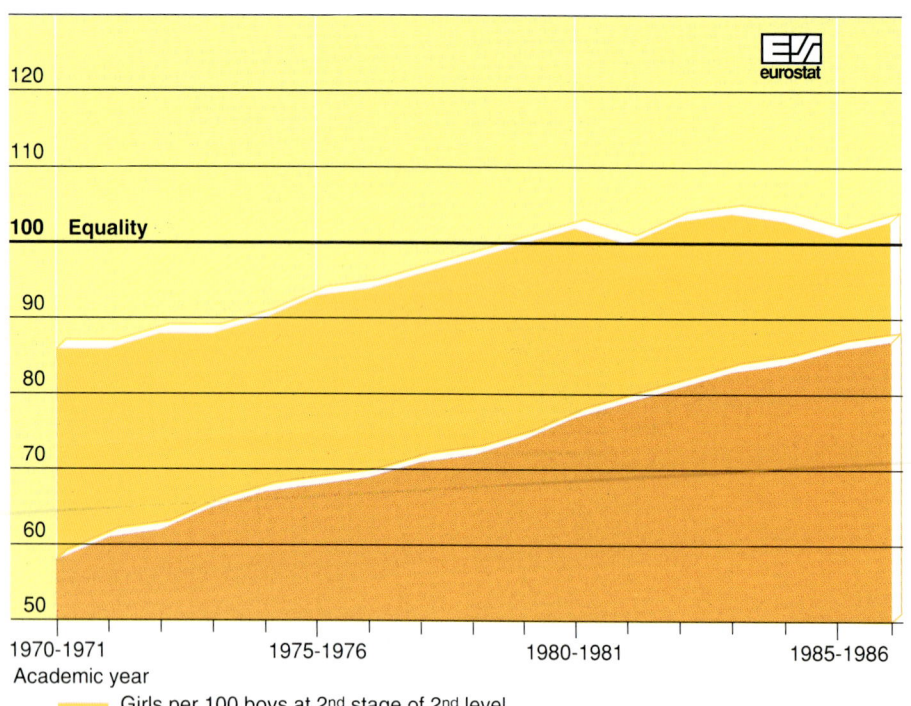

Since primary education is compulsory, the number of boys and girls is the same. The slight inequality shown in the figures for the trend since 1970 is due entirely to the fact that slightly more boys are born each year than girls.

In secondary education, equality was achieved gradually during the 1970s and 1980s. Only at the third level is there now a slight difference, despite the substantial growth in female numbers. In 1986/87, 46% of third-level students in the Community as a whole were female; women accounted for 50% or more of the total in countries such as Denmark, Spain, France and Portugal, but for only 41% in the Federal Republic of Germany and the Netherlands.

EDUCATION

LANGUAGES AND COMPUTER STUDIES

The study of languages is one of the priorities of the European Community's action programme. Statistics on language teaching at secondary level show English to be the first foreign language learnt by pupils, since more than 50% learn English in all regions other than the French-speaking area of Belgium. Next comes French (more than 50% of pupils in the Flemish-speaking area of Belgium, England and Wales, Scotland, Ireland and Luxembourg, and 25-50% in the remaining regions).

Knowledge of computers is fast becoming a necessity in today's society. 47% of young Europeans claim to be able to use a computer. The figure falls to 19% in Greece and Portugal, while 69% of young Danes, Luxembourgers and Britons are computer-literate.

3.9. Language teaching at second level (percentage of pupils following language courses) **February 1988**

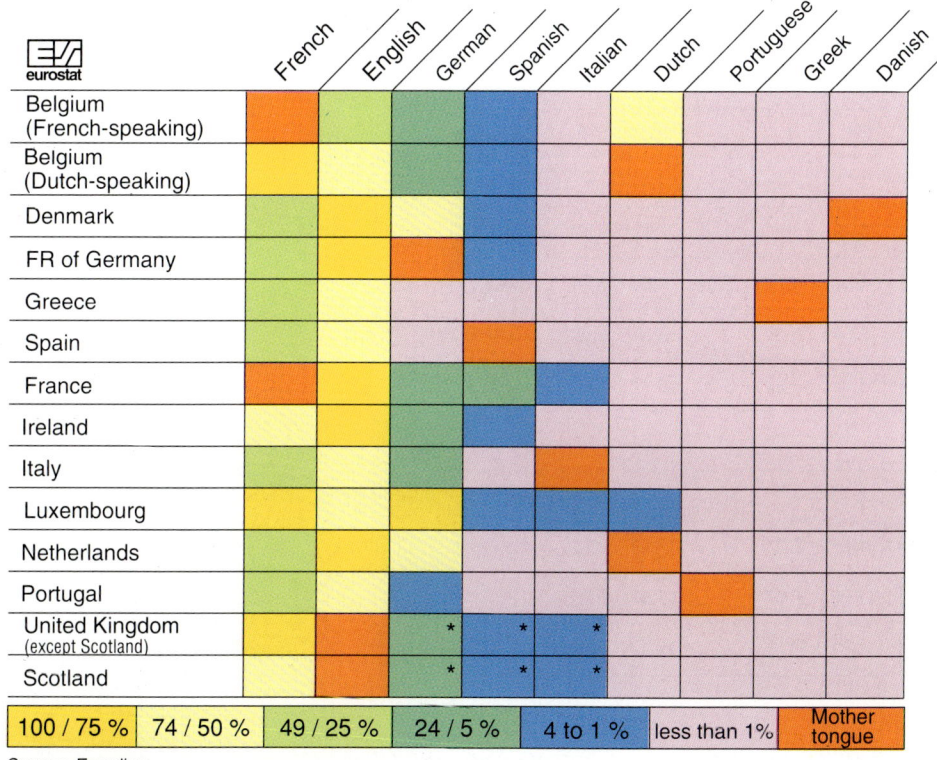

Source: Eurydice.

3.10. Knowledge to computers — percentage of persons aged 15 to 24 claming to know how to use a computer — 1987

EUR 12	B	DK	D	GR	E	F	IRL	I	L	NL	P	UK
47	47	69	45	19	28	58	50	30	69	64	19	69

Source: Eurobarometer.

EDUCATION
EXPENDITURE

3.11. Public expenditure on education per head of population — 1985 (PPS)

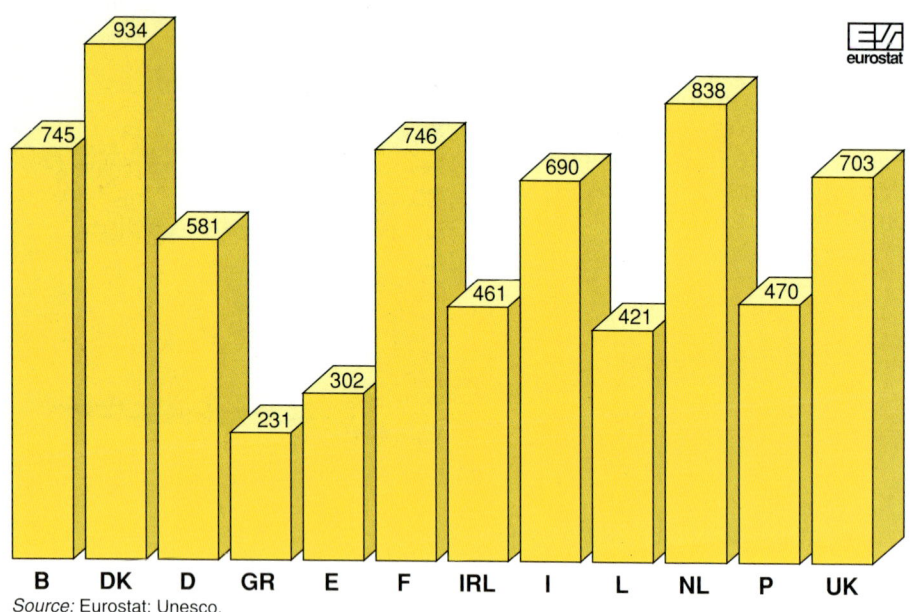

Source: Eurostat; Unesco.

Public expenditure is merely indicative of Member States' expenditure on education. The figures exclude private initiatives, which vary from one country to the next.

The expenditure of households likewise can be no more than a rough indication, since it takes no account of the schooling provided free of charge in some educational sectors.

3.12. Trends in public expenditure on education

	B	DK	D	GR	E	F	IRL	I	L	NL	P	UK
% of GDP											
1982	6,13	6,98	4,64	2,42	2,48	5,74	6,28	:	8,31	7,62	4,58	5,39
1983	6,23	6,76	4,83	2,42	:	5,77	6,82	4,77	7,51	7,62	3,96	5,23
1984	5,90	6,31	4,45	2,64	3,22	5,94	5,66	5,05	:	6,66	4,06	5,17
1985	6,08([1])	6,03	4,57	3,40	3,29	5,73	5,65	4,97	3,36	6,77	3,99([1])	4,96
% of general government expenditure											
1982	10,30	12,01	10,00	:	6,89	12,89	11,73	:	16,23	13,13	10,88	12,91
1983	10,50	11,54	10,68	:	:	12,68	11,58	10,31	14,79	12,63	8,42	12,49
1984	10,06	11,04	9,92	:	8,49	12,91	11,05	10,97	:	11,67	8,71	12,17
1985	10,50([1])	10,75	10,29	:	8,05	12,34	10,81	10,58	:	12,10	7,99([1])	11,98

[1] Ministry of Education.   Sources: Eurostat, Unesco.

3.13. Trends in the expenditure of households on education as a proportion of total expenditure (%)

	B	DK	D	GR	E	F	IRL	I	L	NL	P	UK
1980	:	1,3	:	1,6	1,9	0,4	2,2	0,4	:	0,3	0,9	0,8
1987	:	1,6	:	1,7	1,8([1])	0,5	2,7([2])	0,7	:	0,3	1,4([1])	0,8

([1]) 1985.   ([2]) 1986.

EDUCATION
OPINIONS

The opinions of young people aged 15 to 24 explain the statistical trend in the subjects chosen for study at third level: the overwhelming reasons for a particular choice of subject are that it leads to a desired occupation (46%) or is of special interest (42%). A better chance of a job comes no higher than third place (33%). The level of income expected from a future job is less important (18%), and other people's wishes have a very marginal effect (8%). One remarkable factor is the small variation from country to country, which implies a homogeneity in the opinions of young Europeans on their future careers.

3.14. Opinions of young people aged 15 to 24 on their reasons for choice of subjects for study — 1987 (%)

	EUR 12	B	DK	D	GR	E	F	IRL	I	L	NL	P	UK
Special interest	42	39	39	27	40	46	41	40	47	55	38	50	61
Leads to desired occupation	46	43	47	46	43	33	48	44	51	51	48	57	48
Leads to a well-paid job	18	13	11	20	20	5	21	15	19	29	18	18	20
Offers a better chance of a job	33	27	20	37	21	23	38	34	39	29	32	20	28
Other people's wishes	8	10	4	13	9	11	8	11	10	4	5	3	3
Other reasons	4	8	7	3	1	4	4	5	3	3	13	1	2

Source: Eurobarometer.
Total more than 100 owing to multiple replies.

3.15. Opinions of young people aged 15 to 24 on their reasons for choice of subjects for study according to age — EUR 12 — 1987 (%)

	15-16 years	17-18 years	19-20 years	21-22 years	23-24 years
Special interest	36	37	49	59	54
Leads to desired occupation	43	46	47	50	50
Leads to a well-paid job	14	19	20	21	23
Offers a better chance of a job	32	35	42	31	21
Other people's wishes	13	9	4	5	1
Other reasons	4	5	3	2	5

Source: Eurobarometer.
Total more than 100 owing to multiple replies.

EDUCATION
FOR FURTHER INFORMATION

Definitions

Levels of education

The various types of national education have been broken down as follows according to the levels defined in the ISCED, which are now used in all the Member States of the Community:

Pre-school (ISCED 0): education prior to the beginning of compulsory schooling. As a rule it begins around the age of 3 and 4 and finishes around the age of 6.

First level (ISCED 1): elementary education, compulsory in all cases and as a rule lasting five years.

Second level, first stage (ISCED 2): this is also compulsory and lasts three years in the majority of cases.

Second level, second stage (ISCED 3): begins around the age of 14 or 15, lasts for three years in the majority of cases and leads to the level required for admission to university or any other form of higher education. Depending on the country, this level may begin at the end or still be a part of compulsory schooling.

Third level (ISCED 5, 6, 7): comprises universities and all other types of higher education.

Public expenditure

Total public expenditure means all expenditure on goods and services, wages and salaries, transfers etc. borne by general government, comprising central and local government and social security funds (ESA code S60).

Expenditure on education and training

Public expenditure on education and training means expenditure by central and local government on education and training, usually excluding registration fees and other charges paid by students or their parents. It comprises the following:

Teaching and administration

(a) *Current expenditure* comprises the wages and salaries and the social security contributions of teachers and other persons, purchases of goods and services, rents, etc.

(b) *Capital expenditure* comprises purchases of land, buildings and durable equipment.

(c) *Transfers to households*: grants, loans and other forms of direct aid.

(d) *Other expenditure of a social nature* comprises school transport, medical services, meals, accommodation, etc.

References

Eurostat
Education and training, 1985.

Eurobarometer
The Young Europeans in 1987.

EMPLOYMENT AND UNEMPLOYMENT

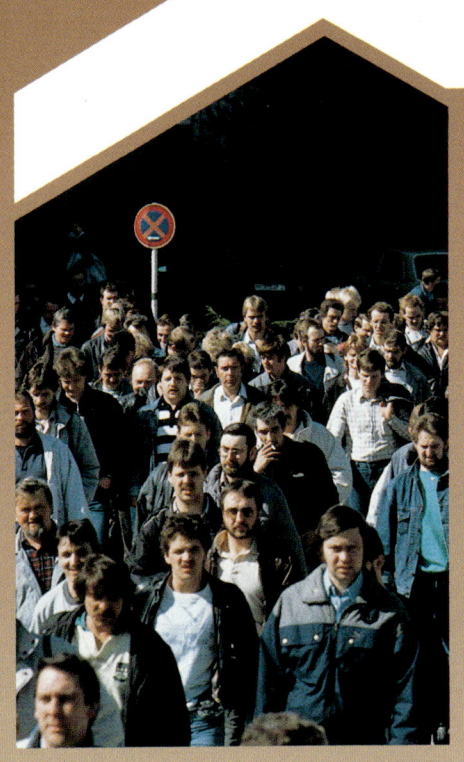

The activity rate for women aged between 14 and 64 rose in the Community from 46.6% in 1983 to 51.0% in 1988, but it is still well below that for men (78.5%) (4.8).

Married men have a higher activity rate than single men (87.1% compared with 64.5%), while married women are 'less economically active' than single women (49.1% compared with 54.5%) (4.11).

The services sector accounts for approximately 60% of total employment in the Community, while agriculture accounts for less than 8% (4.15).

There were 12.7 million unemployed persons in the Community in 1989, i.e. 9% of the active population (4.20) (4.21).

The unemployment rate for women in the Community (11.9%) is higher than that for men (7.0%), while for young persons under 25 it is 17.4% (4.21).

In 1988 over half of all unemployed persons, both men (51.7%) and women (52.5%), fell within the category of long-term unemployed (i.e. persons unemployed for more than one year) (4.28).

90% of foreign workers (from both Community and non-Community countries) have the occupational status of employee (4.32).

The majority of male foreign workers are employed in industry and the majority of their female counterparts in the services sector (4.36).

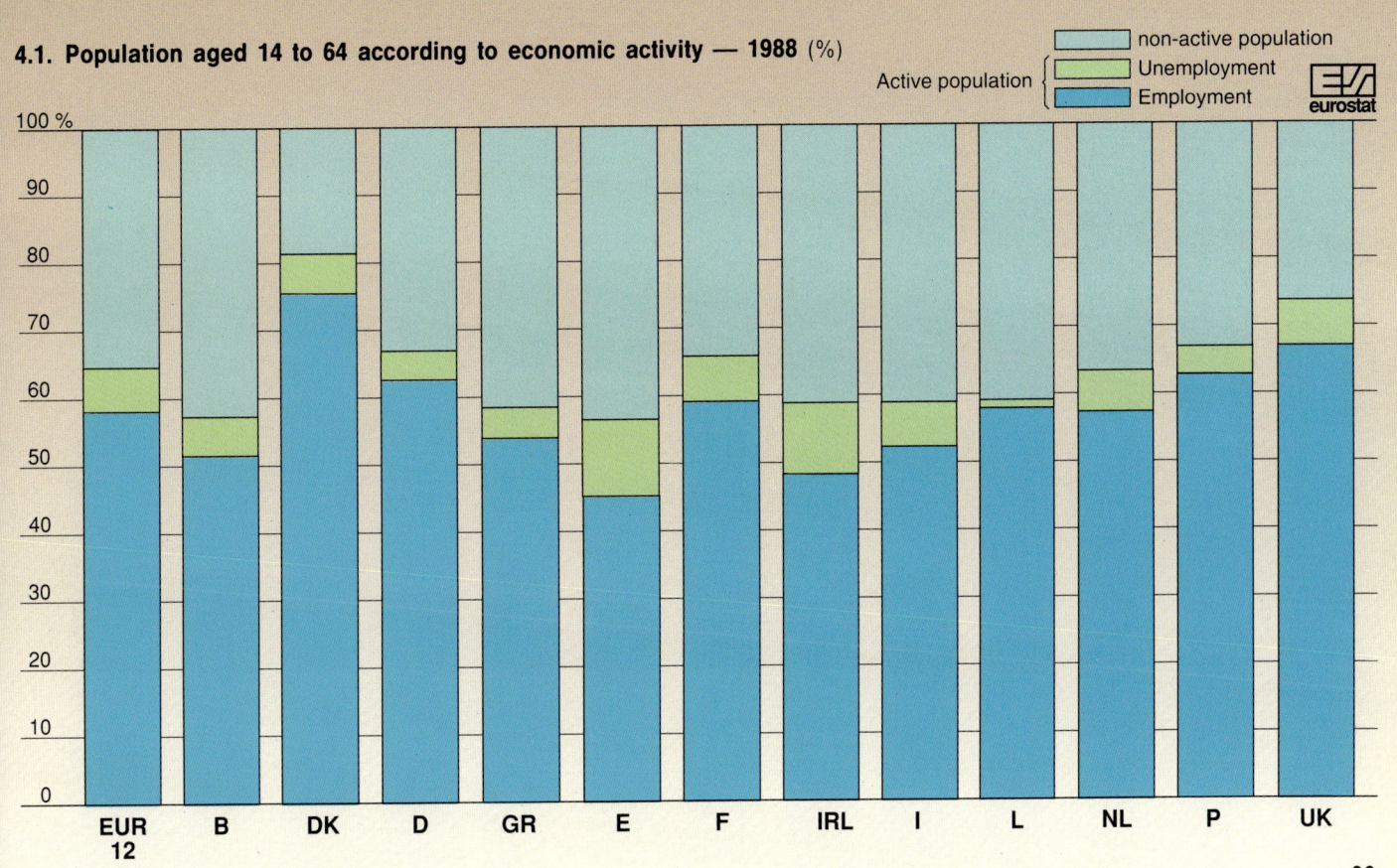

4.1. Population aged 14 to 64 according to economic activity — 1988 (%)

Active population { Employment, Unemployment }; non-active population

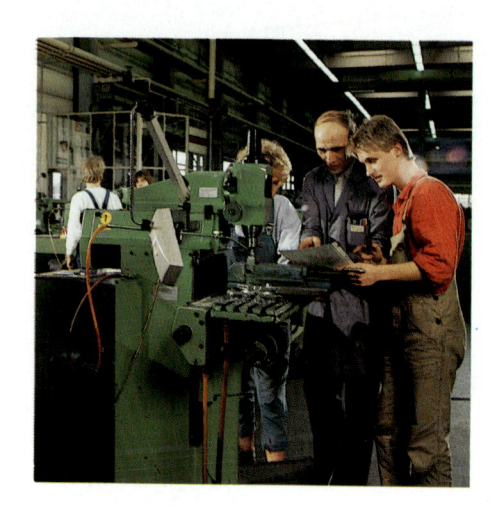

EMPLOYMENT AND UNEMPLOYMENT
LABOUR MARKET

The period between 1975 and 1988 saw a steady growth of approximately 10% in the Community's active population, matching the approximately 10% growth in the population aged between 14 and 64. Following the onset of a downward trend in 1980, employment rates began to recover from 1984 onwards, rising by 1.8% in 1988 compared with 1987. Unemployment rose between 1975 and 1984, gradually until 1980 and then more abruptly, as can be seen on the graph in the diverging curves for the active population and employment. From 1985 the two curves reconverge to become virtually parallel, indicating a gradual steadying of unemployment.

The growth in the active population over 14 years of age is due chiefly to an increase in the number of women

4.2. Changes in the structure of the population aged 14 to 64 — EUR 12
(millions)

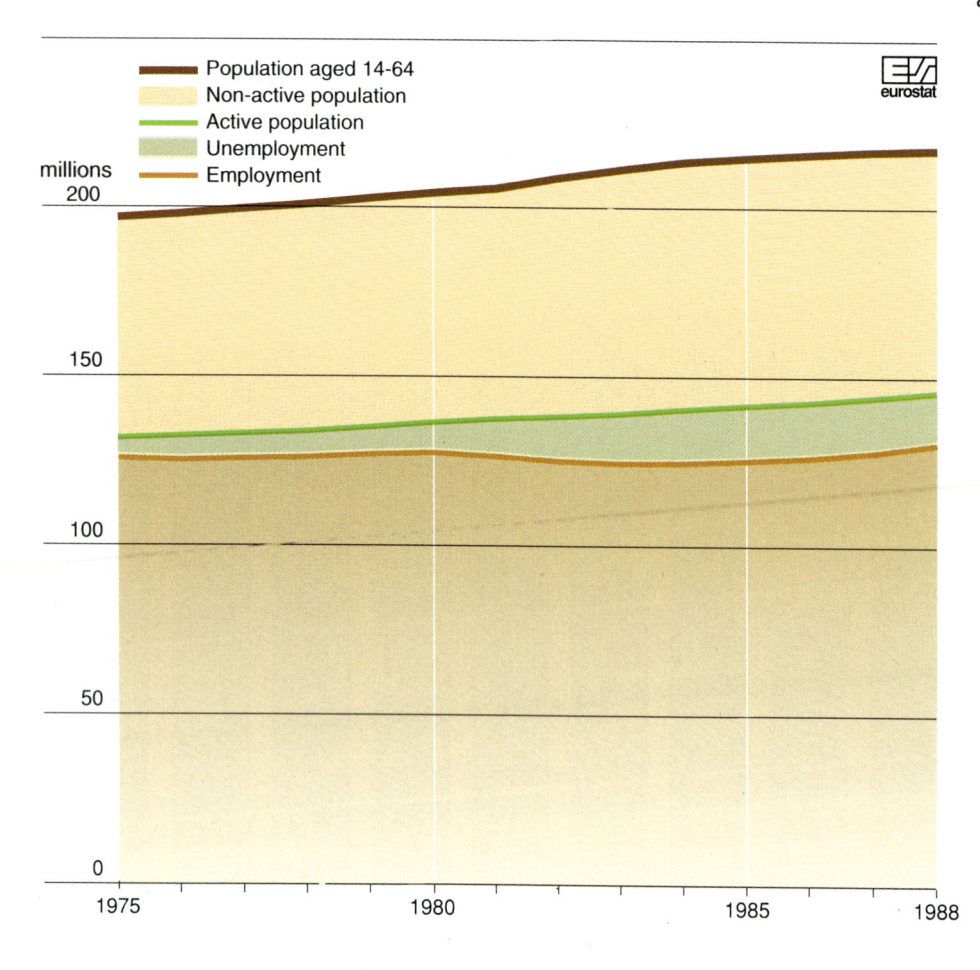

EMPLOYMENT AND UNEMPLOYMENT
LABOUR MARKET

4.3. Changes in principal characteristics of the population — EUR 12 (1 000)

	1983 Male	1983 Female	1983 Total	1985 Male	1985 Female	1985 Total	1988 Male	1988 Female	1988 Total
Total population (private households)	151 776	161 692	313 468	152 928	163 143	316 071	154 269	164 123	318 393
Population aged over 14	120 331	131 499	251 830	122 577	134 096	256 673	126 441	137 573	264 016
Active population aged over 14	83 733	50 812	134 545	84 508	52 967	137 475	86 110	56 629	142 739
Persons in employment	76 640	44 972	121 612	76 540	46 155	122 695	79 006	49 396	128 403
Persons seeking employment	7 093	5 840	12 933	7 946	6 749	14 695	7 104	7 233	14 336
Non-active	36 598	80 687	117 285	38 069	81 129	119 198	40 331	80 946	121 277
Non-active in job training	12 119	11 950	36 019	11 992	11 703	23 695	12 104	11 985	24 088

on the labour market. In 1988 women accounted for approximately 40% of the labour force (56.6 million out of 142.7 million), although quite a high proportion of these women were working part-time. The proportion of women in the labour force has risen more swiftly, particularly in recent years, than that of men. Between 1983 and 1988, for example, the labour force expanded by almost six million women compared with just over two million men. During the same period the number of women employed rose by over four million, whereas male employment increased by only a little over two million. The increase in the number of women unemployed was also greater than for their male counterparts (+1.4 million women in 1988 compared with 1983, as against an increase of barely 11 000 men during the same period).

The age pyramid for the active population shows the asymmetric distribution of the two sexes at the various working ages, with women recording consistently lower percentages than men. Participation in economic activity is highest for both sexes between the ages of 20 and 40.

4.4. Structure of the population by age and sex — EUR 12 — 1988

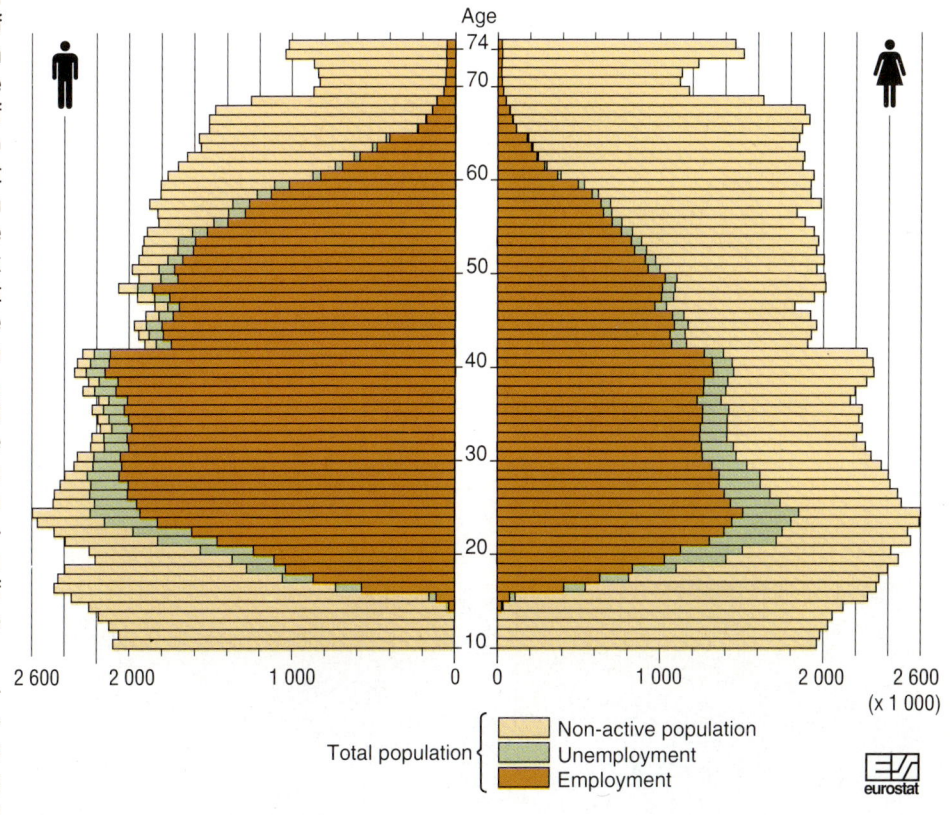

Total population { Non-active population / Unemployment / Employment }

EMPLOYMENT AND UNEMPLOYMENT
ACTIVE POPULATION

4.5. Distribution of population by age, sex and economic situation — EUR 12 — 1988

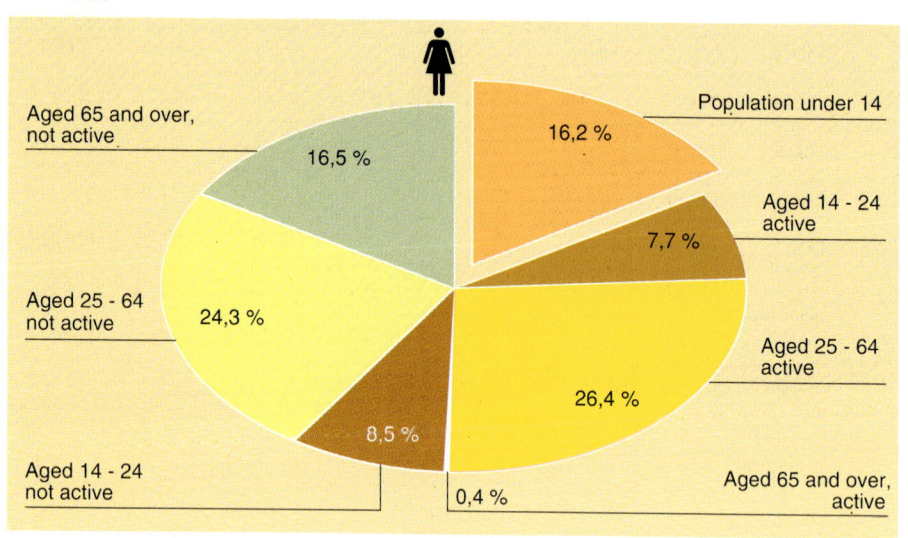

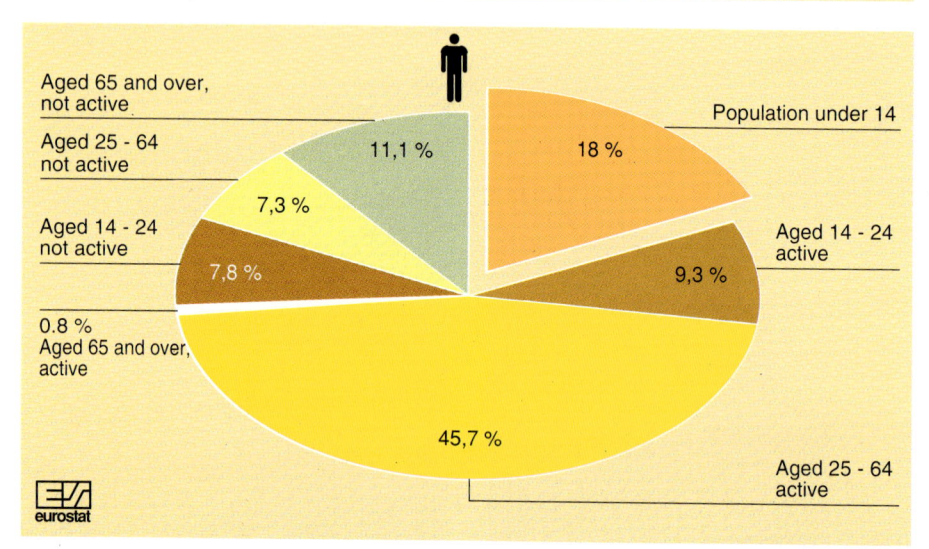

Female:
- Aged 65 and over, not active: 16,5 %
- Population under 14: 16,2 %
- Aged 14 - 24 active: 7,7 %
- Aged 25 - 64 active: 26,4 %
- Aged 65 and over, active: 0,4 %
- Aged 14 - 24 not active: 8,5 %
- Aged 25 - 64 not active: 24,3 %

Male:
- Aged 65 and over, not active: 11,1 %
- Population under 14: 18 %
- Aged 14 - 24 active: 9,3 %
- Aged 25 - 64 active: 45,7 %
- Aged 65 and over, active: 0,8 %
- Aged 14 - 24 not active: 7,8 %
- Aged 25 - 64 not active: 7,3 %

eurostat

The population of the Community can be analysed according to activity, and this activity is directly related to age and sex. Thus, the female population has the following characteristics: 26.4 % of women are aged between 25 and 64 and economically active, 24.3 % are aged between 25 and 64 but non-active, and the remainder are young persons under 25 (32.4 %) and retired persons (16.9 %), whether active or non-active.

The distribution is different for the male population. 45.7 % of men are aged between 25 and 64 and active, 7.3 % are aged between 25 and 64 and non-active, 35.1 % are young persons under 25 and 11.9 % are retired persons, whether active or non-active.

EMPLOYMENT AND UNEMPLOYMENT
ACTIVE POPULATION

In 1988 the activity rate for the population aged between 14 and 64 was 64.6% for the Community as a whole. The rate is higher for men (78.5%) than for women (51.0%) and varies from one country to another. For example, it is well below the Community average in Spain (56.5%), Belgium (57.3%), Greece (58.5%), Ireland (58.8%), Italy (58.8%) and Luxembourg (59.1%) but as high as 73.7% in the United Kingdom and 81.4% in Denmark. This latter figure is explained by the very high activity rate for women in Denmark (76.2%), which is without parallel in any other EC Member State.

Women are becoming increasingly involved in economic activity. The increase in the overall activity rate for the population aged between 14 and 64 during the period 1983 to 1988 was due to a rise in the activity rate for women from 46.6% to 51.0%, the rate for men having dropped from 79.1% to 78.5%.

4.6. Activity rate of population aged 14 to 64, by country and by sex — 1988 (%)

	EUR 12	B	DK	D	GR	E	F	IRL	I	L	NL	P	UK
Male	78,5	70,1	86,6	80,4	76,6	75,4	75,6	77,9	76,2	77,7	77,5	79,9	84,8
Female	51,0	44,5	76,2	53,2	41,8	38,1	56,5	39,3	42,0	41,5	49,0	56,0	62,7
Total	64,6	57,3	81,4	66,8	58,5	56,5	66,0	58,8	58,8	59,1	63,4	67,0	73,7

4.7. Active population aged 14 to 64, by country and by sex — 1988 (1 000)

	Male	Female	Total
EUR 12	84 872	56 023	140 895
B	2 364	1 493	3 857
DK	1 519	1 313	2 832
D	17 214	11 340	28 554
GR	2 420	1 422	3 842
E	9 525	4 930	14 455
F	13 404	10 371	23 775
IRL	861	424	1 285
I	14 887	8 453	23 340
L	101	54	155
NL	3 988	2 476	6 464
P	2 614	1 945	4 559
UK	15 975	11 802	27 777

4.8. Changes in activity rate of population aged 14 to 64, by sex — EUR 12

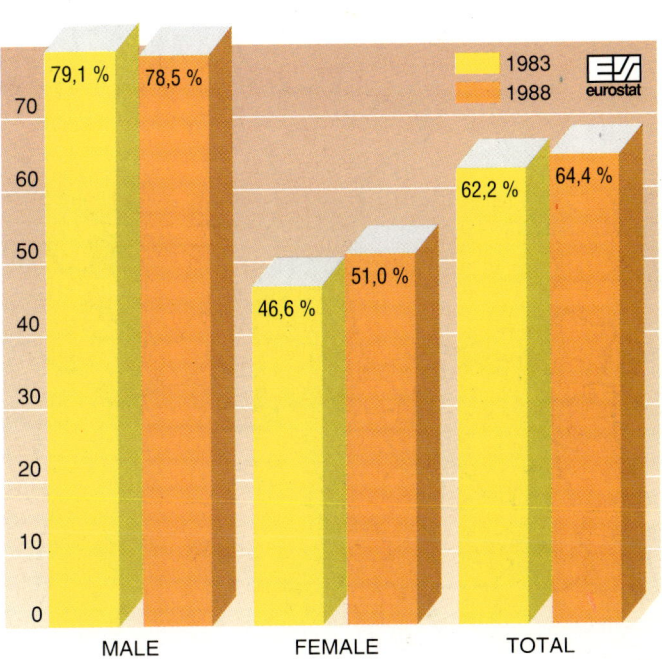

- 1983: Male 79,1%, Female 46,6%, Total 62,2%
- 1988: Male 78,5%, Female 51,0%, Total 64,4%

EMPLOYMENT AND UNEMPLOYMENT
ACTIVITY — REGIONAL DISTRIBUTION

The activity rate varies widely from one region to another, depending partly on the economic situation in each region but also on mentalities and customs. It is below 60% in the Mezzogiorno, most regions of Spain, Greece and Ireland and in Belgium and Luxembourg. In most other regions it lies between 60% and 70%, but in Denmark, most regions of the United Kingdom and in Bavaria it is particularly high (above 70%).

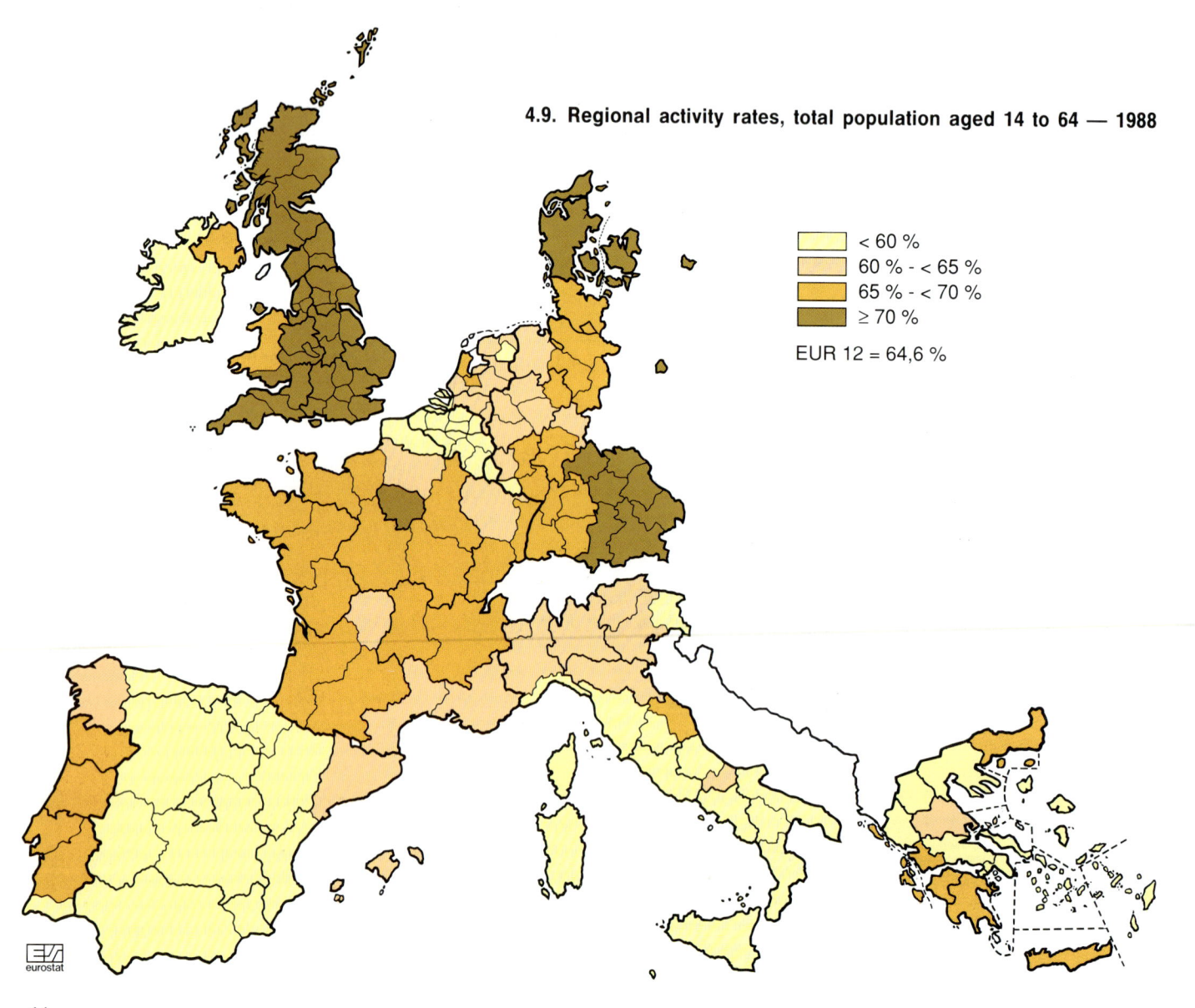

4.9. Regional activity rates, total population aged 14 to 64 — 1988

- < 60 %
- 60 % - < 65 %
- 65 % - < 70 %
- ≥ 70 %

EUR 12 = 64,6 %

EMPLOYMENT AND UNEMPLOYMENT

ACTIVITY REGIONAL DISTRIBUTION

In overall terms, the rate of activity for women shows the same distribution as that for both sexes, but the level is lower (between 40% and 60%). In Spain, southern Italy and the islands, the Greek Islands and Ireland it does not exceed 40%, while in the United Kingdom, Denmark, some regions of the Federal Republic of Germany and certain urban regions (Paris, London, Berlin) it is above 60%. Thus, with a number of slight discrepancies (the Autonomous Community of Valencia, Asturias, etc.), the same north-south disparity applies as in the overall activity rate.

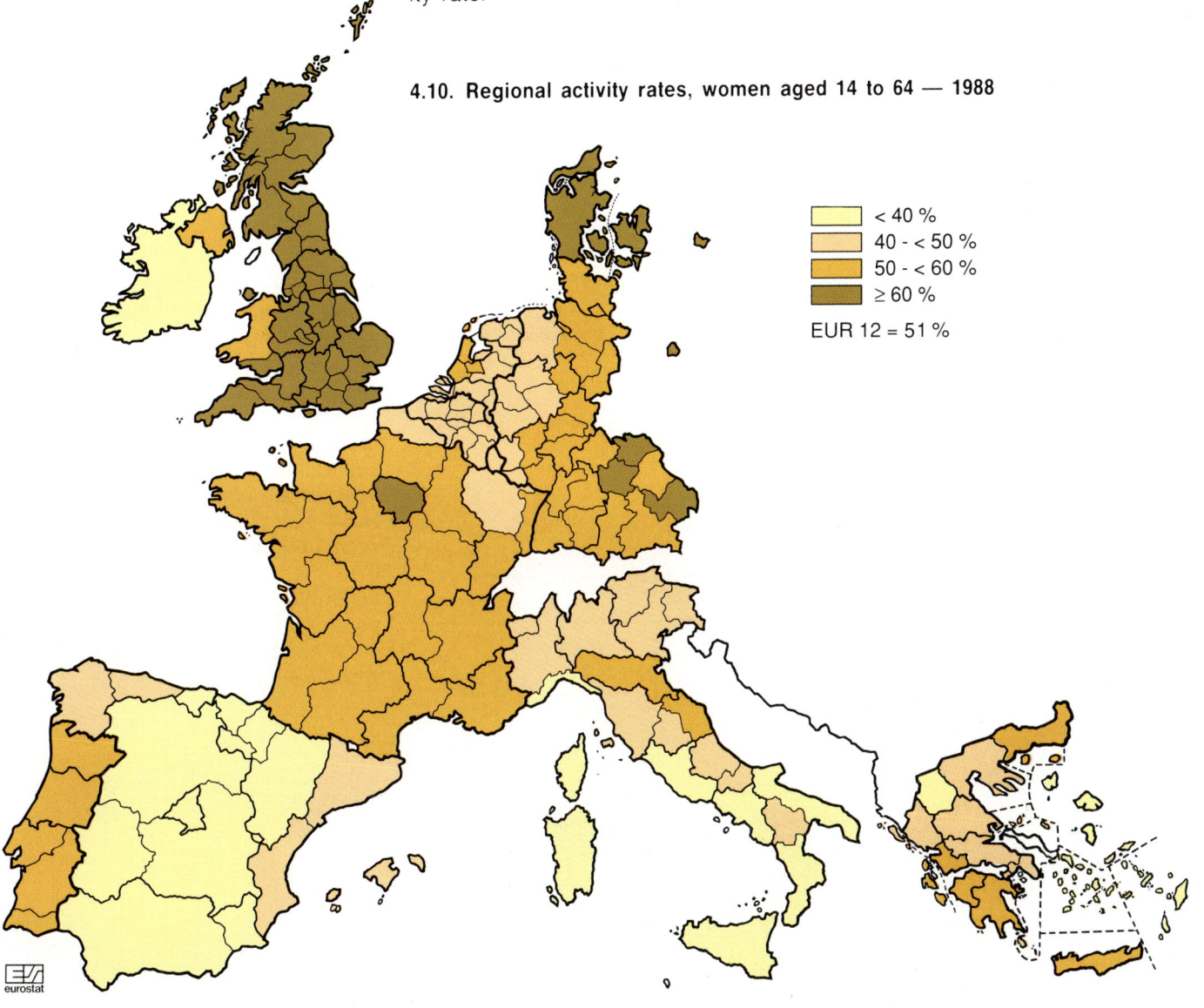

4.10. Regional activity rates, women aged 14 to 64 — 1988

< 40 %
40 - < 50 %
50 - < 60 %
≥ 60 %

EUR 12 = 51 %

EMPLOYMENT AND UNEMPLOYMENT
ACTIVITY AND MARITAL STATUS

4.11. Activity rate, population aged 14 to 64, by marital status and sex — EUR 12 — 1988

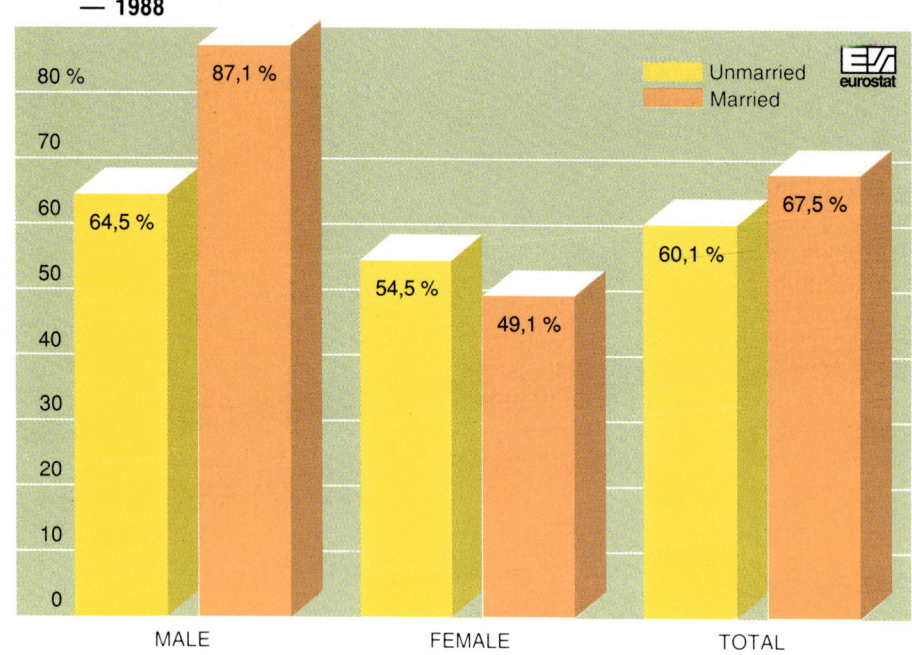

Legend: Unmarried / Married

MALE: Unmarried 64,5 % — Married 87,1 %
FEMALE: Unmarried 54,5 % — Married 49,1 %
TOTAL: Unmarried 60,1 % — Married 67,5 %

4.12. Activity rate, population aged 14 to 64, by marital status, sex and age — EUR 12 — 1988 (%)

	Male		Female		Total	
	Unmarried	Married	Unmarried	Married	Unmarried	Married
14-24 years	52.2	95.3	45.5	58.2	49.1	68.1
25-34 years	89.1	97.9	84.1	59.1	87.2	76.4
35-44 years	90.2	97.9	82.9	58.5	87.5	78.1
45-54 years	82.9	93.1	74.0	48.1	79.2	71.0
55-64 years	52.2	57.1	37.9	23.1	44.6	40.9
Aged 14-24	64.5	87.1	54.5	49.1	60.1	67.5

The activity rate varies according to marital status. For the Community as a whole in 1988, the rate between the ages of 14 and 64 was 60.1 % for single persons and 67.5 % for married persons. However, the gap is greater if the sexes are considered separately. Married women have an activity rate of 49.1 % compared with 54.5 % for single women, this difference perhaps being due to the fact that many mothers with children leave their employment at least temporarily. For married men, on the other hand, the activity rate is 87.1 % and for single men 64.5 %.

EMPLOYMENT AND UNEMPLOYMENT
ACTIVITY AND MARITAL STATUS

The differences are even more marked if age as well as marital status is taken into account. Married men within all age groups have a higher activity rate than single men, while activity rates for women vary more according to age. For example, up to 24 years of age the activity rate for married women is relatively low, although nevertheless higher than for single women (58.2% compared with 45.5%); in the subsequent age groups, on the other hand, married women are far less 'economically active' than single women (59.1% compared with 84.1% between the ages of 25 and 34).

Broadly speaking, the positions described for the Community as a whole hold true for individual Member States, albeit with minor disparities due to each country's specific economic and cultural circumstances.

It is worth noting the high activity rate for married women in Denmark, which up to 54 years of age is higher than that for single women and exceeds 90% between the ages of 25 and 44.

4.13. Activity rate, women, by marital status and age group — EUR 12 — 1988(%)

	Unmarried					Married				
	Aged 14-24	Aged 25-34	Aged 35-44	Aged 45-54	Aged 55-64	Aged 15-24	Aged 25-34	Aged 35-44	Aged 45-54	Aged 55-64
EUR 12	45,5	84,1	82,9	74,0	37,9	58,2	59,1	58,5	48,1	23,1
B	25,9	84,3	79,0	63,5	22,1	72,3	71,9	57,9	33,3	9,6
DK	67,6	84,3	89,1	81,2	48,7	76,4	90,1	90,7	82,0	43,3
D	53,9	84,7	89,9	87,0	43,4	59,7	68,5	57,5	51,5	23,2
GR	30,4	83,1	72,3	49,1	29,5	36,1	50,0	49,3	40,6	29,1
E	40,1	84,4	78,9	67,3	51,6	45,0	46,0	33,6	25,9	16,2
F	35,4	87,8	86,8	82,0	45,3	67,1	68,5	69,1	58,8	25,6
IRL	42,0	87,6	77,1	65,9	40,2	51,4	45,5	29,7	25,6	13,5
I	40,5	78,2	76,9	63,9	22,7	45,6	54,5	49,4	34,8	14,8
L	45,6	87,9	84,6	75,3	49,9	58,9	46,5	39,0	25,1	8,9
NL	46,8	79,9	78,8	62,6	44,8	66,3	72,0	66,2	49,9	30,9
P	52,3	88,6	85,4	76,4	34,8	56,9	50,5	52,4	41,4	14,3
UK	59,8	83,2	80,3	76,3	34,8	62,6	64,5	74,5	69,9	36,8

EMPLOYMENT AND UNEMPLOYMENT
EMPLOYMENT

4.14. Fluctuations in employment according to economic sector — EUR 12

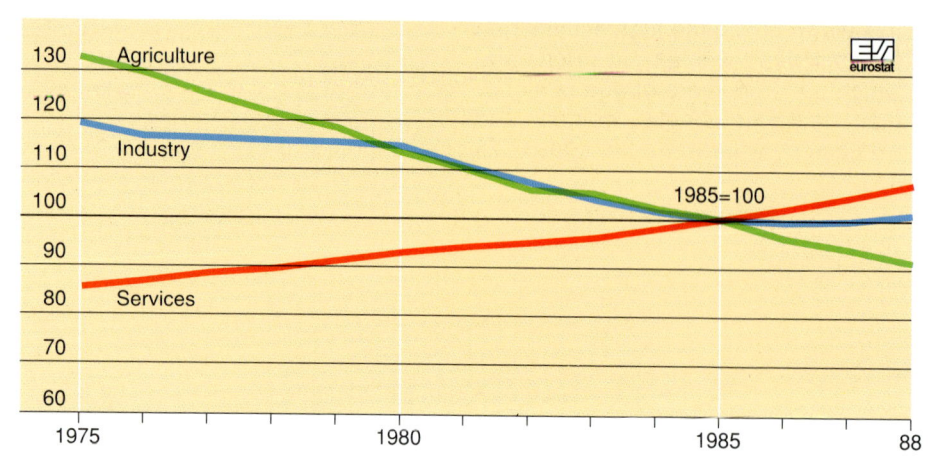

4.15. Share of each economic sector in total employment — 1988

Index	Agriculture (1 000)	%	Industry (1 000)	%	Services (1 000)	%	Total (1 000)	%
EUR 12	9 736	7.6	42 539	33.2	75 844	59.2	128 119 [1]	100.0
B	110	3.2	1 092	31.3	2 281	65.5	3 483	100.0
DK	154	5.8	723	27.1	1 790	67.1	2 667 [1]	100.0
D	1 202	4.5	10 941	40.5	14 856	55.0	26 999	100.0
GR	972	26.6	928	25.4	1 757	48.0	3 657	100.0
E	1 671	14.3	3 813	32.6	6 224	53.1	11 708	100.0
F	1 547	7.2	6 426	30.0	13 436	62.8	21 409 [1]	100.0
IRL	171	15.8	311	28.6	604	55.6	1 086 [1]	100.0
I	2 071	9.8	6 796	32.2	12 233	58.0	2 100	100.0
L	6	3.9	44	29.0	102	67.1	152 [1]	100.0
NL	286	4.8	1 564	26.6	4 041	68.6	5 891	100.0
P	944	21.2	1 540	34.6	1 962	44.2	4 446 [1]	100.0
UK	602	2.4	8 361	32.8	16 558	64.8	25 521 [1]	100.0

[1] The total does not correspond to the overall employment figures because a number of workers have not replied to the question concerning the economic sectors.

In 1988 there were 128.4 million persons employed in the Community, 6.8 million more than in 1983. However, this improvement does not extend to all sectors of the economy. In agriculture, for example, employment continues to decline, and in 1988 a mere 9.7 million persons (7.6% of total employment) were employed in this sector. Growth in employment is most marked in the services sector, which employs 75.8 million persons (59.2% of total employment). Employment in the industrial sector, which experienced a rapid decline from 1980 onwards, has to some extent steadied since 1985, and in 1988 this sector employed 42.5 million persons (33.2% of total employment).

The distribution of employment across the three sectors of the economy varies from one Member State to another. In Greece and Portugal, for example, a large number of persons are still employed in agriculture (26.6% and 21.2% of total employment respectively). In the Federal Republic of Germany industry accounts for 40.5% of total employment, while employment in the services sector is highest in the Netherlands, Luxembourg and Denmark (over 67% of total employment).

4.16. Employment according to economic sector and sex — EUR 12 — 1988

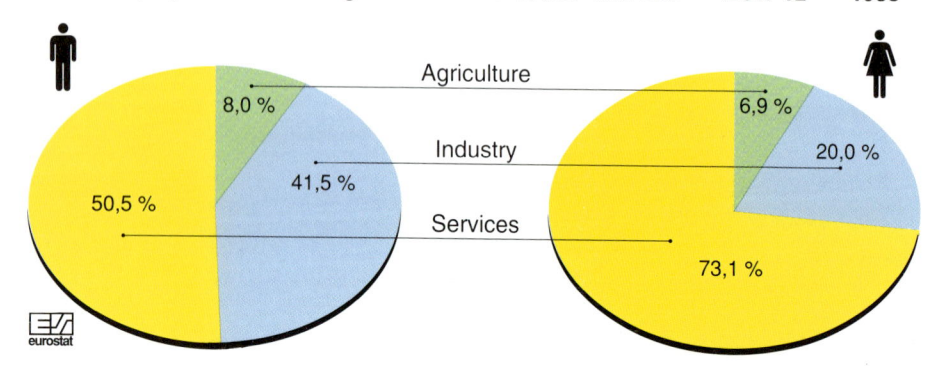

Men: Agriculture 8,0 %; Industry 41,5 %; Services 50,5 %
Women: Agriculture 6,9 %; Industry 20,0 %; Services 73,1 %

EMPLOYMENT AND UNEMPLOYMENT
EMPLOYMENT

In 1988 almost three-quarters (73.1%) of the Community's female labour force was employed in the services sector and one-fifth (20%) in industry. The distribution was different for the male labour force, of which 50.5% was employed in the services sector and 41.5% in industry. Employees accounted for a major share of persons employed, especially in industry (89%) and the services sector (83.3%).

Employees accounted for 79% of male employment and 84% of female employment, with family workers accounting for a substantial share (6.2%) in the latter.

In all the Member States the majority of employees are employed in the services sector and only a small percentage in agriculture (ranging between 0.4% in Belgium and Luxembourg and 6.4% in Spain).

4.17. Employment, by occupational status and economic sector — EUR 12 — 1988

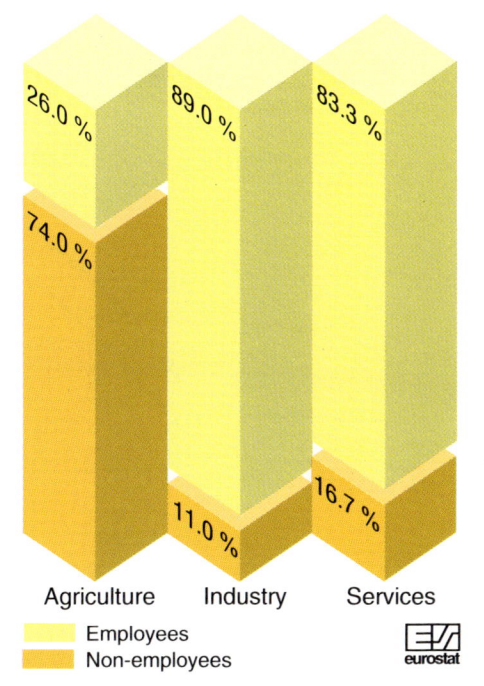

Agriculture: Employees 26.0%, Non-employees 74.0%
Industry: Employees 89.0%, Non-employees 11.0%
Services: Employees 83.3%, Non-employees 16.7%

4.18. Employment, by occupational status and sex — EUR 12 — 1988 (%)

Male			
Self-employed with employees	Wage or salary earner	Family worker	Total
19.5	79.0	1.4	100.0

Female			
Self-employed with employees	Wage or salary earner	Family worker	Total
10.0	83.8	6.2	100.0

Total			
Self-employed with employees	Wage or salary earner	Family worker	Total
15.9	80.8	3.2	100.0

4.19. Percentage of wage or salary earners in each economic activity — 1988

	Agriculture	Industry	Services	Total
EUR 12	2,4	36,5	61,0	100,0
B	0,4	34,7	64,9	100,0
DK	2,2	28,1	69,7	100,0
D	1,2	43,5	55,4	100,0
GR	1,9	36,4	61,6	100,0
E	6,4	38,9	54,7	100,0
F	1,4	32,4	66,2	100,0
IRL	2,8	34,4	62,8	100,0
I	5,3	37,7	57,0	100,0
L	0,4	31,0	68,4	100,0
NL	1,8	28,6	69,6	100,0
P	5,1	63,8	51,0	100,0
UK	1,3	32,9	65,7	100,0

EMPLOYMENT AND UNEMPLOYMENT

UNEMPLOYMENT RATE

4.20. Fluctuations in unemployment according to sex — EUR 12 (%)

In 1977 there were five million unemployed in the Community as a whole, while in 1986 the figure was 14.9 million and in 1989 12.7 million. Although falling, unemployment is still one of the most worrying features of the labour market, accounting for 9 % of the working population and affecting more women (11.9 %) than men (7.0 %).

Unemployment rates are highest in Ireland and Spain (17.0 %). In the Federal Republic of Germany the rate has fallen to 5.5 %, in Portugal to 5.0 % and in Luxembourg to 1.8 %. Unemployment among women is highest in Spain (25.2 %), Ireland (18.8 %) and Italy (17.4 %), and among men in Ireland (16.1 %) and Spain (12.7 %). 17.4 % of young persons under 25 are unemployed in the Community; the corresponding rate in Spain is 33.8 %, in Italy 32.1 %, in Greece 26.1 % and in Ireland 23.6 %. The proportion of young women unemployed in these same countries is very high (42.1 % in Spain, 38.8 % in Italy and 36.2 % in Greece).

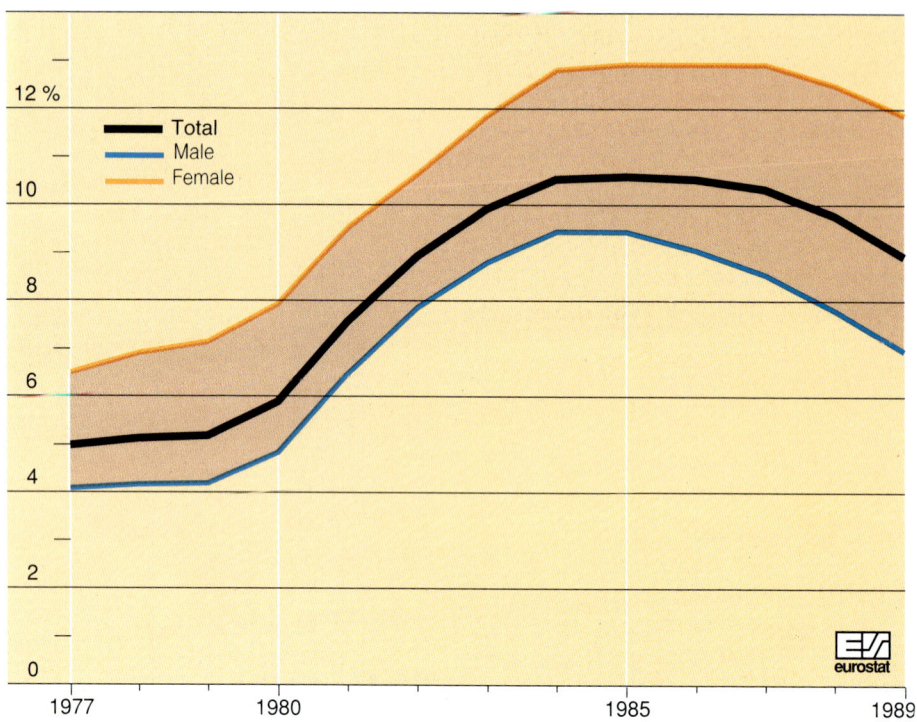

4.21. Percentage unemployment rates by sex and age band — EUR 12 — 1989

	\multicolumn{3}{c}{Total}	\multicolumn{3}{c}{Under-25s}	\multicolumn{3}{c}{Over-25s}
	M	F	T	M	F	T	M	F	T
EUR 12	7,0	11,9	9,0	14,9	20,1	17,4	9,6	5,5	7,1
B	5,4	13,3	8,5	12,7	21,8	17,0	5,5	12,9	7,2
DK	5,8	7,8	6,7	7,9	9,2	8,5	5,0	7,2	6,2
D	4,4	7,3	5,5	4,5	5,9	5,1	4,3	7,7	5,6
GR	4,9	12,7	7,8	17,2	36,2	26,1	3,4	7,3	5,0
E	12,7	25,2	17,0	27,0	42,1	33,8	9,7	12,9	12,7
F	7,1	12,7	9,5	16,1	24,1	20,1	5,7	10,4	7,8
IRL	16,1	18,8	17,0	24,9	21,9	23,6	14,1	17,3	15,0
I	7,4	17,4	11,1	26,3	38,8	32,1	4,2	11,1	6,6
L	1,4	2,7	1,8	3,6	3,9	3,7	1,0	2,3	1,4
NL	6,8	13,2	9,3	12,9	14,5	13,7	5,6	12,8	8,1
P	3,4	7,2	5,0	8,5	15,4	11,6	2,1	4,9	3,3
UK	7,1	6,1	6,7	11,2	8,3	9,9	6,0	5,5	5,8

50

EMPLOYMENT AND UNEMPLOYMENT
UNEMPLOYMENT RATE

4.22. Numbers employed, by sex — EUR 12 — 1989 (1 000)

	Male	Female	Total
EUR 12	5 998	6 701	12 699
B	130	202	332
DK	90	103	193
D	751	832	1 583
GR	122	182	303
E	1 211	1 278	2 488
F	956	1 334	2 290
IRL	142	81	224
I	1 101	1 494	2 596
L	1	1	3
NL	273	332	604
P	93	148	241
UK	1 128	713	1 842

4.23. Main types of unemployed seeking work, by sex — EUR 12 — 1988 (%)

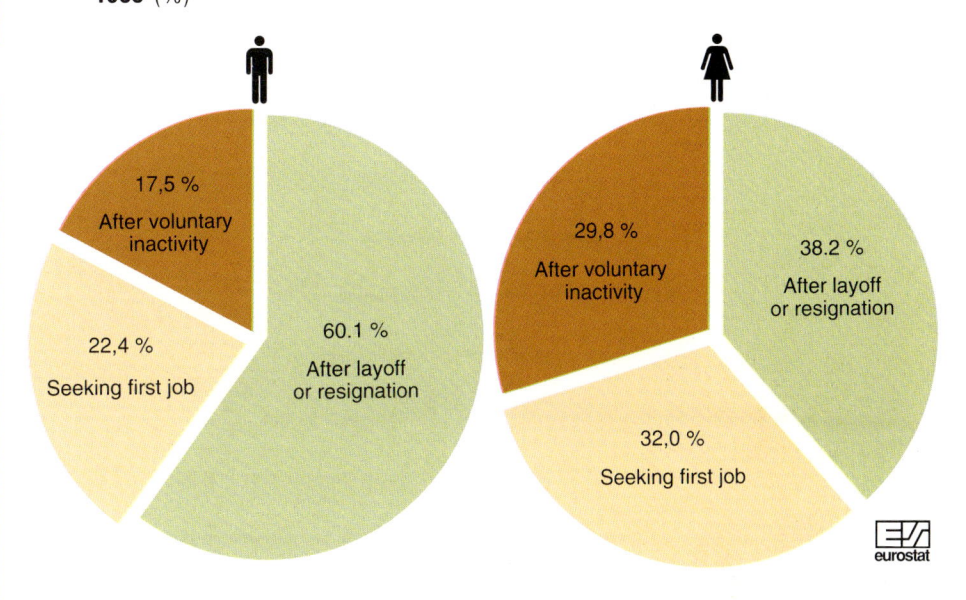

Male:
- 17,5 % After voluntary inactivity
- 22,4 % Seeking first job
- 60,1 % After layoff or resignation

Female:
- 29,8 % After voluntary inactivity
- 32,0 % Seeking first job
- 38.2 % After layoff or resignation

4.24. Regional unemployment rates in the Community — 1988 (%)

Legend:
- < 6 %
- 6 - 9 %
- 9 - 12 %
- 12 - 15 %
- ≥ 15 %

EUR 12 = 9,0 %

Over one-quarter of all persons seeking employment are first-time jobseekers, i.e. young persons seeking to begin their working life after leaving school, further or higher education or an apprenticeship.

Unemployment rates tend to be high at the Community's northern and southern extremities (Ireland and Northern Ireland on the one hand and certain regions of Spain and the Mezzogiorno on the other), in the north of France and the south-east of Belgium, i.e. chiefly in underdeveloped regions or regions whose traditional industries are in decline (e.g. steel-producing regions etc.).

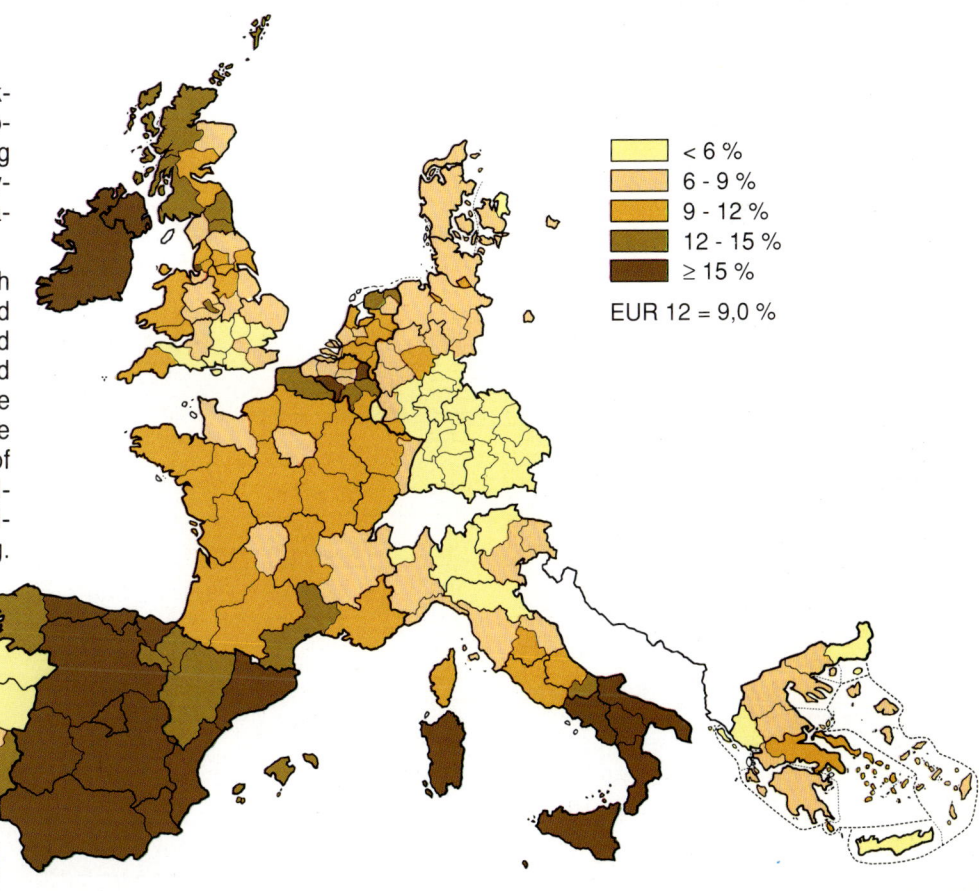

EMPLOYMENT AND UNEMPLOYMENT
STRUCTURE OF UNEMPLOYMENT

4.25. Age structure of unemployment — EUR 12 — 1988

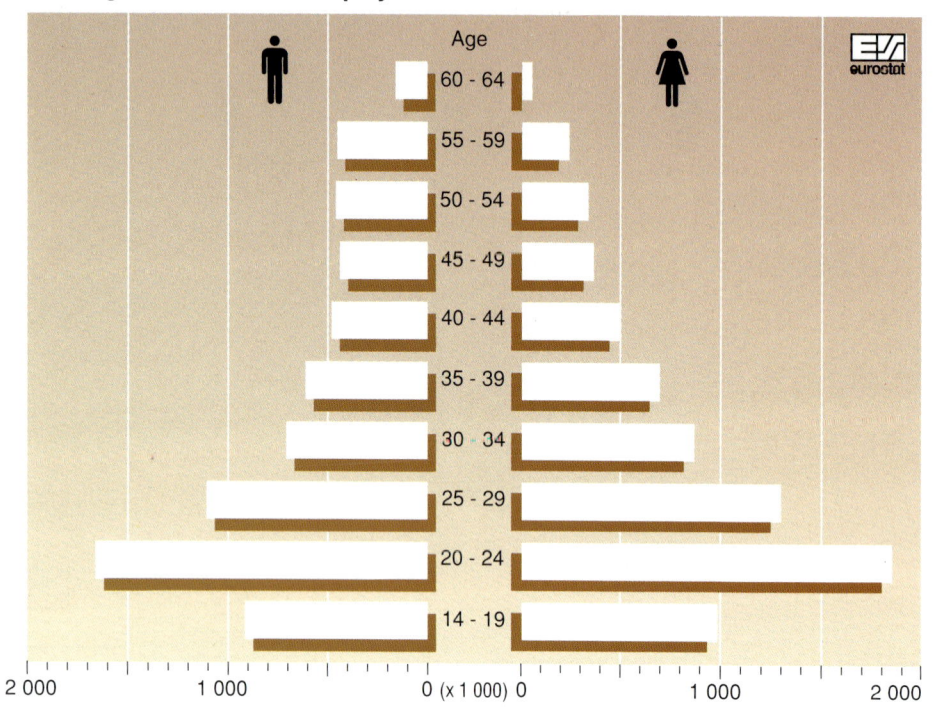

Generally speaking, those hardest hit by unemployment are young persons between the ages of 20 and 34. In 1988 the average age of unemployed persons throughout the Community was 31.7. This average is lowest in the southern countries (i.e. 26.8 in Italy, 28.4 in Portugal, 29.4 in Greece and 29.6 in Spain) and highest (37.2) in the Federal Republic of Germany.

Unemployed women are on average younger (30.5) than unemployed men (32.9). This applies to all Community countries except Italy, the Netherlands and Luxembourg, where the average age is the same for both sexes.

4.26. Average age of the unemployed and of the active population, by sex — 1988

	Unemployed		
	Male	Female	Total
EUR 12	32,9	30,5	31,7
B	35,3	31,4	33,0
DK	34,2	33,8	34,0
D	38,1	36,3	37,2
GR	31,5	28,1	29,4
E	31,6	27,4	29,6
F	33,6	32,3	32,9
IRL	33,4	30,6	32,4
I	26,8	26,8	26,8
L	29,0	29,1	29,1
NL	31,9	31,9	31,9
P	30,0	27,3	28,4
UK	35,0	32,5	34,0

	Active population		
	Male	Female	Total
EUR 12	38,4	36,1	37,5
B	37,9	34,5	36,6
DK	37,9	36,6	37,3
D	38,9	36,7	38,0
GR	41,2	38,6	40,3
E	38,5	34,4	37,1
F	37,9	36,8	37,4
IRL	37,8	32,5	36,1
I	39,2	35,4	37,8
L	37,4	33,5	36,1
NL	36,8	33,6	35,6
P	39,0	37,3	38,3
UK	37,5	36,5	37,1

EMPLOYMENT AND UNEMPLOYMENT
STRUCTURE OF UNEMPLOYMENT

For EUR 12 as a whole, the average age of unemployed persons (32.9 for men and 30.5 for women, giving an overall average of 31.7) is lower than the average age of the labour force, which is 37.5 (38.4 for men and 36.1 for women).

The map shows clearly the scale of youth unemployment in Spain, southern Italy and the Islands, Greece, Ireland, northern, western and southern France and southern and eastern Belgium.

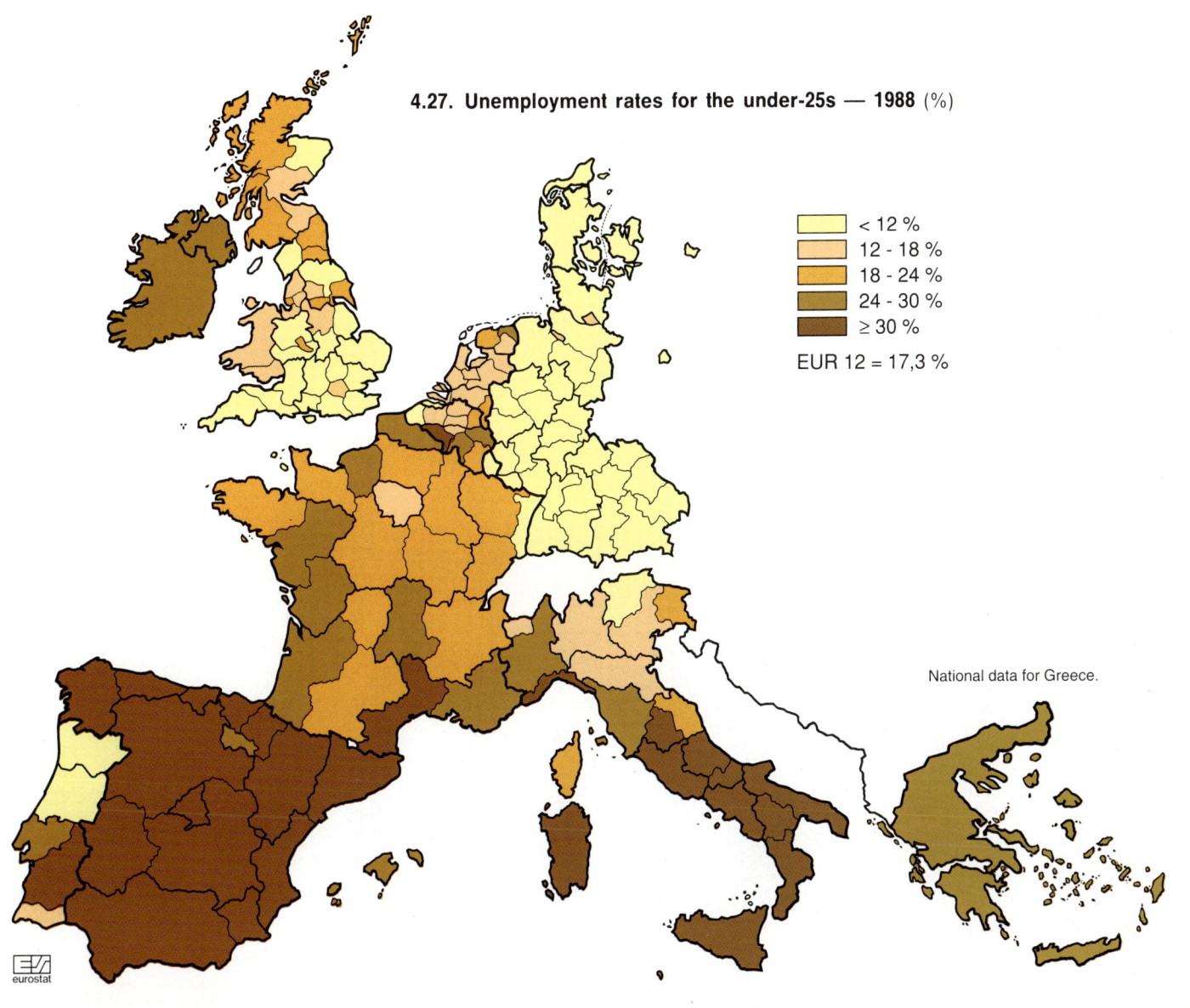

4.27. Unemployment rates for the under-25s — 1988 (%)

- < 12 %
- 12 - 18 %
- 18 - 24 %
- 24 - 30 %
- ≥ 30 %

EUR 12 = 17,3 %

National data for Greece.

EMPLOYMENT AND UNEMPLOYMENT
LONG-TERM UNEMPLOYMENT

4.28. Fluctuations in long-term unemployment as % of total unemployment, by sex

	1983			1988		
	Male	Female	Total	Male	Female	Total
EUR 12	:	:	:	51,7	52,5	52,1
B	57,7	69,0	64,1	73,0	77,5	75,6
DK	27,3	37,4	32,2	20,6	25,0	22,9
D	39,7	36,8	38,4	46,7	44,6	45,6
GR	22,2	42,0	32,3	35,3	53,0	45,9
E	:	:	:	50,4	64,9	57,4
F	36,4	42,2	39,6	42,0	46,7	44,6
IRL	40,8	24,2	35,2	67,6	54,9	63,3
I	52,1	56,6	54,6	67,2	67,8	67,5
L	34,8	30,8	32,7	35,5	27,1	31,1
NL	46,2	48,0	46,9	51,7	42,3	46,8
P	:	:	:	42,2	50,8	47,2
UK	50,4	34,6	44,8	51,7	28,4	42,2

The persisting high level of unemployment in the Community brings with it a serious social problem, i.e. that of long-term unemployment. A growing number of unemployed persons now find themselves in a precarious situation and experience great difficulty in re-entering the employment market.

In 1988 over half (52.1%) of all unemployed persons had been unemployed for more than 12 months, this figure applying to both men (51.7%) and women (52.5%) alike. The proportion of long-term unemployed was particularly high in Belgium (75.6%), Italy (67.5%) and Ireland (63.3%). Between 1983 and 1988 the number of long-term unemployed rose in most Member States, Denmark being the only country to record a decline (from 32.2% to 22.9%). In Luxembourg, the United Kingdom and the Netherlands the number of long-term unemployed remained fairly stable.

In 1988, 49.1% of the long-term unemployed were men and 50.9% women. In Ireland the proportion of women was 70.4% and in Greece 69.1%. Among the long-term unemployed, men outnumbered women only in the Netherlands and the United Kingdom (53% and 72.6% respectively).

4.29. Long-term unemployed, by sex — 1988 (%)

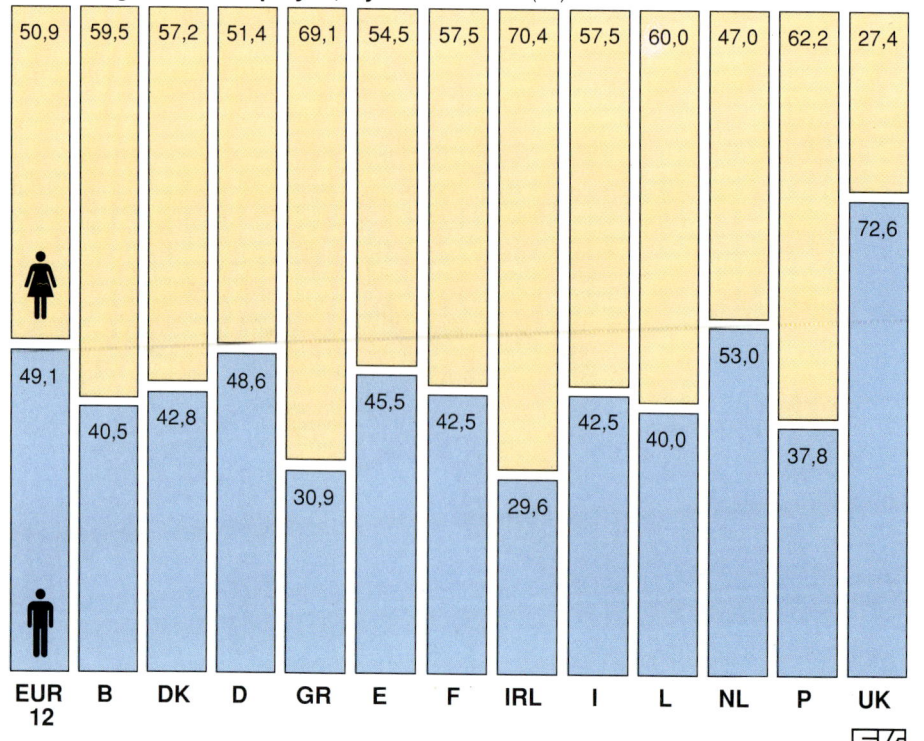

	EUR 12	B	DK	D	GR	E	F	IRL	I	L	NL	P	UK
Female	50,9	59,5	57,2	51,4	69,1	54,5	57,5	70,4	57,5	60,0	47,0	62,2	27,4
Male	49,1	40,5	42,8	48,6	30,9	45,5	42,5	29,6	42,5	40,0	53,0	37,8	72,6

EMPLOYMENT AND UNEMPLOYMENT
UNEMPLOYMENT AND HOUSEHOLDS

In 1988, 33.7% of unemployed persons in the Community were heads of household, 22.9% spouses of heads of household and 38.9% children of heads of household. These percentages varied from one country to another. In Italy, Portugal, Spain and Greece, for example, the percentage of unemployed heads of household was lowest (less than 25%), while the children of heads of household accounted for over 50% of all unemployed persons. In Denmark, on the other hand, unemployed heads of household accounted for 81.9% of all unemployed persons, while the children of heads of household accounted for a mere 3.9%.

In the same year approximately 10% of households in the Community as a whole contained at least one unemployed person, while in 4% of such households the entire family was unemployed. These rates were higher in Ireland (18.1% and 9.1% respectively) and Spain (20.4% and 6.6% respectively), but very low in Luxembourg (where 2.1% of households contained at least one unemployed person), Denmark (5.9%) and the Federal Republic of Germany (6.3%).

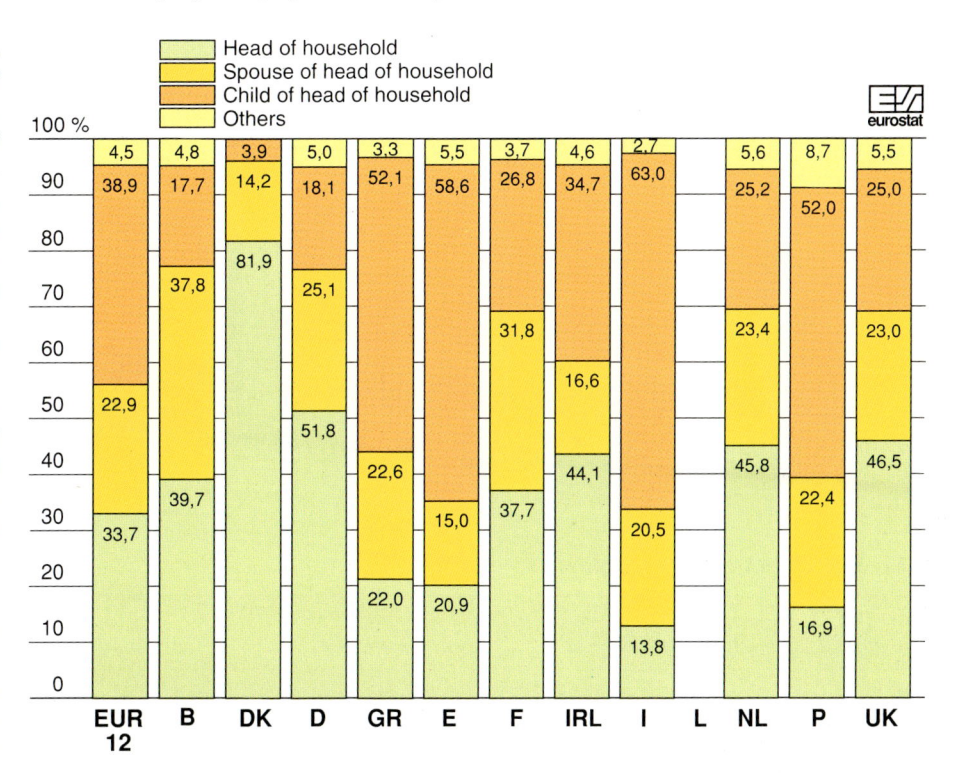

4.30. Unemployment, by relationship to head of household — 1988 (%)

Legend:
- Head of household
- Spouse of head of household
- Child of head of household
- Others

	EUR 12	B	DK	D	GR	E	F	IRL	I	L	NL	P	UK
Others	4,5	4,8	3,9	5,0	3,3	5,5	3,7	4,6	2,7		5,6	8,7	5,5
Child	38,9	17,7	14,2	18,1	52,1	58,6	26,8	34,7	63,0		25,2	52,0	25,0
Spouse	22,9	37,8		25,1	22,6	15,0	31,8	16,6	20,5		23,4	22,4	23,0
Head	33,7	39,7	81,9	51,8	22,0	20,9	37,7	44,1	13,8		45,8	16,9	46,5

4.31. Household membership, according to the household's relationship with the employment market — 1988 (%)

	Household with no unemployed	Household with one or more unemployed	
		One other person in employment	No one in employment
EUR 12	89,9	6,1	4,0
B	90,6	4,9	4,4
DK	94,1	1,7	4,2
D	93,7	3,1	3,2
GR	91,8	5,5	2,7
E	79,6	13,8	6,6
F	89,6	6,5	3,9
IRL	81,9	9,0	9,1
I	89,7	7,5	2,8
L	97,9	1,5	0,6
NL	90,1	5,2	4,7
P	92,1	6,5	1,5
UK	90,1	5,3	4,7

EMPLOYMENT AND UNEMPLOYMENT
FOREIGN WORKERS

4.32. Employment by occupational status and nationality — EUR 12 — 1988 (%)

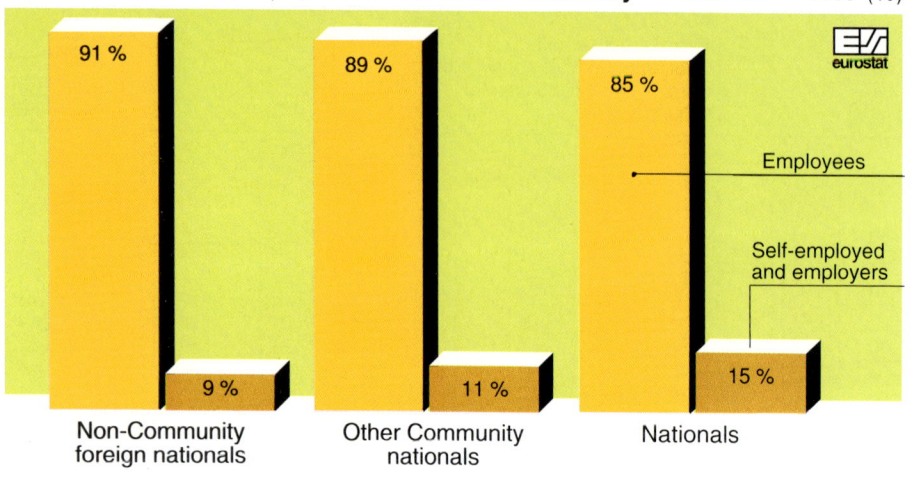

- Non-Community foreign nationals: 91% Employees, 9% Self-employed and employers
- Other Community nationals: 89% Employees, 11% Self-employed and employers
- Nationals: 85% Employees, 15% Self-employed and employers

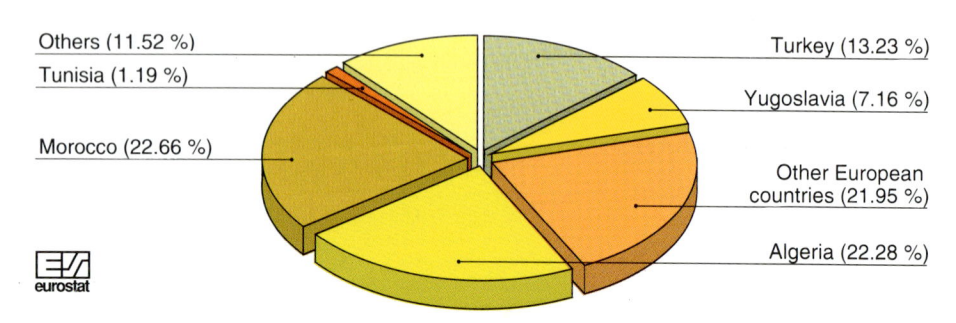

The occupational status of most foreign workers resident in Community countries is that of employee; this status is shared by proportionately more foreign workers than Community nationals (i.e. Community citizens employed in their own country): 91% for workers from non-Community countries and 89% for 'foreign' workers from Community Member States, compared with 85% for Community 'nationals'.

Foreign employees are largely concentrated in three countries, i.e. the Federal Republic of Germany (1 557 000), France (1 131 000) and the United Kingdom (821 000).

In Luxembourg and Belgium the majority of foreign employees are from Community countries (61 000 out of 64 000 and 130 000 out of 177 000 respectively). In the Federal Republic of Germany and the United Kingdom, on the other hand, foreign employees from non-Community countries outnumber those from Community countries (1 074 000 compared with 484 000 in the Federal Republic of Germany, and 423 000 compared with 398 000 in the United Kingdom). In France the two categories of foreign employees are evenly balanced.

While a substantial percentage of employees from non-Community countries are from countries in Europe, e.g. Turkey (13.2%), Yugoslavia (7.2%) and other European countries (21.9%), a high proportion (46.1%) are from the Maghreb countries.

4.33. Number of foreign employees — 1988 (1 000)

Country of residence	Total of foreign employees	Non-Community	Community
B	176.6	46.8	129.8
DK	47.1	32.3	14.0
D	1 557.1	1 073.6	483.5
GR	24.9	18.3	6.6
E	:	:	:
F	1 130.7	561.7	569.0
IRL	19.9	3.7	16.0
I	:	:	:
L	64.1	3.1	60.7
NL	176.0	91.0	85.0
P	35.2	25.5	9.7
UK	820.9	422.6	398.2

4.34. Foreign employees from non-Community countries — EUR 12 — 1988

- Others (11.52%)
- Tunisia (1.19%)
- Morocco (22.66%)
- Turkey (13.23%)
- Yugoslavia (7.16%)
- Other European countries (21.95%)
- Algeria (22.28%)

EMPLOYMENT AND UNEMPLOYMENT
FOREIGN WORKERS

Generally speaking, foreign employees account for only a small percentage of the total number of employees in the various Member States, the most notable exception being Luxembourg, where foreign employees account for 33.2% of all employees. In the Federal Republic of Germany the proportion is 7.7% and in Belgium and France 6.4%.

Very few foreign workers from non-Community countries are employed in agriculture (1.1% of women and 2% of men), whereas the share of 'nationals' in this sector varies between 6.6% and 8% for both sexes.

Examination of the breakdown by sex shows that there is a higher concentration of male foreign workers than male 'nationals' in industry (58.9% compared with 41.5%). On the other hand, the distribution of female foreign workers by economic sector is comparable to that of female 'nationals', i.e. they are employed chiefly in the services sector in a breakdown of 70.7% from non-Community countries and 73.0% from Community countries, compared with 74.3% 'nationals'.

4.35. Employees by nationality — 1988 (%)

Country of residence	Foreign nationals Non-Community	Community	Nationals	Total
B	1.6	4.8	93.6	100
DK	0.9	0.5	98.6	100
D	5.0	2.7	92.3	100
GR	0.7	0.2	99.1	100
E	0.1	0.1	99.8	100
F	3.3	3.1	93.6	100
IRL	0.5	2.2	97.3	100
I	:	:	:	100
L	2.2	31.0	66.8	100
NL	1.6	1.5	96.9	100
P	0.5	0.1	99.4	100
UK	2.6	1.6	95.8	100

4.36. Employment by sector of economic activity, sex and nationality — EUR 12 — 1988 (%)

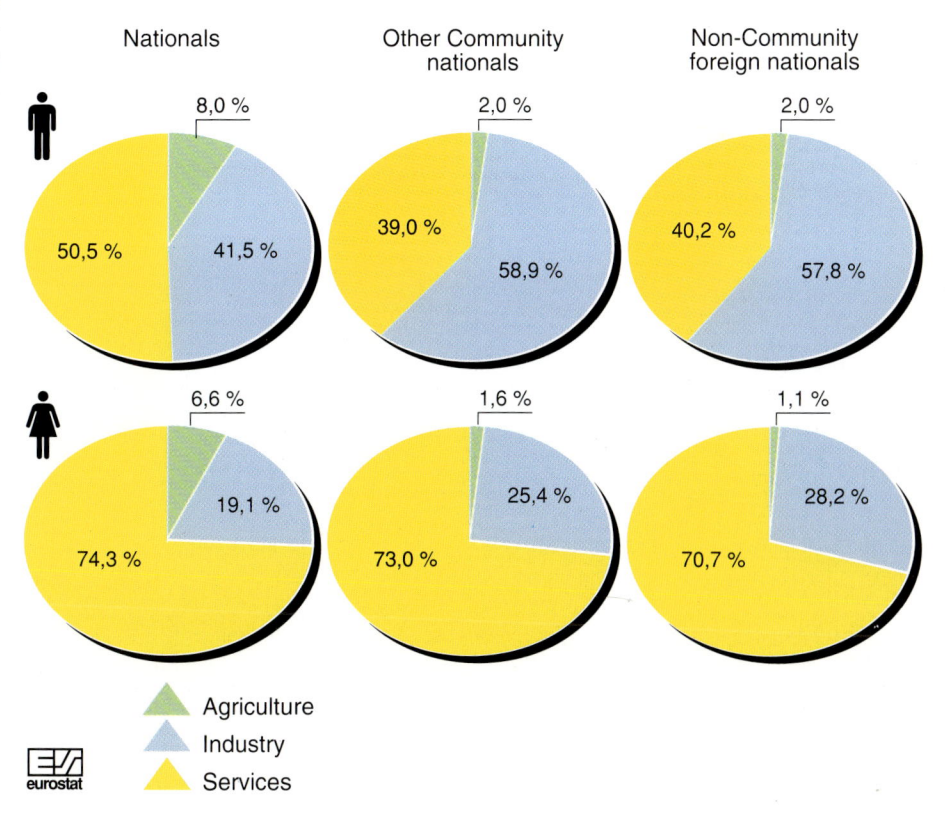

Men:
- Nationals: Agriculture 8.0%, Industry 41.5%, Services 50.5%
- Other Community nationals: Agriculture 2.0%, Industry 58.9%, Services 39.0%
- Non-Community foreign nationals: Agriculture 2.0%, Industry 57.8%, Services 40.2%

Women:
- Nationals: Agriculture 6.6%, Industry 19.1%, Services 74.3%
- Other Community nationals: Agriculture 1.6%, Industry 25.4%, Services 73.0%
- Non-Community foreign nationals: Agriculture 1.1%, Industry 28.2%, Services 70.7%

▲ Agriculture
▲ Industry
● Services

eurostat

EMPLOYMENT AND UNEMPLOYMENT

FOR FURTHER INFORMATION

Definitions

LFS: Community labour force survey. This survey is conducted once a year in spring. The new version of the LFS, in force since 1983, represents a major source of statistics on the Community's labour force. The definitions used are common to all the Member States and are based on the international recommendations of the ILO. The survey covers the whole of the population resident in private households but excludes persons living in collective households, such as homes, boarding schools, hospitals, religious institutions, etc.

The active population (or labour force): this comprises all persons in employment and unemployed persons.

The non-active population: this comprises all persons classified neither as in employment nor as unemployed.

Family workers: these are persons who assist on a regular basis, without direct remuneration, in the running of farms or businesses.

Unemployed persons: these are persons aged 14 or over who are without work, actively seeking work and currently available for work.

The activity rate: this represents the labour force as a percentage of the population of working age living in private households. The figures given here relate principally to the population aged between 14 and 64.

The unemployment rate: this represents the number of unemployed persons as a percentage of the labour force.

Employment: this term covers all persons in gainful employment or self-employed during the reference period. It also covers family workers.

Long-term unemployment: this term is used to describe persons unemployed for more than 12 months.

References

Eurostat
– Labour force survey results, 1988

Eurostat databank
– Cronos
– Regio

WORKING CONDITIONS

In 1988 the average working week in the EC for persons employed full-time was 42.5 hours (43.4 hours for men and 40.5 hours for women) (5.2) (5.5).

People employed part-time worked on average 19.4 hours per week; in agriculture this figure was 22.5 hours, in industry 20.7 hours and in the services sector 18.9 hours (5.2).

Those employed in agriculture worked an average of 43.6 hours per week in 1988, compared with 40.9 hours in industry and 40.4 hours in the services sector (5.4).

Part-time work increased in the EC between 1983 and 1988, when 13.2 % of employed persons worked part-time. More women than men work part-time (28.1 % of women in work compared with 3.9 % of men). The highest proportions of women working part-time are in the Netherlands, the United Kingdom and Denmark (between 57.7 % and 41.5 %) (5.6) (5.7).

In 1988, 9.6 % of employed persons in the EC had a temporary contract; most of them were men (54.7 %) and over half (51.2 %) were young people under 25 (5.13) (5.14) (5.15).

The most frequent cause of hours lost through absence from work is annual leave and public holidays (43.7 % of hours lost); sickness and accidents (24.3 %) take second place (5.17).

5.1. Employees with a temporary contract as % of total employees — 1988

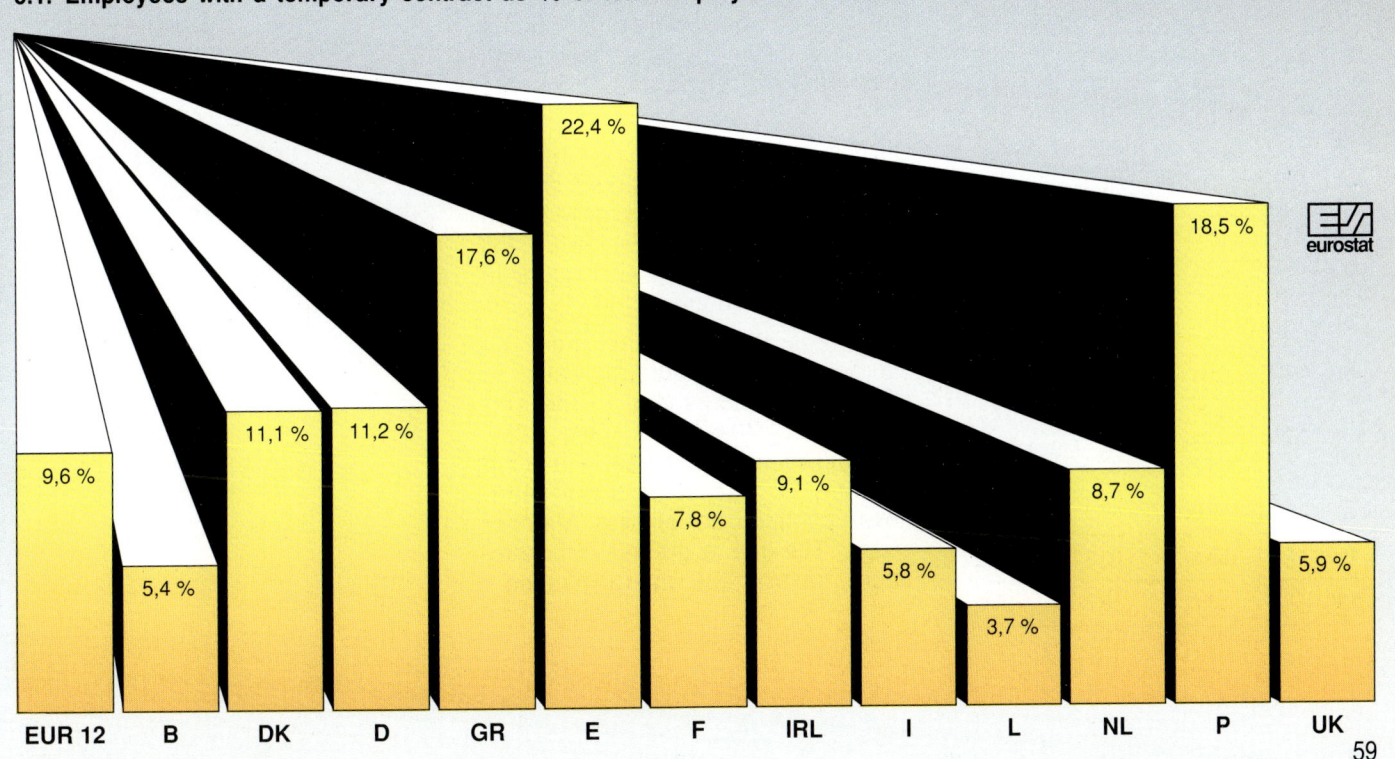

EUR 12	B	DK	D	GR	E	F	IRL	I	L	NL	P	UK
9,6 %	5,4 %	11,1 %	11,2 %	17,6 %	22,4 %	7,8 %	9,1 %	5,8 %	3,7 %	8,7 %	18,5 %	5,9 %

WORKING CONDITIONS
WORKING HOURS

5.2. Hours usually worked per week, 1988 — EUR 12

	Part-time	Full-time
Self-employed	18.4	50.8
Employees	19.4	40.7
Unpaid family workers	20.3	48.4
Agriculture	22.5	50.9
Industry	20.7	41.6
Services	18.9	42.0
Men	19.7	43.4
Women	19.4	40.5
Total	19.4	42.5

5.3. Hours usually worked per week by full-time self-employed persons, 1988

	Men	Women	Total
EUR 12	51.5	48.2	50.8
B	56.7	51.1	55.2
DK	54.1	49.7	53.5
D	56.5	51.9	55.6
GR	51.0	46.7	50.3
E	47.5	45.3	47.0
F	56.9	51.6	55.7
IRL	61.4	52.6	60.5
I	46.1	43.6	45.6
L	55.2	53.5	54.8
NL	59.0	52.0	58.1
P	52.1	53.2	52.6
UK	53.7	50.7	53.2

Data on weekly working hours and the distinction between part-time and full-time workers can be obtained from the Community labour force survey.

In 1988 the average number of hours worked part-time per week in the EC was 19.4 hours usually worked, which applied almost equally to men and women. Longer hours were worked in agriculture (22.5 hours) than in industry (20.7 hours) or the services sector (18.9 hours).

For self-employed persons working part-time, the average number of hours worked per week was less (18.4 hours) than for employed persons (19.4 hours) and unpaid family workers (20.3 hours).

The average number of hours worked per week by persons employed full-time was 42.5 for the EC as a whole; it was a little less for women than for men (40.5 compared with 43.4).

The longest average full-time working week is in agriculture: 50.9 hours; this compares with 42 hours in the services sector and 41.6 hours in industry.

Self-employed persons working full-time worked an average of 50.8 hours per week in the EC as a whole, with 60.5 hours in Ireland and 45.6 hours in Italy.

On the other hand, in all the EC countries employees worked shorter hours than the self-employed: an average of 40.7 hours in the EC (38 hours in Belgium and 43.6 hours in the United Kingdom).

Employees in agriculture work an average of 43.6 hours a week, in industry 40.9 hours and in the services sector 40.4 hours. This difference between the three sectors of the economy is, with some small variations, common to all the Member States. The gap is greater in Luxembourg, for example, than in France.

On the whole, women, whether employees or self-employed, worked shorter hours than men in 1988: 39.1 hours a week compared with 41.5 hours for employees and 48.2 hours compared with 51.5 hours for the self-employed.

These shorter working hours for women apply to all three economic sectors and to all the Member States. The only exception is the Federal Republic of Germany, where in the agricultural sector women worked slightly longer hours than men: 44.6 hours compared with 43.7 hours a week.

Similarly, in all age groups the number of hours per week usually worked by women is, throughout the EC, slightly less than that worked by men.

WORKING CONDITIONS
PART-TIME WORK

5.4. Hours usually worked per week by full-time employees — 1988

	Agriculture			Industry			Services			Total		
	Men	Women	Total	Men	Women	Total	Men	Women	Total	Men	Women	Total
EUR 12	44,3	41,0	43,6	41,2	39,7	40,9	41,6	38,2	40,4	41,5	39,1	40,7
B	40,4	39,0	40,3	38,9	38,3	38,8	38,1	36,4	37,5	38,5	36,8	38,0
DK	44,7	39,8	43,9	39,7	33,0	39,5	40,5	39,1	39,8	40,2	39,1	39,8
D	43,7	44,6	43,9	39,7	39,3	39,6	41,7	40,5	41,2	40,7	40,2	40,5
GR	47,1	44,6	46,6	41,1	40,7	41,0	40,9	38,0	39,8	41,1	38,9	40,4
E	44,5	40,3	44,0	40,5	40,2	40,5	41,4	39,8	40,8	41,2	39,9	40,9
F	43,0	39,7	42,5	40,3	39,3	40,0	40,9	38,6	39,8	40,7	38,8	39,9
IRL	49,5	43,9	49,1	41,2	39,5	40,8	41,4	38,1	39,9	41,7	38,5	40,5
I	41,3	37,7	40,3	40,6	39,7	40,4	38,7	35,2	37,3	39,7	36,5	38,6
L	50,7	41,0	49,4	40,4	39,4	40,3	40,2	38,4	39,5	40,4	38,5	39,8
NL	42,1	39,7	41,9	38,9	38,2	38,9	39,7	38,4	39,3	39,5	38,4	39,2
P	49,4	45,5	48,2	44,0	43,2	43,7	42,0	38,6	40,4	43,4	40,5	42,3
UK	49,9	44,5	49,0	45,2	40,0	44,1	45,5	40,0	43,2	45,4	40,0	43,6

5.5. Hours usually worked per week full-time by age group and sex — EUR 12 — 1988

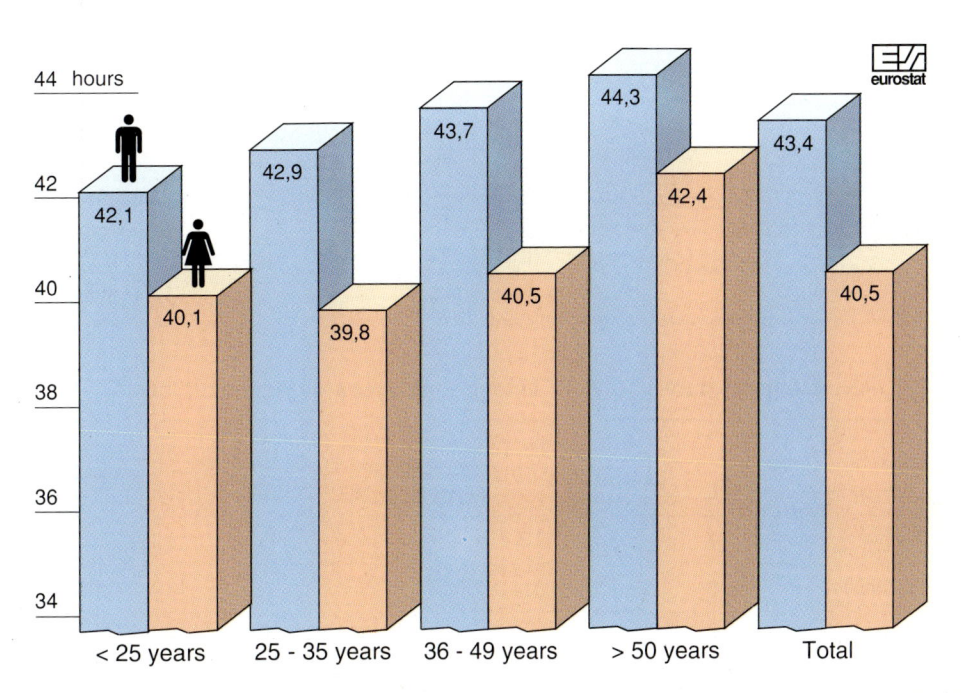

Age group	Men	Women
< 25 years	42,1	40,1
25 - 35 years	42,9	39,8
36 - 49 years	43,7	40,5
> 50 years	44,3	42,4
Total	43,4	40,5

WORKING CONDITIONS
PART-TIME WORK

5.6. Part-time work as % of total employment

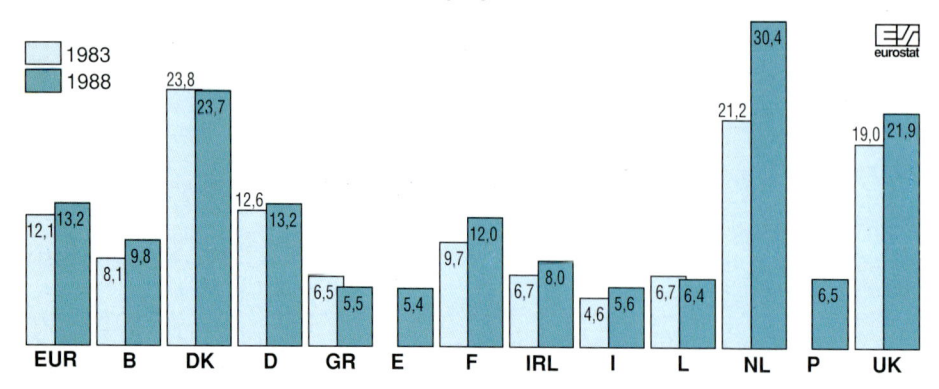

	1983	1988
EUR	12,1	13,2
B	8,1	9,8
DK	23,8	23,7
D	12,6	13,2
GR	6,5	5,5
E		5,4
F	9,7	12,0
IRL	6,7	8,0
I	4,6	5,6
L	6,7	6,4
NL	21,2	30,4
P		6,5
UK	19,0	21,9

5.7. Part-time work as % of the number of men/women in employment — 1988

	EUR 12	B	DK	D	GR	E	F	IRL	I	L	NL	P	UK
Men	3,9	2,0	8,9	2,1	2,9	2,1	3,4	3,7	3,2	1,9	14,5	3,6	5,5
Women	28,1	23,4	41,5	30,6	10,3	13,0	23,8	17,0	10,4	15,0	57,7	10,5	44,2
Total	13,2	9,8	23,7	13,2	5,5	5,4	12,0	8,0	5,6	6,4	30,4	6,5	21,9

5.8. Part-time work as % of the number of employees/self-employed — 1988

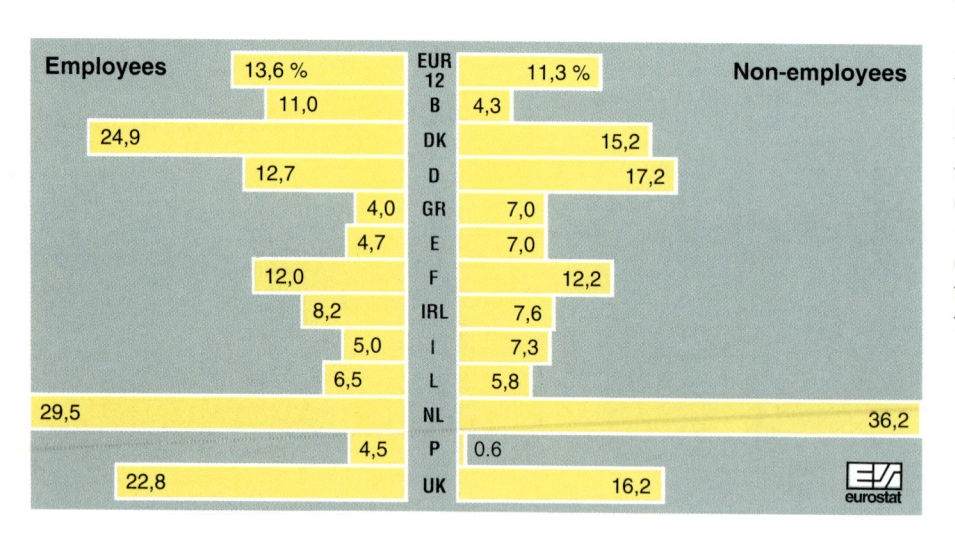

Employees			Non-employees
13,6 %	EUR 12	11,3 %	
11,0	B	4,3	
24,9	DK	15,2	
12,7	D	17,2	
4,0	GR	7,0	
4,7	E	7,0	
12,0	F	12,2	
8,2	IRL	7,6	
5,0	I	7,3	
6,5	L	5,8	
29,5	NL	36,2	
4,5	P	0,6	
22,8	UK	16,2	

5.9. Percentage of part-time work among employees by economic sector — 1988

	EUR 12	B	DK	D	GR	E	F	IRL	I	L	NL	P	UK
Agriculture	14,8	:	18,0	9,0	12,2	2,4	12,9	:	23,0	:	28,3	10,8	20,9
Industry	5,3	3,3	11,2	6,1	2,5	1,7	3,8	3,4	3,0	3,0	13,2	1,7	7,7
Services	18,6	15,1	30,5	18,0	4,7	7,1	16,0	10,9	4,7	8,0	36,3	6,2	30,4
Total	13,6	11,0	24,9	12,7	4,0	4,7	12,0	8,2	5,0	6,5	29,5	4,5	22,8

In 1988, 13.2% of employed persons in the EC worked part-time; the percentage was 30.4% in the Netherlands but only 5.4% in Spain. On the whole, part-time working increased in the Community between 1983 and 1988; a decrease was recorded only in Greece (from 6.5% to 5.5%), whereas the level remained stable in Luxembourg and Denmark.

28.1% of working women worked part-time in 1988 as against 3.9% of men. There is a similar gap between the sexes in all the Member States, but the percentage of women working part-time is particularly high in the Netherlands (57.7%), the United Kingdom (44.2%) and Denmark (41.5%), while it is lower in Greece (10.3%), Italy (10.4%) and Portugal (10.5%).

Part-time work is common to both employees and the self-employed (13.6% and 11.3% respectively). In some countries such as Belgium, Denmark and the United Kingdom, more employees work part-time than the self-employed. Part-time work is particularly widespread in the services sector (18.6%) and in agriculture (14.8%); only 5.3% of employees in industry work part-time. In Italy, Portugal and Greece, more employees work part-time in agriculture than in the other economic sectors.

WORKING CONDITIONS
PART-TIME WORK

More women than men work part-time: over 80% of persons employed part-time in 1988 were women, of whom 63.6% were married; the figure for men was only 18.2%. In comparison, 68.1% of persons employed full-time were men. Women accounted for the largest proportion of persons working part-time in the Federal Republic of Germany (90.5%), of whom 75% were married, while in Italy the figure was only 62.2%, of whom 45.4% were married.

In 1988 part-time employees worked, in the EC as a whole, an average of a little over 19 hours a week (19.3 for men and 19.4 for women). These figures vary from one country to another: they are highest in Luxembourg for men (35.1 hours) and in Italy for women (23.1 hours).

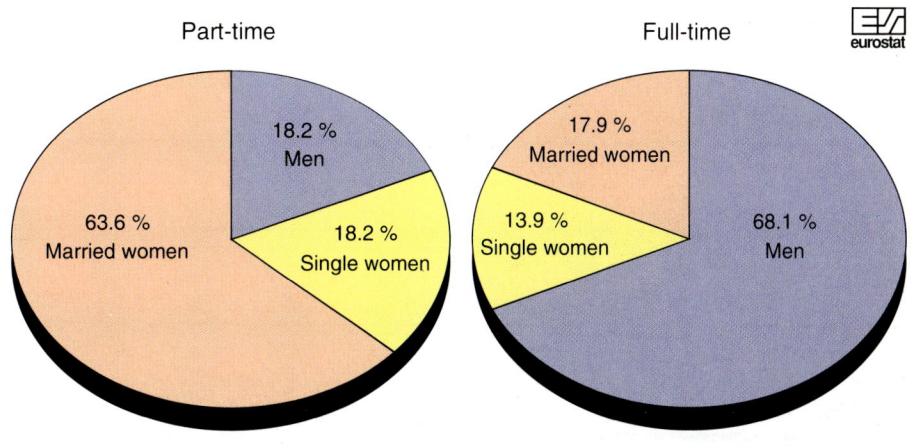

5.10. Men/women breakdown of part-time work (compared with full-time) — EUR 12 — 1988

Part-time: 18.2% Men, 63.6% Married women, 18.2% Single women

Full-time: 17.9% Married women, 13.9% Single women, 68.1% Men

5.11. Men/women breakdown of part-time work by country — 1988 (%)

	Total	Men	Women	Of whom married
EUR 12	100,0	18,2	81,8	63,6
B	100,0	12,9	87,1	68,4
DK	100,0	20,5	79,5	51,1
D	100,0	9,5	90,5	75,0
GR	100,0	34,2	65,8	49,2
E	100,0	26,3	73,7	48,3
F	100,0	16,3	83,7	59,8
IRL	100,0	31,6	68,4	50,1
I	100,0	37,8	62,2	45,4
L	100,0	19,4	80,6	60,0
NL	100,0	30,2	69,8	47,9
P	100,0	32,9	67,1	43,6
UK	100,0	14,3	85,7	71,2

5.12. Hours usually worked part-time per week by employees according to sex — 1988

	EUR 12	B	DK	D	GR	E	F	IRL	I	L	NL	P	UK
Men	19,3	20,5	12,7	19,3	22,0	19,4	22,8	20,0	30,8	35,1	16,6	29,4	16,2
Women	19,4	18,7	21,6	20,9	21,6	17,8	21,6	17,6	23,1	20,5	16,7	17,8	17,9
Total	19,4	20,1	19,8	20,8	21,8	18,1	21,7	18,2	25,7	23,2	16,7	19,6	17,7

WORKING CONDITIONS
TEMPORARY CONTRACT

5.13. Employees with a temporary contract as % of total employees by sex — 1988

	Men	Women	Total
EUR 12	8,7	10,9	9,6
B	3,5	8,6	5,4
DK	10,6	11,6	11,1
D	10,4	12,5	11,2
GR	18,5	15,7	17,6
E	20,5	20,6	22,4
F	7,3	8,5	7,8
IRL	7,3	11,9	9,1
I	4,6	8,0	5,8
L	2,4	6,2	3,7
NL	6,9	11,9	8,7
P	17,1	20,6	18,5
UK	4,7	7,5	5,9

5.14. Employees with a temporary contract by age — 1988 (%)

	Under 25	25-44	45-64	over 65	Total
EUR 12	51.2	36.5	11.5	0.8	100.0
B	42.2	52.8	5.0	—	100.0
DK	62.6	28.3	8.0	1.1	100.0
D	66.2	26.1	7.5	0.1	100.0
GR	24.5	50.8	24.0	0.7	100.0
E	43.9	41.8	14.1	0.2	100.0
F	60.7	33.0	6.1	0.2	100.0
IRL	46.5	40.8	12.0	0.7	100.0
I	34.2	44.6	20.0	1.2	100.0
L	60.0	34.1	5.6	0.3	100.0
NL	48.2	43.7	6.9	1.2	100.0
P	49.3	38.3	11.4	1.0	100.0
UK	38.9	41.0	16.5	3.6	100.0

In 1988, 9.6 % of employees in the EC had a temporary employment contract. The figure was higher in Greece (17.6 %), Portugal (18.5 %) and Spain (22.4 %) and much lower in Luxembourg (3.7 %), Belgium (5.4 %), Italy (5.8 %) and the United Kingdom (5.9 %).

In the EC the majority of employees with a temporary contract are men (54.7 %); this also applies to most of the Member States except Luxembourg, Belgium and the United Kingdom, where women account for 60.0 %, 58.7 % and 56.9 % respectively of employees with a temporary contract.

More than half of those in this employment category (51.2 %) are young people under 25, particularly in the Federal Republic of Germany (66.2 %), Denmark (62.6 %), France (60.7 %) and Luxembourg (60.0 %). In Belgium, Greece, Italy and the United Kingdom, however, persons aged between 25 and 44 make up the largest group of employees with a temporary contract (41 to 53 %).

5.15. Temporary contract distribution by sex — 1988 (%)

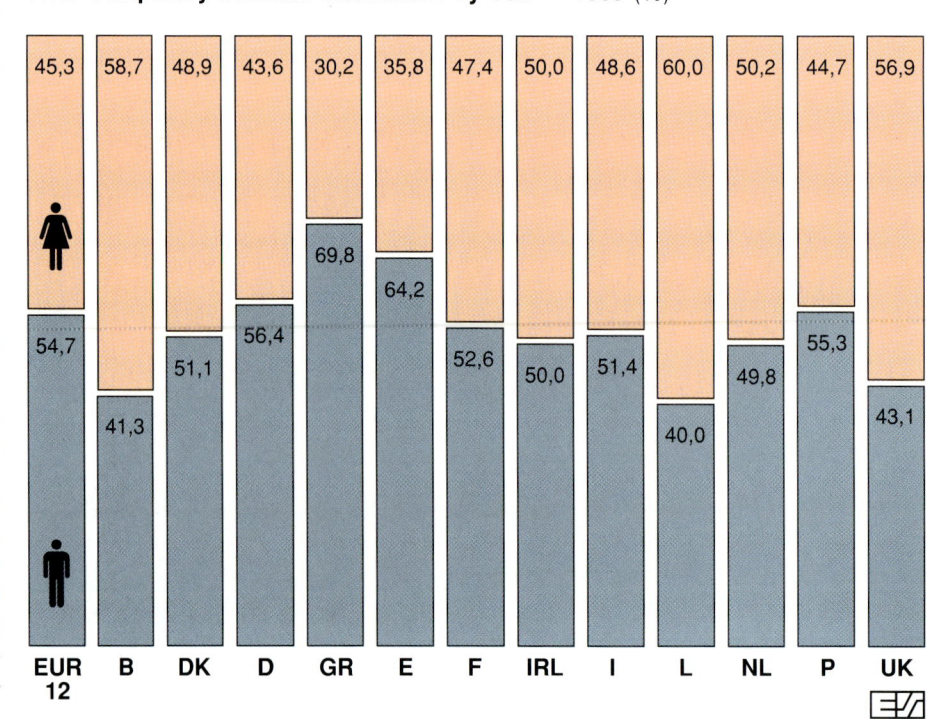

	EUR 12	B	DK	D	GR	E	F	IRL	I	L	NL	P	UK
Women	45,3	58,7	48,9	43,6	30,2	35,8	47,4	50,0	48,6	60,0	50,2	44,7	56,9
Men	54,7	41,3	51,1	56,4	69,8	64,2	52,6	50,0	51,4	40,0	49,8	55,3	43,1

WORKING CONDITIONS
HOURS LOST

5.16. Hours usually worked during the reference week and hours lost, 1988 (million)

	Hours usually worked	Hours lost	%
EUR 12	4 871.1	380.0	7.8
B	128.1	3.0	2.3
DK	96.3	13.2	13.7
D	1 059.0	48.4	4.6
GR	156.8	13.2	8.4
E	476.8	43.7	9.2
F	730.4	56.5	7.7
IRL	42.4	1.8	4.3
I	813.2	34.2	4.2
L	6.1	0.2	3.3
NL	197.3	26.4	13.4
P	185.9	10.6	5.7
UK	978.8	128.6	13.1

During the reference week of the spring 1988 survey, approximately 4 900 million hours usually worked per week were recorded for the EC as a whole, of which approximately 380 million hours (i.e. 7.8%) were lost, i.e. were not used to produce goods and services owing to absence from work during all or part of the week in question.

The highest percentages of hours lost were recorded in Denmark (13.7%), the Netherlands (13.4%) and the United Kingdom (13.1%). They were lower in Belgium (2.3%), Luxembourg (3.3%), Italy (4.2%), Ireland (4.3%) and the Federal Republic of Germany (4.6%).

The most common reason for absence from work is leave (43.7% of hours lost). The second most common reason is sickness or accident (24.3%). Next in line, but with smaller percentages, are variable working hours (4.4%), short-time working for technical or economic reasons (4.0%), maternity leave (3.6%), bad weather (3.5%) and staff training (1.9%).

5.17. Reasons for absence — EUR 12 — 1988 (%)

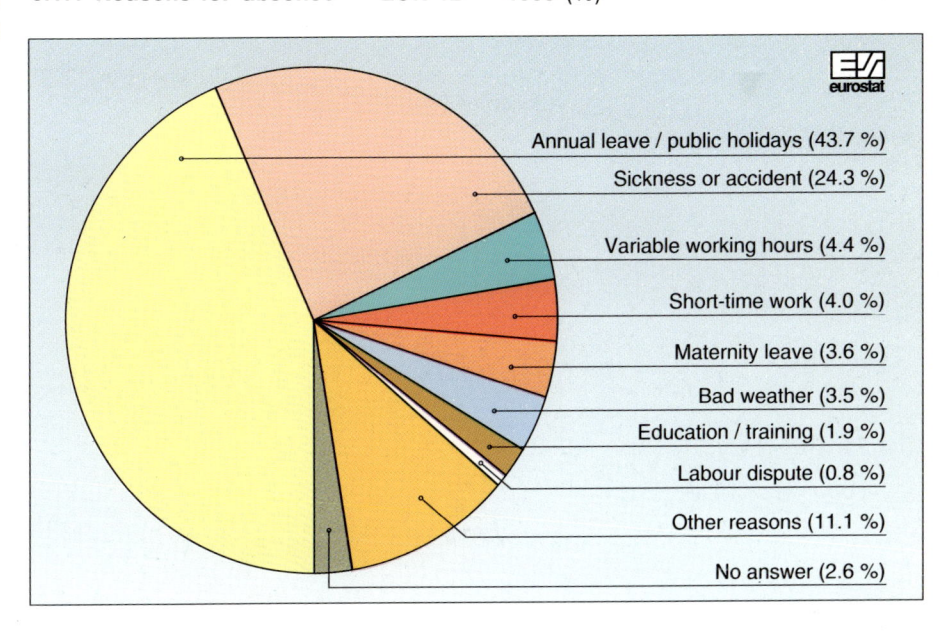

- Annual leave / public holidays (43.7 %)
- Sickness or accident (24.3 %)
- Variable working hours (4.4 %)
- Short-time work (4.0 %)
- Maternity leave (3.6 %)
- Bad weather (3.5 %)
- Education / training (1.9 %)
- Labour dispute (0.8 %)
- Other reasons (11.1 %)
- No answer (2.6 %)

WORKING CONDITIONS
FOR FURTHER INFORMATION

Definitions

LFS: Community labour force survey. This survey is carried out annually in the spring. The new version of the LFS, introduced in 1983, is an important source of statistics on the labour force in the Community. The definitions used are the same for all the Member States and are based on the international recommendations of the ILO. The survey covers the entire population living in private households. It does not cover persons living in collective households such as homes, boarding schools, hospitals, religious institutions, etc.

Part-time: the distinction between full-time and part-time is made on the basis of a spontaneous reply by the interviewee. In principle, a person works part-time when he/she works fewer hours than the norm for the particular type of job. The only exception is in the Netherlands, where part-time workers are those who work fewer than 35 hours a week.

Temporary contract: this covers temporary work and only concerns employed persons. A job is regarded as temporary when there is an agreement between the employer and the employee that the cessation of employment is determined by objective conditions such as the expiry of a given period, the completion of a task or the return of a temporarily replaced employee.

This category includes:

(i) persons engaged by an employment agency on behalf of a third party in order to perform a 'work task' (unless there is a written employment contract of unlimited duration with the employment agency);

(ii) persons with specific training contracts.

References

Eurostat
– Labour-force survey results, 1988

Eurostat databank
– Cronos

STANDARD OF LIVING

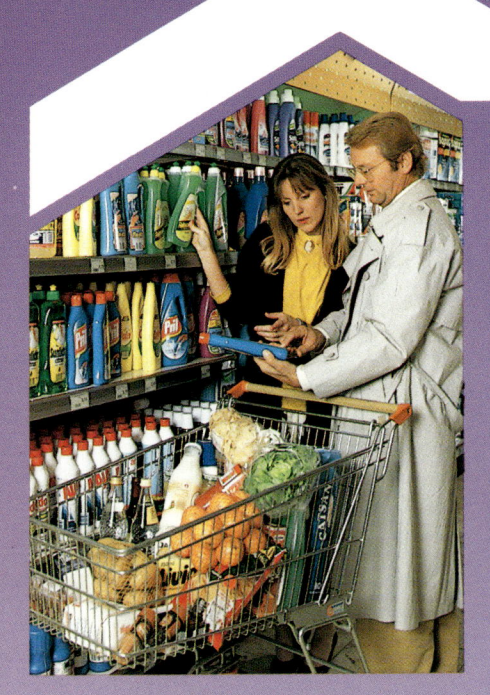

In the European Community, average per capita gross domestic product in 1988 was almost 16 000 PPS. It ranged from 8 553 PPS in Portugal to a little more than double at 19 130 in Luxembourg (6.2).

Per capita GDP has risen virtually without interruption since 1970. The only exceptions were two slight downturns in 1975 and 1981 (6.3).

Of the 13 882 PPS of per capita net national income in the Community in 1988, on average 12 429 PPS were spent (89.5%) and 1 453 saved (10.5%) (6.19).

Average income from employment in 1988 was 25 119 PPS, ranging from 14 250 PPS in Portugal to 30 168 in the Netherlands — almost exactly double (6.10).

Over the period 1970-88, the pattern of consumption changed. The share of income spent on food, beverages and tobacco fell from 29.8% to 21.3%, and that on clothing and footwear from 9.2% to 7.8%. Meanwhile, expenditure on transport and communication rose rapidly from 11.9% to 14.9%, on medical care and health services (private consumption) from 5.1% to 7.4%, and on housing, fuel and power from 15.0% to 16.8% (6.25) (6.26).

6.1. Net disposable national income per head of population — 1988 (in PPS)

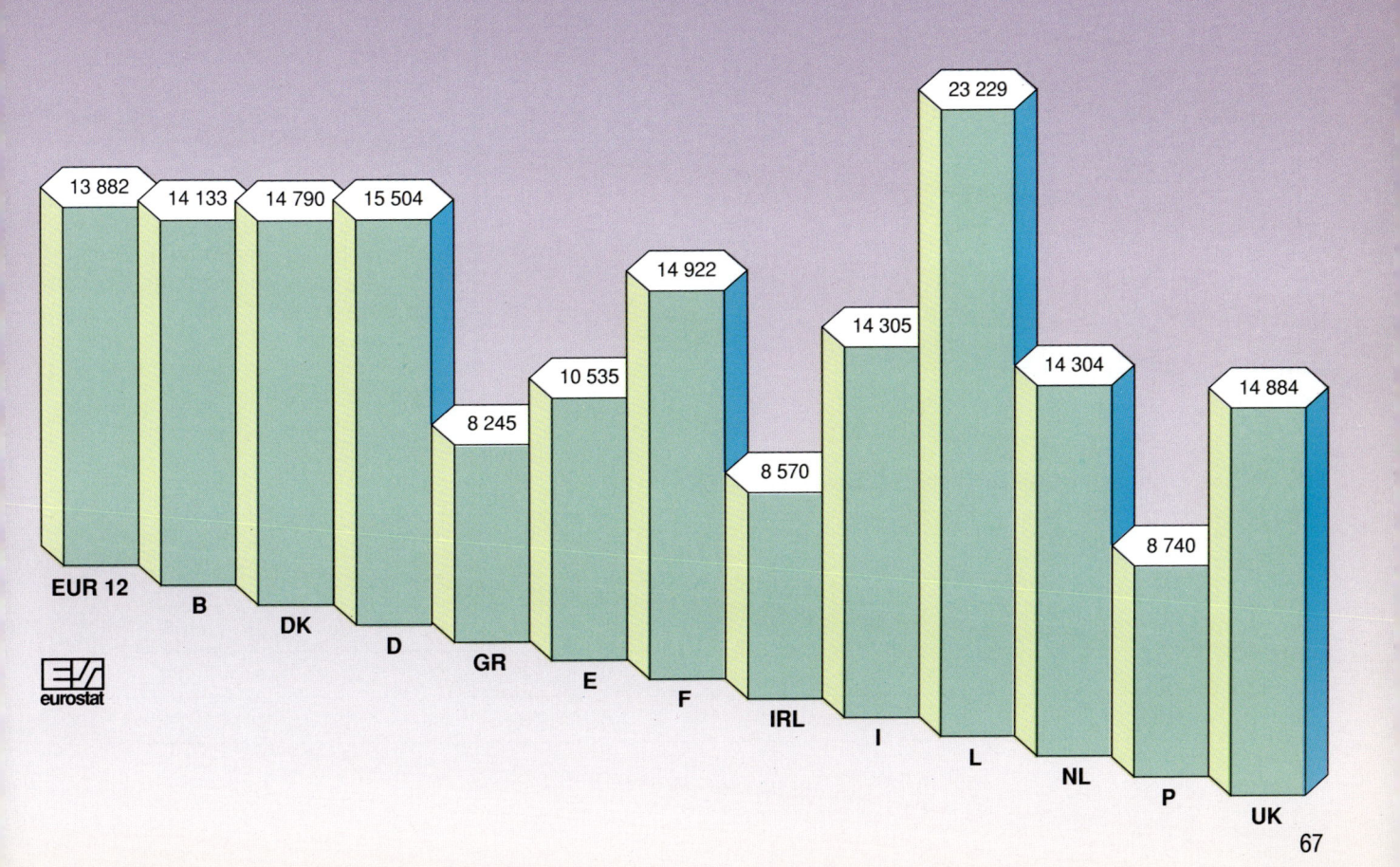

EUR 12	B	DK	D	GR	E	F	IRL	I	L	NL	P	UK
13 882	14 133	14 790	15 504	8 245	10 535	14 922	8 570	14 305	23 229	14 304	8 740	14 884

STANDARD OF LIVING
GDP

6.2. GDP per head of population — 1988 (in PPS)

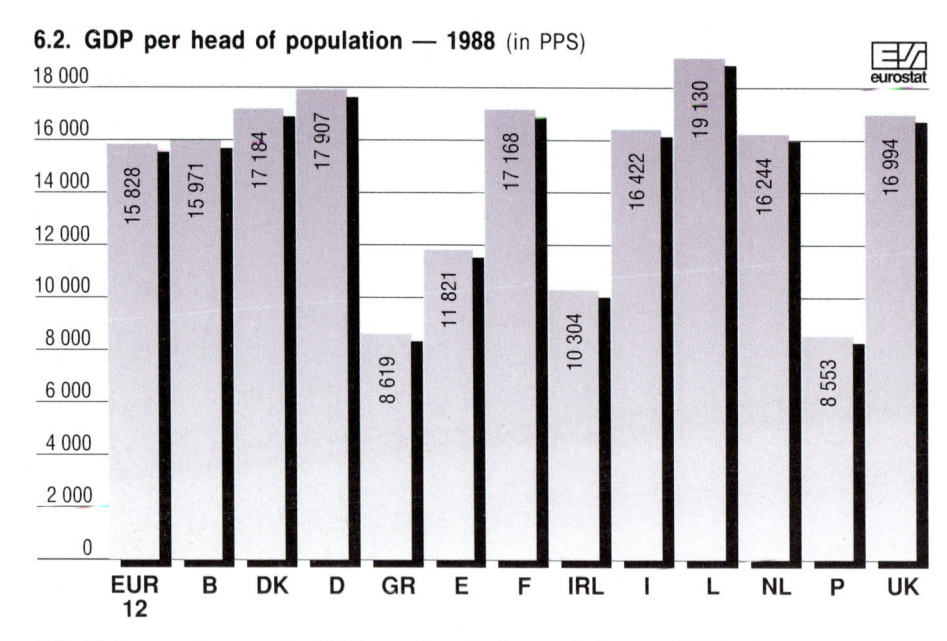

EUR 12	15 828
B	15 971
DK	17 184
D	17 907
GR	8 619
E	11 821
F	17 168
IRL	10 304
I	16 422
L	19 130
NL	16 244
P	8 553
UK	16 994

6.3. Volume changes in GDP per head of population — EUR 12 (in PPS at 1985 prices and purchasing power parities)

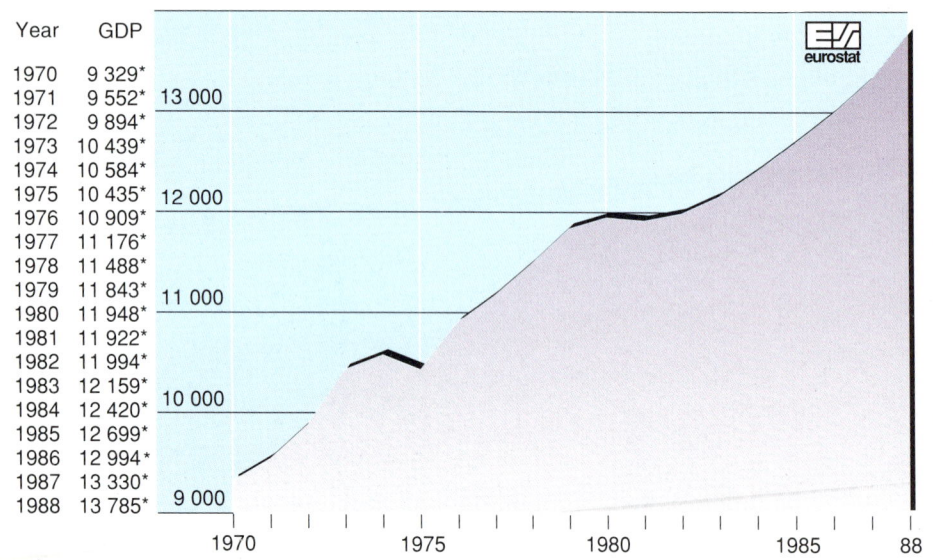

Year	GDP
1970	9 329*
1971	9 552*
1972	9 894*
1973	10 439*
1974	10 584*
1975	10 435*
1976	10 909*
1977	11 176*
1978	11 488*
1979	11 843*
1980	11 948*
1981	11 922*
1982	11 994*
1983	12 159*
1984	12 420*
1985	12 699*
1986	12 994*
1987	13 330*
1988	13 785*

The standard of living can be measured in a number of ways, not all of which are entirely objective. This chapter considers only the financial aspects of the standard of living, and takes no account of the markets in goods and services. Neither does it show figures other than annual flows (GDP, income, consumption, saving), and despite its importance it ignores the question of accumulated capital. The disparities between countries are shown systematically, but those between socio-economic categories cannot be shown since internationally-comparable statistics do not exist. However, changes over time are shown in addition to current levels, since it would appear that changes themselves are a significant element in evaluating the standard of living. All data are calculated in purchasing power standards (PPS), since this allows data to be presented after correction for differences in price levels between countries.

Per capita gross domestic product at market prices (per capita GDP) is the most comprehensive indicator of the wealth produced each year in the Community. In 1988 per capita GDP averaged 15 828 PPS (the value of the PPS in national currencies is shown in the table on the last page). Disparities between countries remain considerable, ranging from a per capita GDP of 8 553 PPS in Portugal to rather more than twice as much, 19 130, in Luxembourg.

6.4. Volume changes in GDP per head of population — 1985 = 100

	EUR 12	B	DK	D	GR	E	F	IRL	I	L	NL	P	UK
1970	73	72	73	73	67	76	73	67	68	74	79	69	77
1980	94	96	88	94	96	96	95	92	94	89	97	99	91
1985	100	100	100	100	100	100	100	100	100	100	100	100	100
1988	109	108	102	107	104	113	106	108	109	110	104	112	112

STANDARD OF LIVING
GDP

Per capita GDP in the Community has risen steadily each year since 1970, with the exception of a slight downturn in 1975 and again in 1981. At constant prices and in terms of 1985 PPS, per capita GDP rose from 9 329 in 1970 to 13 785 in 1988: an average annual rise over 18 years of 2.2%.

Although the gap between Community countries remains wide, it is narrowing as a result of the higher growth rate recorded by most of the less-wealthy countries. Table 6.4 and Graph 6.5 show this gradual convergence of the economies of the Member States of the European Community.

6.5. Changes in GDP per head of population — 1985-88 (in PPS, at 1985 prices and purchasing power parities)

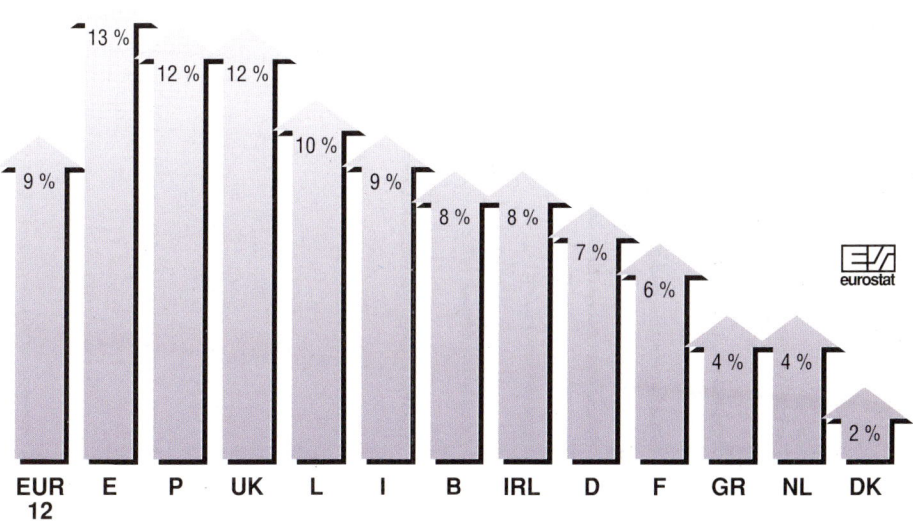

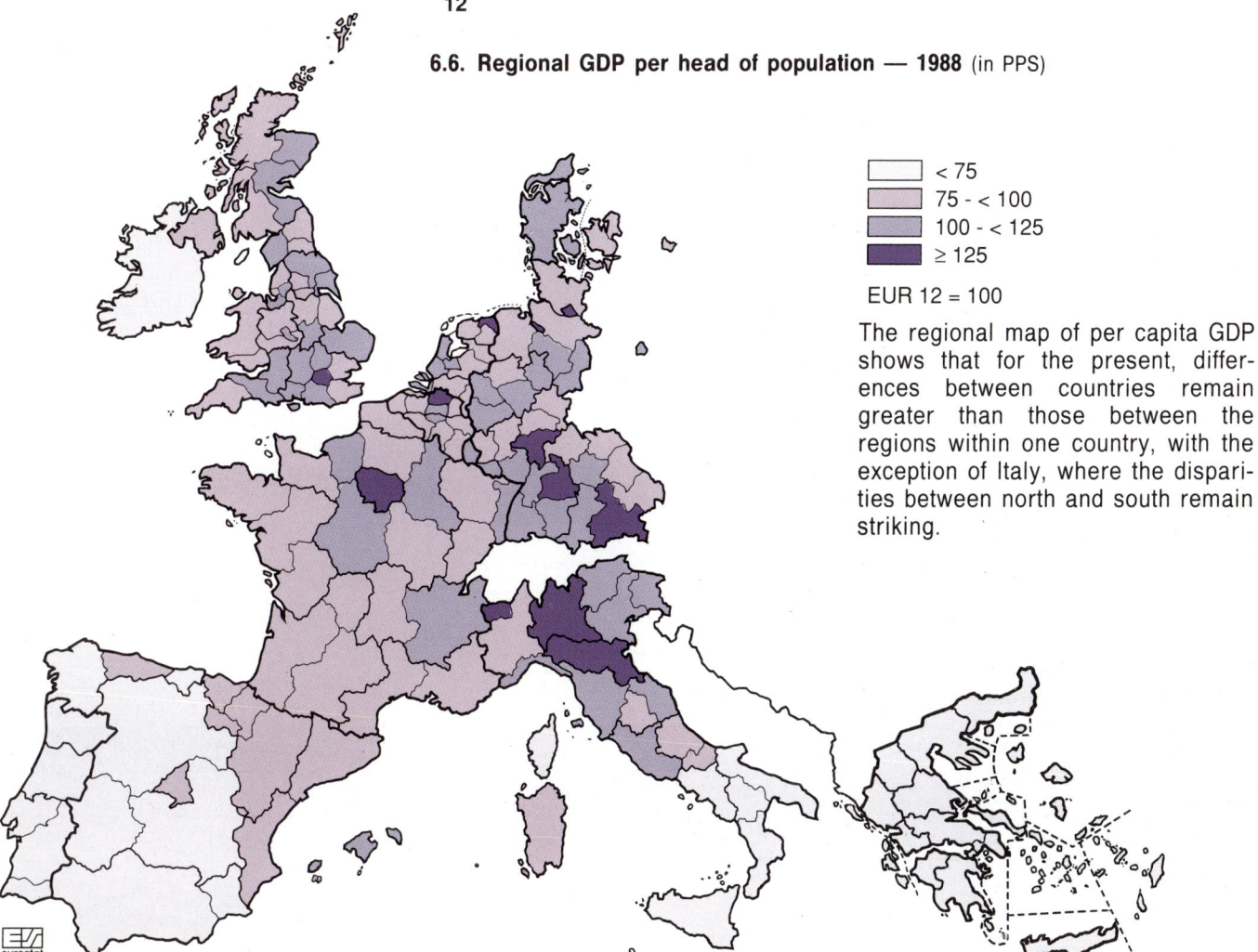

EUR 12	E	P	UK	L	I	B	IRL	D	F	GR	NL	DK
9%	13%	12%	12%	10%	9%	8%	8%	7%	6%	4%	4%	2%

6.6. Regional GDP per head of population — 1988 (in PPS)

- < 75
- 75 - < 100
- 100 - < 125
- ≥ 125

EUR 12 = 100

The regional map of per capita GDP shows that for the present, differences between countries remain greater than those between the regions within one country, with the exception of Italy, where the disparities between north and south remain striking.

STANDARD OF LIVING
INCOME

6.7. National income per head of population — 1988 (in PPS)

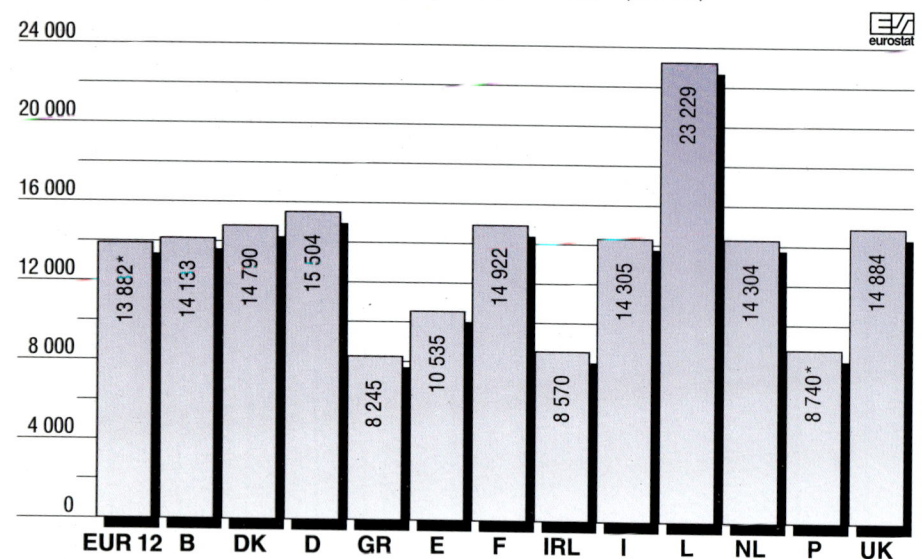

EUR 12	13 882*
B	14 133
DK	14 790
D	15 504
GR	8 245
E	10 535
F	14 922
IRL	8 570
I	14 305
L	23 229
NL	14 304
P	8 740*
UK	14 884

6.8. Volume changes in national income per head of population — EUR 12 (in PPS, at 1985 prices and purchasing power parities)

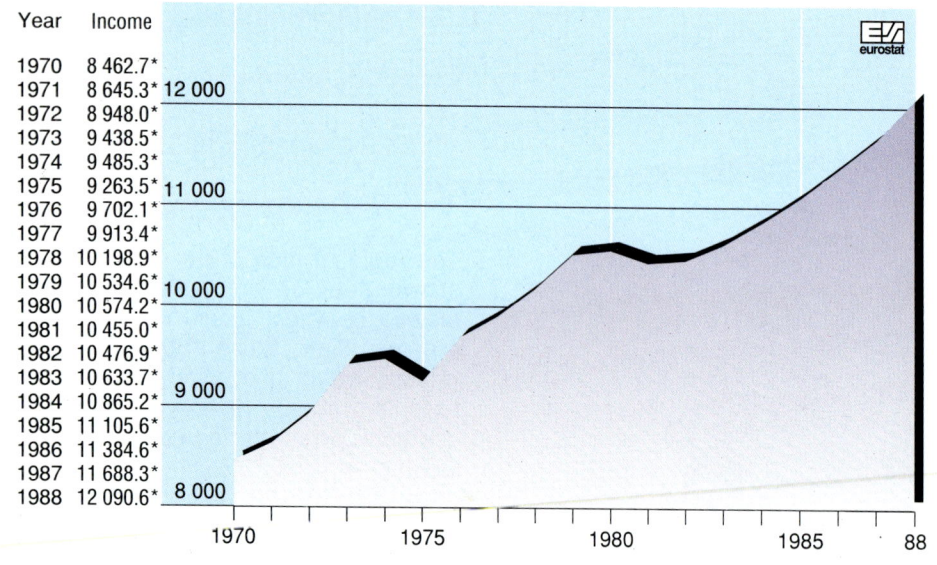

Year	Income
1970	8 462.7*
1971	8 645.3*
1972	8 948.0*
1973	9 438.5*
1974	9 485.3*
1975	9 263.5*
1976	9 702.1*
1977	9 913.4*
1978	10 198.9*
1979	10 534.6*
1980	10 574.2*
1981	10 455.0*
1982	10 476.9*
1983	10 633.7*
1984	10 865.2*
1985	11 105.6*
1986	11 384.6*
1987	11 688.3*
1988	12 090.6*

Net disposable national income ('national income') totalled some 4 500 Mrd PPS (Mrd = thousand million) in 1988 for the whole Community. This amount corresponds to GDP (5 130 Mrd PPS in 1988) less fixed capital consumption (597 Mrd) and the balance on current distributive transactions with the rest of the world (34 Mrd). The net figure is the sum of national income, arising both at home and abroad, and available for either consumption or saving.

The Community per capita average national income in 1988 was 13 822 PPS, with a range from 8 245 in Greece to 15 504 in Germany (Luxembourg's 23 229 is a special case on account of the heavy concentration of banking).

At 1985 constant prices, and constant PPS, per capita national income has grown virtually without interruption since 1970. As with per capita GDP, there was a slight downturn in 1975 and 1981, and on average over the 18 years from 1970 to 1988, national income grew by 2% annually, a little less than per capita GDP.

As with per capita GDP, national income is beginning to converge in the Member States of the Community, since it is the countries with the lowest levels of income which are showing the fastest growth.

6.9. Volume changes in national income — 1985 = 100

	EUR 12	B	DK	D	GR	E	F	IRL	I	L	NL	P	UK
1970	76	73	78	75	70	79	77	76	70	51	82	71	80
1980	95	98	90	94	99	98	97	99	95	76	98	104	91
1985	100	100	100	100	100	100	100	100	100	100	100	100	100
1988	109	108	102	108	105	115	106	107	109	105	103	115	112

STANDARD OF LIVING
COMPENSATION OF EMPLOYEES

Earnings from employment per employee is a rather different indicator of the standard of living, since it depends on paid employment. The 2 600 Mrd PPS distributed in the Community in 1988 are divided not amongst the entire population but amongst the population in employment — each of whom may have one or more dependants not in employment.

Average earnings from employment in the Community in 1988 were 25 119 PPS, ranging from 14 250 PPS in Portugal to 30 168 in the Netherlands. The one is almost exactly double the other, but the countries are far from being in the same order as for GDP and national income.

The average remuneration of the average Community employee has risen regularly and without interruption since 1970: not even during economic crises has it fallen. Taken overall, the average increase of 2.2% from 1970 to 1988 is identical to the increase for per capita GDP.

The tendency towards convergence is still noticeable, though there are exceptions: Luxembourg and Italy on the one hand, Greece on the other.

6.10. Earnings from employment, per employee — 1988 (in PPS)

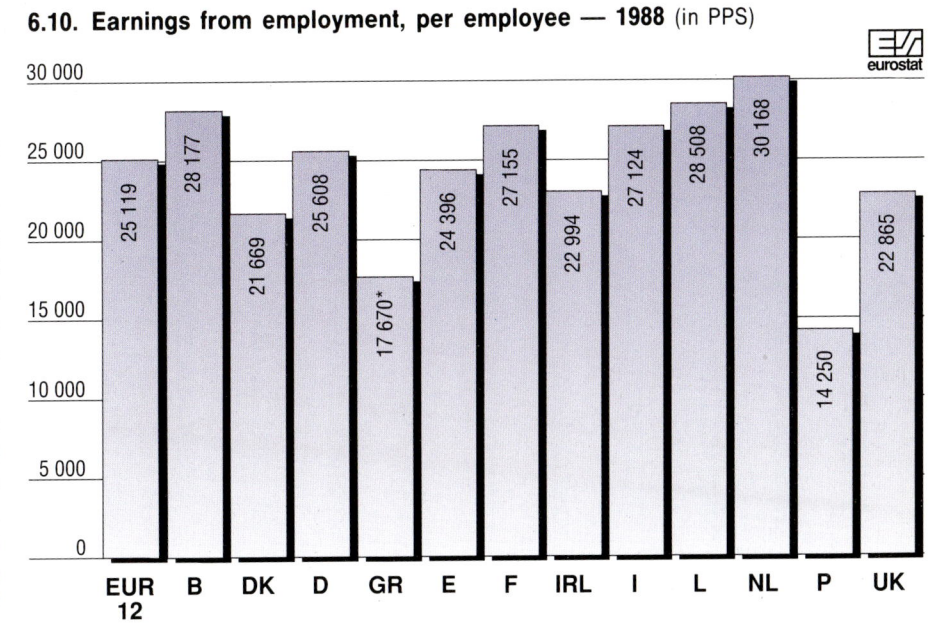

EUR 12	B	DK	D	GR	E	F	IRL	I	L	NL	P	UK
25 119	28 177	21 669	25 608	17 670*	24 396	27 155	22 994	27 124	28 508	30 168	14 250	22 865

6.11. Volume changes in earnings per employee — EUR 12 (in PPS, at 1985 prices and purchasing power parities)

Year	Income
1970	14 883*
1971	15 500*
1972	16 165*
1973	16 940*
1974	17 651*
1975	18 229*
1976	18 776*
1977	19 016*
1978	19 404*
1979	19 807*
1980	20 149*
1981	20 519*
1982	20 652*
1983	20 899*
1984	21 020*
1985	21 201*
1986	21 344*
1987	21 638*
1988	21 877*

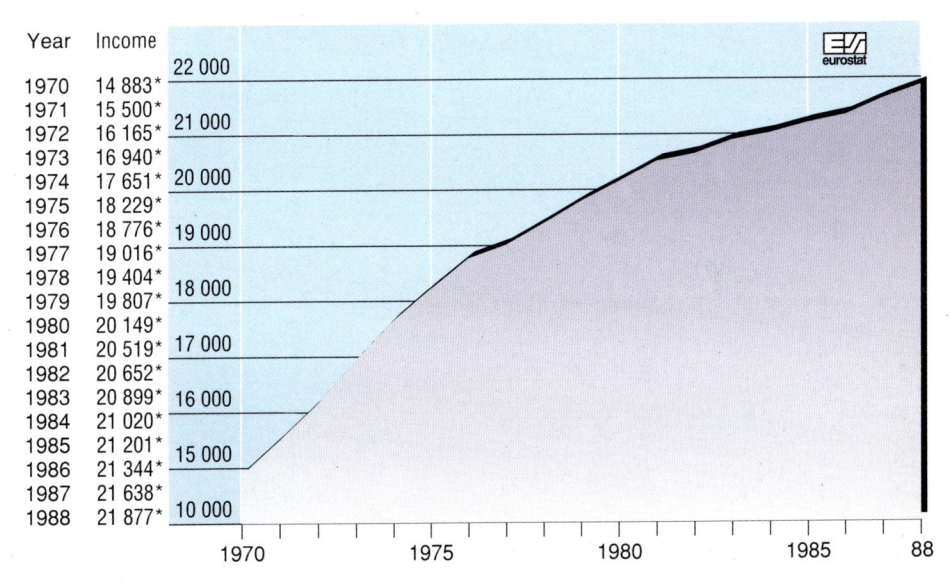

6.12. Volume changes in earnings per employee — 1985 = 100

	EUR 12	B	DK	D	GR	E	F	IRL	I	L	NL	P	UK
1970	70	61	84	71	58	61	66	61	70	68	77	58	77
1980	95	98	99	96	87	95	94	93	95	99	103	101	92
1985	100	100	100	100	100	100	100	100	100	100	100	100	100
1988	103	101	103	104	98	100	100	104	106	107	103	109	106

STANDARD OF LIVING
EARNINGS OF EMPLOYEES

6.13. Average gross hourly earnings of industrial employees — 1988 (in PPS)

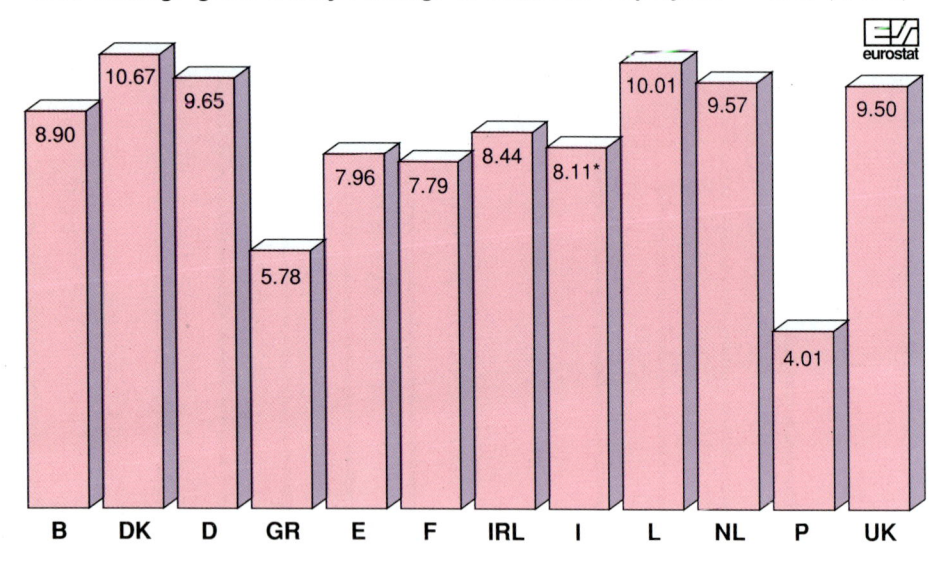

B	DK	D	GR	E	F	IRL	I	L	NL	P	UK
8.90	10.67	9.65	5.78	7.96	7.79	8.44	8.11*	10.01	9.57	4.01	9.50

6.14. Effective changes in gross hourly earnings of industrial employees — October 1985 = 100

	B	DK	D	GR	E	F	IRL	I	L	NL	P	UK
1986	99,6	99,5	104,7	91,0	100,1	101,0	102,0	:	104,3	102,0	105,3	103,6
1987	100,1	105,9	107,8	86,3	103,9	102,1	103,9	:	105,7	103,9	110,1	105,8
1988	101,2	108,0	110,8	92,5	106,8	103,3 (¹)	104,9	:	109,1	104,9	112,3	106,8
1989	101,6 (¹)	107,2 (¹)	111,9	:	107,5 (¹)	:	105,9	:	:	105,9	108,2 (¹)	108,0

¹ April 1989.

6.15. Average gross monthly earnings of employees — 1988 (in PPS)

Industrial employees / Distributive trades employees

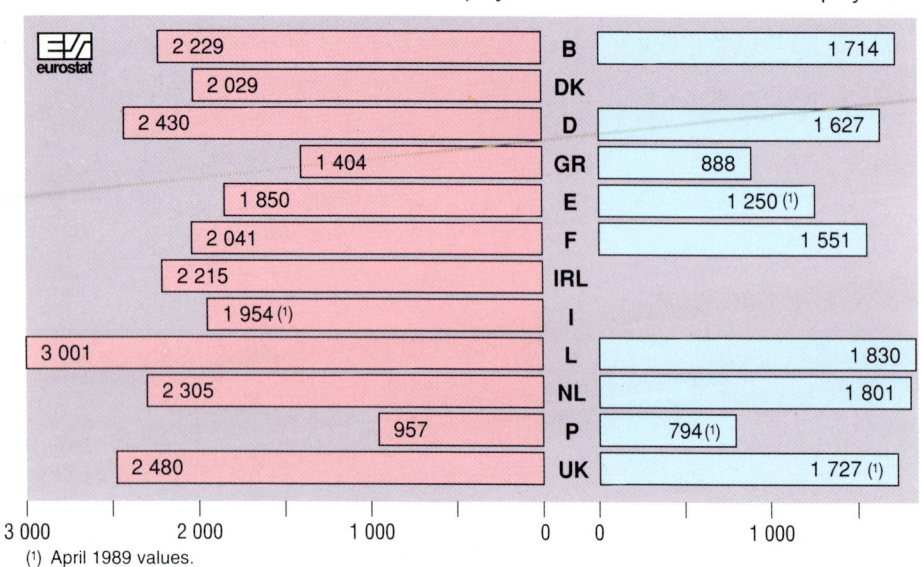

Country	Industrial	Distributive trades
B	2 229	1 714
DK	2 029	
D	2 430	1 627
GR	1 404	888
E	1 850	1 250 (¹)
F	2 041	1 551
IRL	2 215	
I	1 954 (¹)	
L	3 001	1 830
NL	2 305	1 801
P	957	794 (¹)
UK	2 480	1 727 (¹)

(¹) April 1989 values.

In October 1988 the average gross hourly wage of industrial workers (expressed in PPS for the purposes of comparison between countries) ranged from 10.67 PPS in Denmark to 4.01 PPS in Portugal. Hourly earnings are relatively high (between 10.67 and 9.50 PPS) in five countries: Denmark, Luxembourg, Germany, the Netherlands and the United Kingdom. They are 5.78 PPS in Greece, and 4.01 PPS in Portugal.

Between 1986 and 1989, and after deflation by the consumer price index, average hourly earnings of industrial workers showed a general trend towards growth throughout the Community except in Greece. However, a slight fall can be noted in certain countries (Denmark and Portugal) in 1989, and in Greece workers' earnings fell in both 1986 and 1987, to start rising again only in 1988.

The gross monthly earnings of employees in the distributive trades are generally at least 20% lower than those in industry. The gap between the two depends on the country: it is widest in Luxembourg and narrowest in Portugal. The earnings of industrial employees are highest in Luxembourg (3 001 PPS) and lowest in Portugal (957 PPS), elsewhere the range is from 2 480 PPS in the United Kingdom to 1 404 in Greece. The gap is narrower for employees in the distributive trades: from 1 830 PPS in Luxembourg to 794 PPS in Portugal.

The differences between earnings in the different countries narrow if in place of gross earnings we consider net earnings (i.e. after tax and social security contributions have been

STANDARD OF LIVING
EARNINGS OF EMPLOYEES

deducted, but including family allowances). The cases of Germany and France in 1987 illustrate this: whilst the gross earnings of a German worker (1 841 PPS) are 56% higher than that of a French worker (1 182 PPS), the net earnings of a couple with one income and two children are only 28% more (1 374 and 1 076 PPS respectively), and the net earnings of a single worker in Germany (1 069 PPS) are just 17% higher than those of a French single worker (910 PPS).

Actual deductions from the gross earnings of a married industrial worker with two children (income tax and soial security contributions) range from 13.9% in Luxembourg to 37.5% in Denmark. In six countries tax accounts for more than social security contributions (Belgium, Denmark, Ireland, Italy, Spain, United Kingdom): in Denmark the proportions are 35.8% tax to 1.7% social security contributions — the result of the fact that the Danish social security system is financed from tax revenues. In France, on the other hand, a worker on average wages pays no income tax, but pays 16.8% of his earnings in social security contributions.

The effect of income tax, social security contributions and family allowances on net earnings varies widely from country to country within the Community. To the earnings of a couple with one income and two children, family allowances add 0.8% in Spain, 3.1% in Ireland, 9.2% in Luxembourg and 11.4% in Belgium, these being the countries where family allowances are lowest and highest.

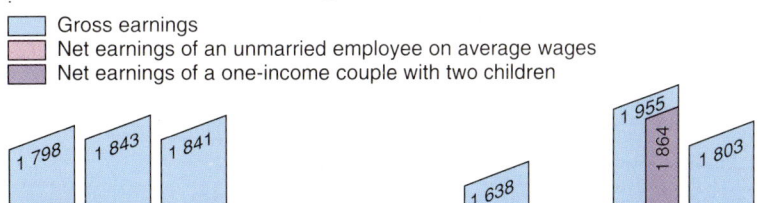

6.16. Gross and net earnings — 1987 (in PPS)

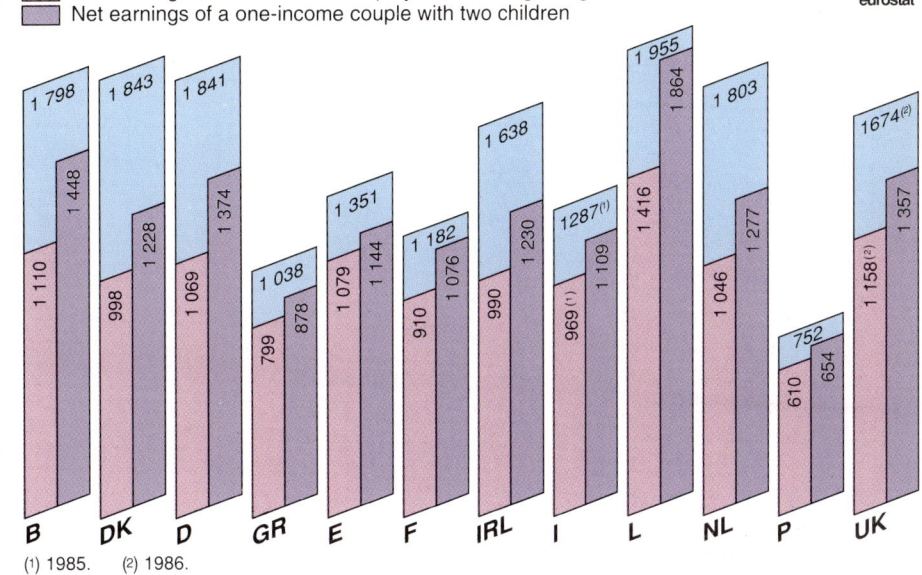

- Gross earnings
- Net earnings of an unmarried employee on average wages
- Net earnings of a one-income couple with two children

(1) 1985.   (2) 1986.

6.17. Changes in the relative proportions of net earnings, income tax and social security deductions in the gross earnings of a one-income couple with two children

Net earnings — 1980 / 1987

Net earnings including family allowances — 1980 / 1987

Deductions — 1980 / 1987
- Social security contributions
- Income tax

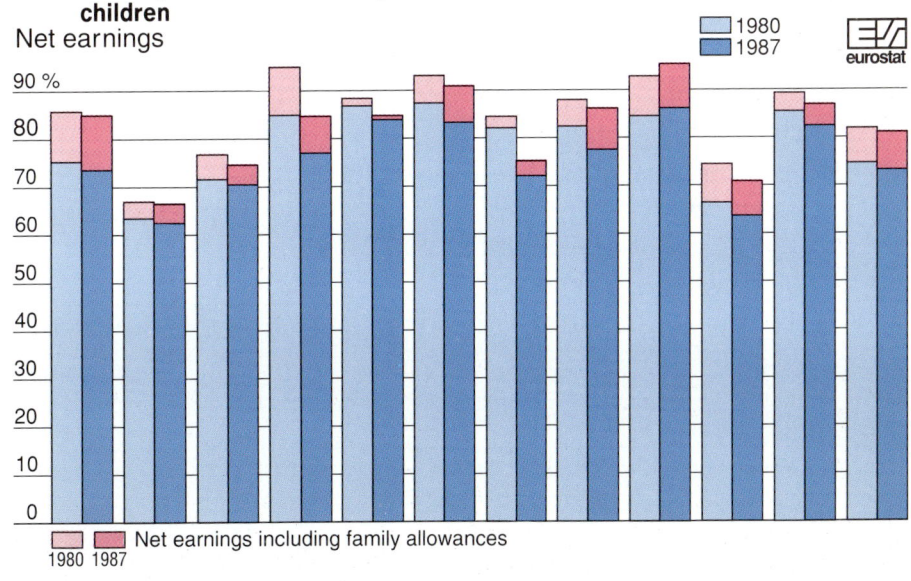

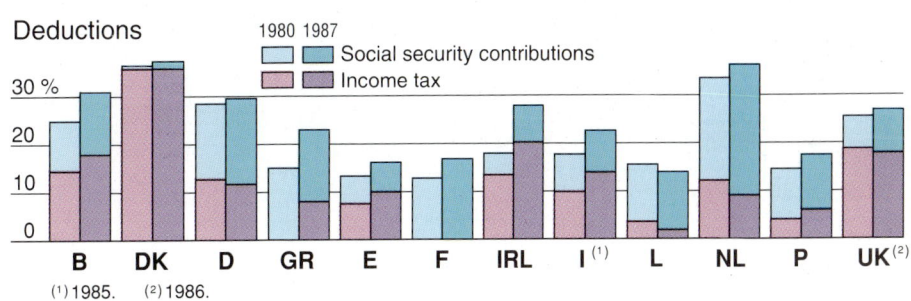

(1) 1985.   (2) 1986.

STANDARD OF LIVING
USE OF INCOME

6.18. Use of net national income per head — 1988 (in PPS)

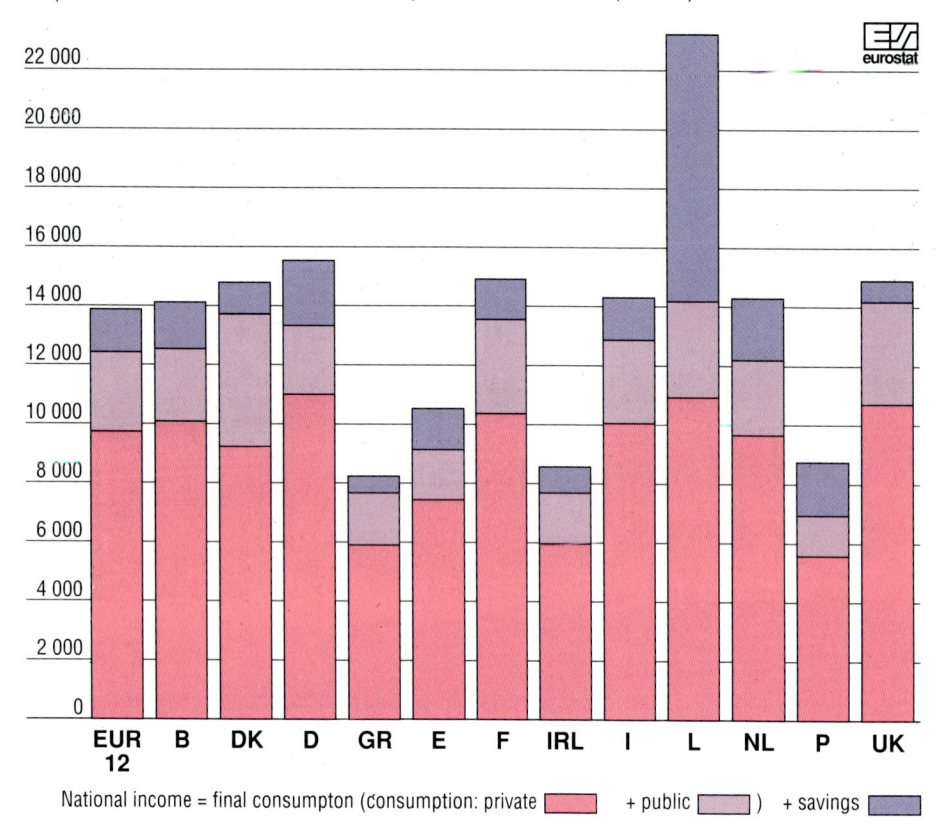

National income = final consumpton (consumption: private ▇ + public ▇) + savings ▇

National income is available either for national final consumption (of households, general government and private non-profit institutions) or for savings (net national saving). Of the 13 822 PPS available to the average European in 1988, 12 429 were spent on national final consumption, and 1 453 PPS (10.5% of income) were saved.

This average figure for saving varies widely from one country to another: from 562 PPS in Greece and 711 in the United Kingdom to 1 798 in Portugal, 2 093 in the Netherlands and 2 198 in Germany. (Luxembourg's figure of 9 039 PPS saved each year results very largely from the heavy concentration of banking activities in the Grand Duchy.) The ratio of one to four is substantially higher than that observed for other indicators.

Per capita national final consumption, which averaged 12 429 PPS, ranged from 6 942 for Portugal to 14 190 in Luxembourg: again, a ratio of close to one to two.

6.19. Use of net national income per head — 1988 (in PPS)

	EUR 12	B	DK	D	GR	E	F	IRL	I	L	NL	P	UK
Final consumption	12 429	12 523	13 697	13 306	7 683	9 136	13 552	7 683	12 867	14 190	12 211	6 942	14 173
private	9 753	10 080	9 231	11 001	5 908	7 444	10 366	5 967	10 048	10 932	9 658	5 570	10 722
public	2 676	2 443	4 466	2 305	1 775	1 692	3 186	1 716	2 819	3 258	2 553	1 372	3 451
Net national saving	1 453	1 610	1 093	2 198	562	1 399	1 370	887	1 438	9 039	2 093	1 798	711
Total (national income)	13 882	14 133	14 790	15 504	8 245	10 535	14 922	8 570	14 305	23 229	14 304	8 740	14 884

6.20. Proportions of saving and consumption in net national income — 1988

	EUR 12	B	DK	D	GR	E	F	IRL	I	L	NL	P	UK
% of private consumption	70,3	71,3	62,4	71,0	71,7	70,7	69,5	69,6	70,2	47,1	67,5	63,7	72,0
% of public consumption	19,3	17,3	30,2	14,9	21,5	16,1	21,4	20,0	19,7	14,0	17,8	15,7	23,2
% of net national saving	10,5	11,4	7,4	14,2	6,8	13,3	9,2	10,4	10,1	38,9	14,6	20,6	4,8
Total (net national income)	100	100	100	100	100	100	100	100	100	100	100	100	100

STANDARD OF LIVING
USE OF INCOME

6.21. Proportions of saving and consumption in net national income — (%)

It can be seen that national rates of saving are not proportionate to national income. Whilst in the United Kingdom the saving rate is 4.8% and in Greece 6.8%, it rises to 13.3% in Spain, 14.2% in the Federal Republic of Germany, 14.6% in the Netherlands and more than 20% in Portugal (not to mention the 38.9% in Luxembourg).

The ratio of final consumption to income is naturally the reverse of the same coin. Final consumption divides into a figure for national private consumption and a figure for the consumption of general government, known for short as 'public consumption'. The split between these two types of consumption varies quite widely from one country to another, since certain high-spending sectors, such as education or health, may in some countries be covered in whole or in part by the State, whilst in other countries the burden borne by the individual may be greater. It may nevertheless be noted that although the level of collective consumption varies widely from one country to another, the proportion of income spent on private consumption is fairly steady, ranging from 68% to 72%, the only exceptions being Denmark (62%) and Portugal (64%), with Luxembourg once again a special case at 47%.

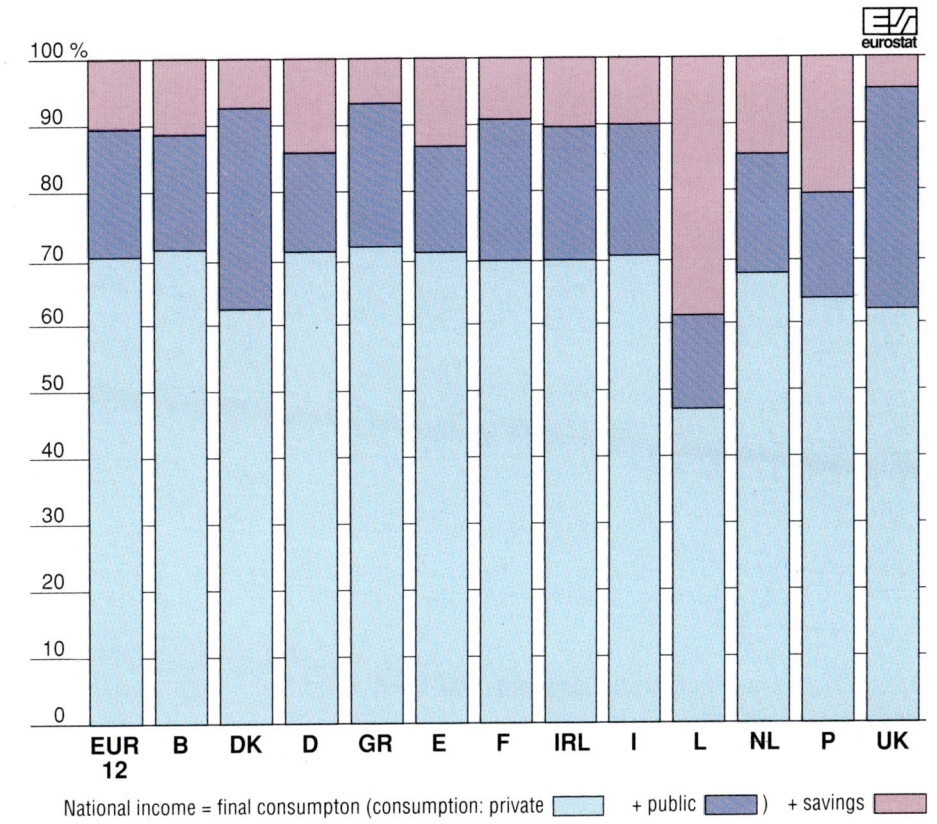

National income = final consumpton (consumption: private + public) + savings

As regards change, convergence of per capita final consumption in the Community as a whole is less evident: certain countries such as the United Kingdom have high consumption and continue to progress faster than the Community average, whilst others such as Greece and, in particular, Ireland are making slower progress at a time when their per capita consumption is below the Community average.

6.22. Volume changes in national final consumption per head — 1985 = 100

	EUR 12 ([1])	B	DK	D	GR	E	F	IRL	I	L	NL	P	UK
1970	71	69	76	70	62	73	71	76	65	69	79	74	74
1980	95	98	91	96	90	98	93	103	92	94	101	101	92
1985	100	100	100	100	100	100	100	100	100	100	100	100	100
1988	110	106	102	108	105	114	107	105	112	107	105	117	114

[1] PPS

STANDARD OF LIVING
PATTERN OF CONSUMPTION

6.23. Final consumption of households per head — 1988 (in national currency)

	Food, beverages and tobacco	Clothing and footwear	Housing, fuel and power	Furnishings, household equipment, household operation	Medical care and health expenses	Transport and communications	Recreation, entertainment, education culture	Other goods and services	Total
B [3]	69 351	25 809	60 050	37 515	38 706	44 990	22 931	53 747	353 099
DK	16 497	4 309	19 365	5 256	1 464	11 564	7 404	8 158	74 017
D	3 361	1 599	3 769	1 780	3 077	2 986	1 857	2 057	20 486
GR	204 271	48 951	62 407	44 651	19 393	65 718	34 721	54 825	534 937
E [1]	163 000	46 000	89 000	44 000	22 000	93 000	41 000	127 000	625 000
F	12 052	4 129	11 504	5 008	5 652	10 303	4 551	8 263	61 462
IRL [1]	1 339	214	362	244	111	395	344	293	3 302
I	2 633	1 113	1 658	1 006	702	1 478	998	1 993	11 581
L	80 327	24 866	76 757	38 749	29 518	66 173	16 334	47 914	380 638
NL	3 313	1 257	3 309	1 451	2 240	1 968	1 726	2 497	17 761
P [2]	114 760	31 704	15 307	26 607	13 895	47 457	17 719	41 491	308 940
UK	846	347	956	336	64	853	457	1 088	4 947

[1] 1987. [2] 1986.
[3] The final consumption of households on the economic territory is not equal to the sum of the various headings: the difference is part of the statistical adjustment made to balance the figures for GDP calculated from each of three points of view (production, income and expenditure).

6.24. Final consumption of households per head — 1988 (in PPS) (private consumption)

	Food, beverages and tobacco	Clothing and footwear	Housing, fuel and power	Furnishings, household equipment, household operation	Medical care and health expenses	Transport and communications	Recreation, entertainment, education culture	Other goods and services	Total
EUR 12*	2 088	763	1 647	791	726	1 459	807	1 539	9 818
B [3]	1 983	738	1 717	1 073	1 107	1 287	656	1 537	10 097
DK	1 883	492	2 211	600	167	1 320	845	931	8 450
D	1 775	845	1 991	940	1 625	1 577	981	1 087	10 822
GR	2 199	527	672	481	209	708	374	590	5 760
E [1]	1 988	561	1 085	537	268	1 134	500	1 549	7 622
F	2 022	693	1 931	840	948	1 729	764	1 387	10 314
IRL [1]	2 224	355	601	405	184	656	571	487	5 485
I	2 324	982	1 463	888	620	1 305	881	1 759	10 222
L	2 452	759	2 343	1 183	901	2 020	499	1 463	11 620
NL	1 799	682	1 796	788	1 216	1 068	937	1 356	9 642
P [2]	1 477	408	197	342	179	611	228	534	3 977
UK	1 737	713	1 963	690	131	1 752	938	2 234	10 158

[1] 1987. [2] 1986.
[3] The final consumption of households on the economic territory is not equal to the sum of the various headings: the difference is part of the statistical adjustment made to balance the figures for GDP calculated from each of three points of view (production, income and expenditure).

STANDARD OF LIVING
PATTERN OF CONSUMPTION

6.25. Changes in the pattern of the final consumption of households (at current prices) (%)

	Food, beverages and tobacco 1970	1988	Clothing and footwear 1970	1988	Housing, fuel and power 1970	1988	Furnishings, household equipment, household operation 1970	1988	Medical care and health expenses 1970	1988	Transport and communications 1970	1988	Recreation, entertainment, education, culture 1970	1988	Other goods and services 1970	1988
EUR 12*	29.80	21.30	9.20	7.80	15.00	16.80	8.80	8.10	5.10	7.40	11.90	14.90	7.70	8.20	12.40	15.70
B[3]	27.95	19.75	8.73	7.35	15.52	17.10	11.69	10.68	6.81	11.02	10.34	12.81	4.71	6.53	13.57	15.31
DK	29.93	22.29	7.68	5.82	18.12	26.16	9.59	7.10	2.01	1.98	14.88	15.62	8.18	10.00	9.62	11.02
D	23.43	16.41	9.62	7.80	15.24	18.40	9.57	8.69	9.47	15.02	13.29	14.58	9.56	9.06	9.83	10.04
GR	41.39	38.19	12.43	9.15	13.99	11.67	7.39	8.35	4.14	3.63	8.34	12.29	4.81	6.49	7.51	10.25
E[1]	32.00*	26.06	8.01*	7.41	18.12*	14.26	7.76*	7.09	2.86*	3.56	10.17*	14.81	5.83*	6.59	11.79*	20.22
F	25.95	19.61	9.54	6.72	15.28	18.72	10.20	8.15	7.12	9.20	13.36	16.76	6.90	7.41	11.66	13.44
IRL[1]	45.04	40.56	9.77	6.47	11.37	10.98	7.59	7.38	2.52	3.37	9.32	11.95	7.77	10.42	6.61	8.88
I	38.56	22.73	8.78	9.61	12.15	14.31	6.96	8.68	3.79	6.06	10.14	12.76	7.74	8.62	11.87	17.21
L	28.40	21.10	9.43	6.53	17.48	20.17	9.43	10.18	5.35	7.75	10.88	17.38	3.99	4.29	15.04	12.59
NL	25.99	18.65	10.67	7.08	12.55	18.63	11.62	8.17	8.47	12.61	9.40	11.08	8.44	9.72	12.86	14.06
P[2]	40.98	37.15	9.05	10.26	6.76	4.95	10.09	8.61	3.93	4.50	12.6	15.36	5.0	5.74	11.58	13.43
UK	26.51	17.09	8.77	7.01	17.11	19.33	7.81	6.79	0.92	1.30	12.63	17.25	8.62	9.24	17.63	21.99

[1] 1987. [2] 1986.
[3] The final consumption of households on the economic territory is not equal to the sum of the various headings: the difference is part of the statistical adjustment made to balance the figures for GDP calculated from each of three points of view (production, income and expenditure).

The way Europeans consume is an interesting indicator of their way of life. Data broken down by purpose are available for per capita final consumption of households on the economic territory, which, from the statistical point of view, is a concept almost identical to national private consumption. These data, which relate to 1988, are given in both PPS and national currency.

Changes in the pattern of consumption are influenced by the differing fluctuations in the prices of goods and services, but they are also indicative of changing priorities in Europeans' private consumption. Between 1970 and 1988 the proportion of income spent on food, beverages and tobacco in the Community dwindled from 29.8% to 21.3%, and that on clothing and footwear from 9.2% to 7.8%. Meanwhile, expenditure on transport and communication rose rapidly from 11.9% to 14.9%, on medical care and health services (private consumption) from 5.1% to 7.4%, and on housing, fuel and power from 15.0% to 16.8%.

6.26. Changes in the pattern of the final consumption of households (at current prices) per head — EUR 12 (%)

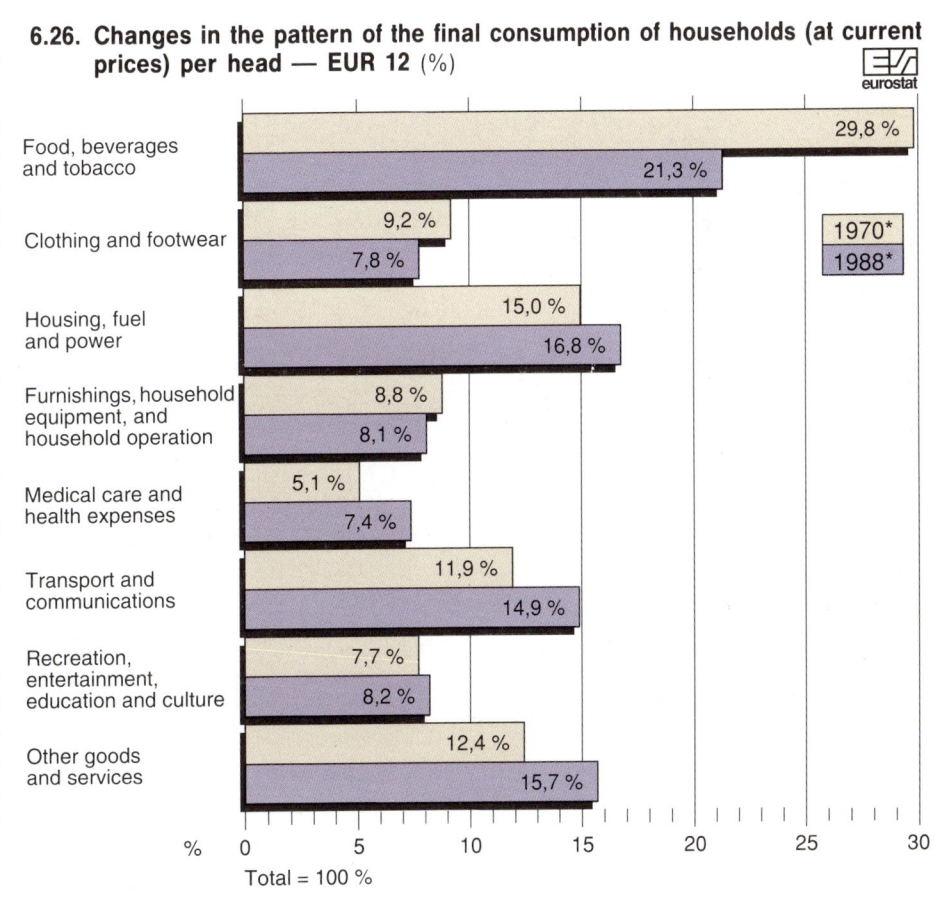

Category	1970*	1988*
Food, beverages and tobacco	29.8%	21.3%
Clothing and footwear	9.2%	7.8%
Housing, fuel and power	15.0%	16.8%
Furnishings, household equipment, and household operation	8.8%	8.1%
Medical care and health expenses	5.1%	7.4%
Transport and communications	11.9%	14.9%
Recreation, entertainment, education and culture	7.7%	8.2%
Other goods and services	12.4%	15.7%

Total = 100%

STANDARD OF LIVING
POVERTY

6.27. Equivalent mean national expenditure (at 1980 prices in ECU)

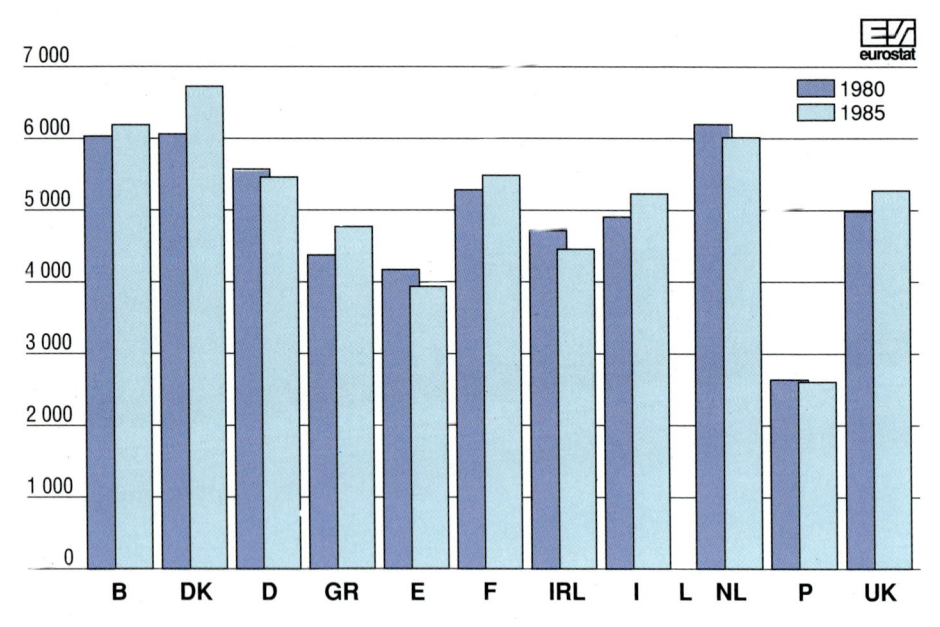

'Equivalent mean national expenditure' is an indicator which may be used to measure relative poverty in different countries. Poverty is defined as having less than 50% of the 'equivalent mean national expenditure of one's country, e.g. less than 50% of Denmark's ECU 6 721 in 1985 or less than 50% of Portugal's ECU 2 618 (at constant 1980 prices). The highest totals are those of France (10.3 million in 1980) and the United Kingdom (10.3 million in 1985). The proportion of poor individuals in the total population varies widely from one country to another: from 5.9% in Belgium (1985) to 32.7% in Portugal. It is around 20% in Ireland, Spain, Greece and the United Kingdom, around 15% in France and Italy, and around 10% in the Netherlands, Germany and Denmark.

6.28. Rates of poverty (households and total population) in the European Community (the poverty threshold is set at 50% of the equivalent mean national expenditure of adults)

Country	1980 Households %	1980 Households ×1 000	1980 Persons %	1980 Persons ×1 000	1985 Households %	1985 Households ×1 000	1985 Persons %	1985 Persons ×1 000
B	6,3	226	7,1	701	5,2	189	5,9	583
DK	8,0	166	7,9	407	8,0	166	8,0	409
D	10,3	2 592	10,5	6 448	9,2	2 306	9,9	6 074
GR	20,5	604	21,5	2 073	17,4	527	18,4	1 817
E	20,3	2 129	20,9	7 829	17,8	1 924	18,9	7 257
F	18,0	3 503	19,1	10 313	14,8	2 947	15,7	8 681
IRL	18,5	167	18,4	625	17,4	162	19,5	684
I	12,0	2 237	14,1	7 941	14,7	2 760	15,5	8 880
L	:	:	:	:	:	:	:	:
NL	6,9	345	9,6	1 363	7,9	403	11,4	1 661
P	31,4	906	32,4	3 167	31,7	948	32,7	3 310
UK	14,1	2 808	14,6	8 226	18,9	3 790	18,2	10 324

STANDARD OF LIVING
POVERTY

6.29. Changes in the percentage of poor amongst the population (%)

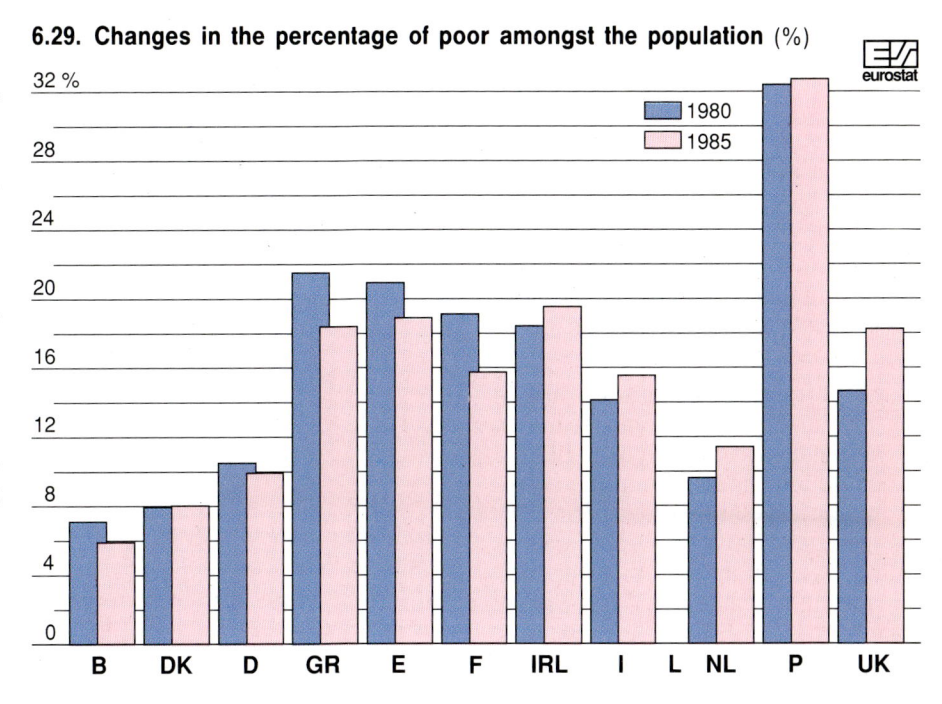

Between 1980 and 1985 the proportion of the poor in the total population increased substantially in the United Kingdom, rising from 14.6% to 18.2%; in France, on the other hand, it fell from 19.1% to 15.7% and in Belgium from 7.1% to 5.9%.

Denmark has 1.6% of the Community's population, but only 0.8% of its poor; Belgium 3.2% of the population but only 1.2% of the poor. The United Kingdom, on the other hand, with 17.6% of the Community's population, has 20.7% of its poor, whilst Portugal has 3.2% of the population and 6.7% of the poor.

6.30. Geographical distribution of poverty (less than 50% of equivalent mean national expenditure) — 1985

Distribution of poverty:
- Belgium (1.2%)
- Denmark (0.8%)
- FR of Germany (12.2%)
- Greece (3.7%)
- Spain (14.6%)
- France (17.5%)
- Ireland (1.4%)
- Netherlands (3.3%)
- Italy (17.9%)
- Portugal (6.7%)
- United Kingdom (20.7%)

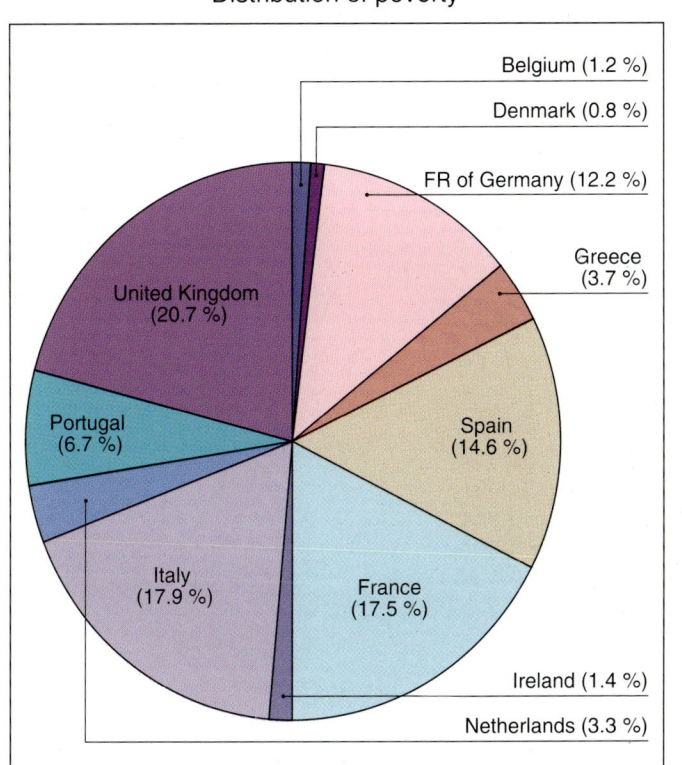

Distribution of the population:
- Belgium (3.1%)
- Denmark (1.6%)
- FR of Germany (19.0%)
- Greece (3.1%)
- Spain (11.9%)
- France (17.1%)
- Ireland (1.1%)
- Italy (17.8%)
- Netherlands (4.5%)
- Portugal (3.2%)
- United Kingdom (17.6%)

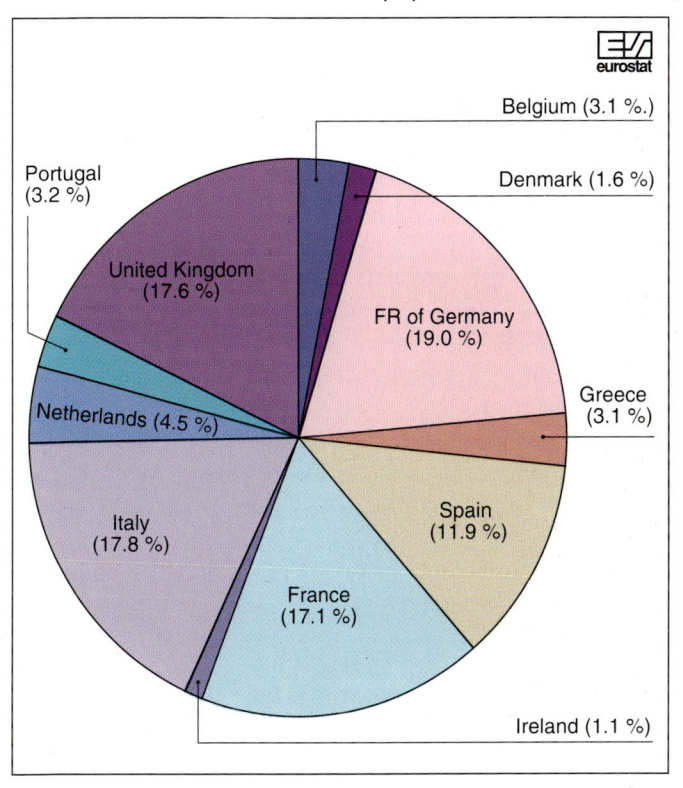

(1) Excluding Luxembourg.

STANDARD OF LIVING
FOR FURTHER INFORMATION

Definitions

Gross domestic product at market prices (GDP): this represents the result of the production activity of resident producer units. It corresponds to the economy's output of goods and services, less intermediate consumption, plus the VAT on products and the taxes linked to imports.

Disposable national income: this is the measure of the income available to the nation for the purposes of final consumption and saving. It corresponds to GDP at market prices, plus the net balance of current transfers with the rest of the world. By deducting the consumption of fixed capital from gross disposable national income, net disposable national income is obtained.

National saving: the part of disposable national income which is not absorbed by final consumption transactions.

Final consumption: the value of goods and services used for the direct satisfaction of human wants, whether individual (final consumption of households) or collective (collective consumption of general government and private non-profit institutions).

The national final consumption shown in this publication refers to the final consumption of residents on the economic territory and **abroad** — the national concept.

Final consumption is broken down into:

(a) private consumption, which is the consumption of households plus that of private non-profit institutions;

(b) public consumption, which is the consumption of general government (central, regional and local government, and social security funds).

It should be noted, however, that the final consumption of households broken down by purpose includes only the consumption effected on the economic territory.

Compensation of employees: this includes all payments in cash and in kind made by employers in remuneration for the work done by their employees during the relevant period.

These payments and benefits include:

(i) gross wages and salaries;
(ii) employers' actual social security contributions;
(iii) imputed social security contributions.

Purchasing power standard (PPS): exchange rates do not necessarily reflect the true purchasing power of a country's currency within its frontiers, and for that reason they cannot be used to give an accurate indication of the volume of goods and services intended for final use in one country or another. Consequently, it is not the ecu which is used as the unit of comparison, but the purchasing power standard (PPS), which eliminates the distortions due to different price levels.

In 1988 one PPS was worth

   34 950 BFR
    8.210 DKR
    1.920 DM
   86.460 DR
   85.900 PTA
    5.910 FF
    0.595 IRL
1 144.000 LIT
   33.780 LFR
    1.880 HFL
   71.900 ESC
    0.477 UKL

Poverty: poverty is defined as having less than 50% of the equivalent mean national expenditure of the country concerned.

References

Eurostat
- National accounts ESA — Aggregates 1970-88
- National accounts ESA — Detailed tables by branch, 1989
- Earnings in industry and services, 1990
- Regions — Statistical yearbook, 1989
- Rapid Reports — Population and Social conditions, 1990-7
- La pauvreté en chiffres: L'Europe au début des années 80

Eurostat databank
- Cronos

SOCIAL PROTECTION

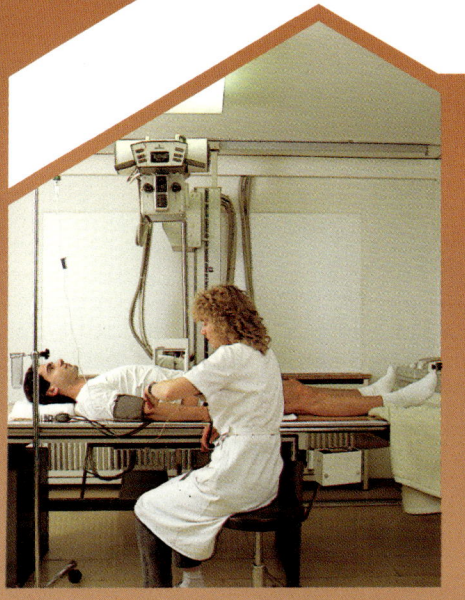

In 1987 the average per capita expenditure on social protection in the European Community [1] was 3 600 PPS (7.1).

The share of social protection in GDP varied between 17.0 % (Portugal) and 30.7 % (the Netherlands), i.e. a ratio of almost 1:2 (7.2).

The largest share of social benefits (over 80 %) is devoted to the old-age and survivors sector (45 %) and the health sector (36 %) (7.6).

In the financing of social protection, the share of contributions from public funds varies between 14 % in the Netherlands and 78 % in Denmark. The share of contributions paid by employers varies between 11 % in Denmark and 53 % in Italy, while that of contributions paid by insured persons (employees etc.) varies between 4 % in Denmark and 36 % in the Netherlands (7.8).

[1] Excluding Greece, for which data are not available.

7.1. Per capita social protection benefits — 1987 (PPS consumption)

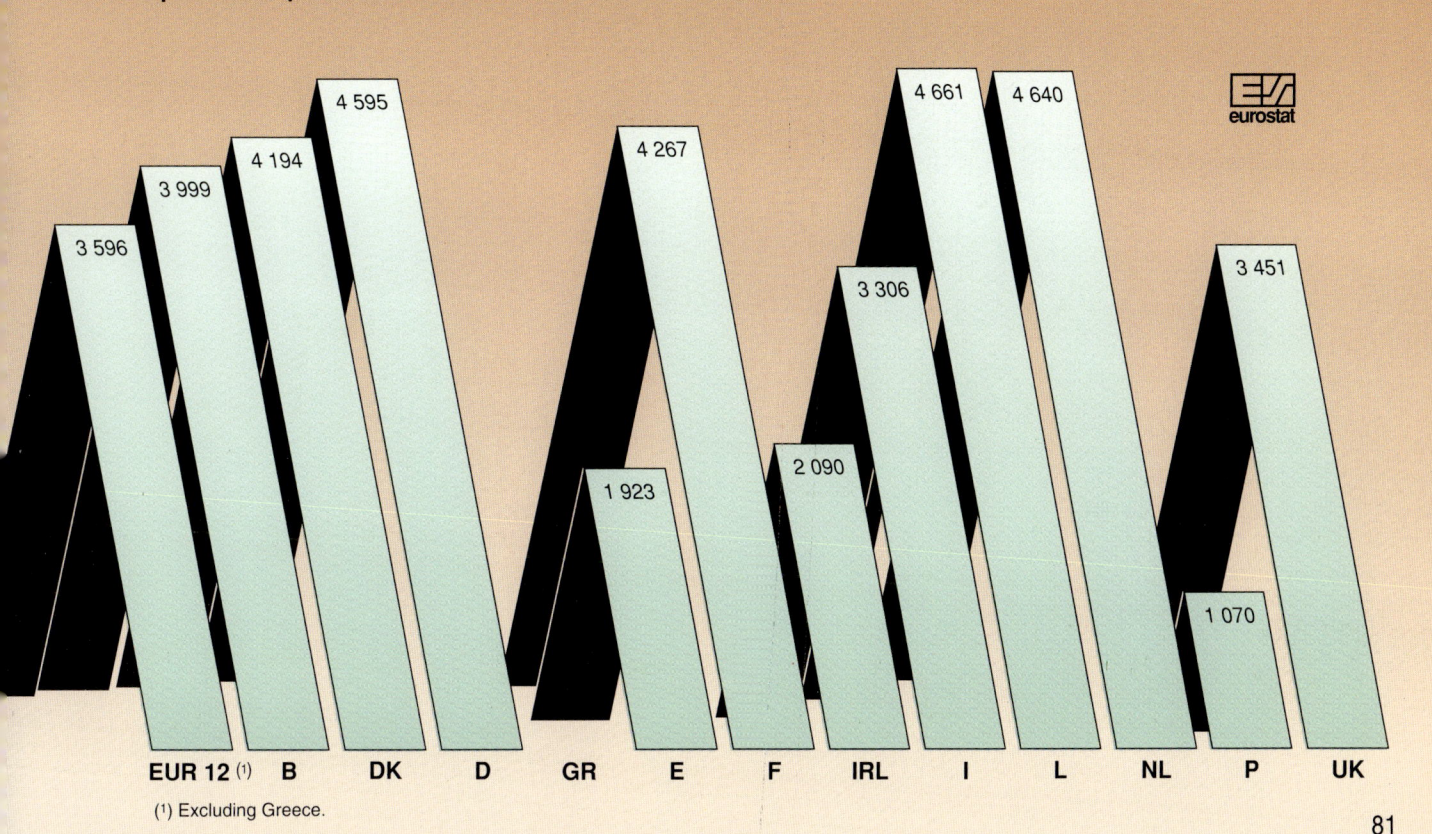

EUR 12 [1]	B	DK	D	GR	E	F	IRL	I	L	NL	P	UK
3 596	3 999	4 194	4 595		1 923	4 267	2 090	3 306	4 661	4 640	1 070	3 451

([1]) Excluding Greece.

SOCIAL PROTECTION
SOCIAL BENEFITS AND GDP

7.2. Social protection expenditure as % of GDP in 1988

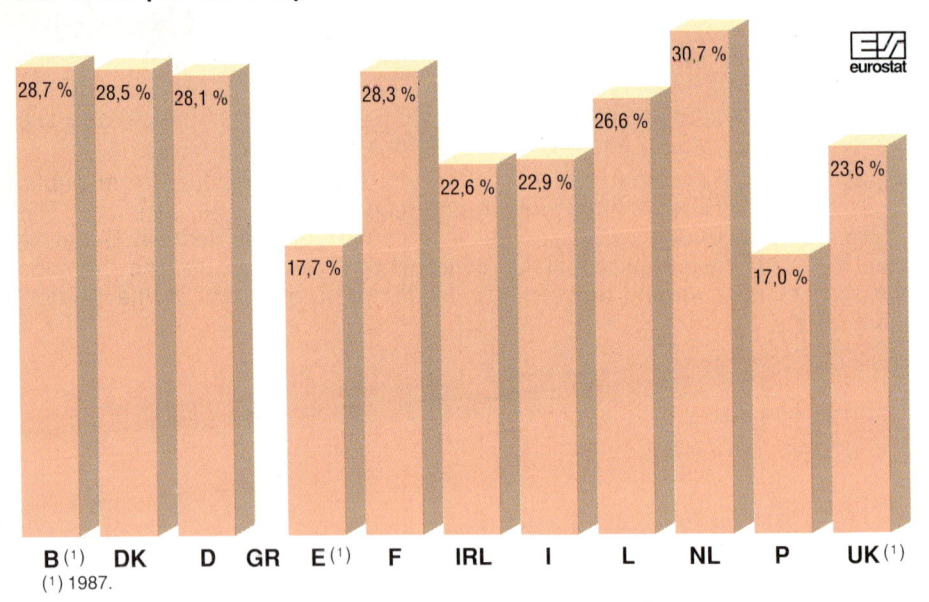

B[1]	DK	D	GR	E[1]	F	IRL	I	L	NL	P	UK[1]
28,7%	28,5%	28,1%		17,7%	28,3%	22,6%	22,9%	26,6%	30,7%	17,0%	23,6%

[1] 1987.

7.3. Percentage of GDP devoted to social protection and per capita GDP in 1988

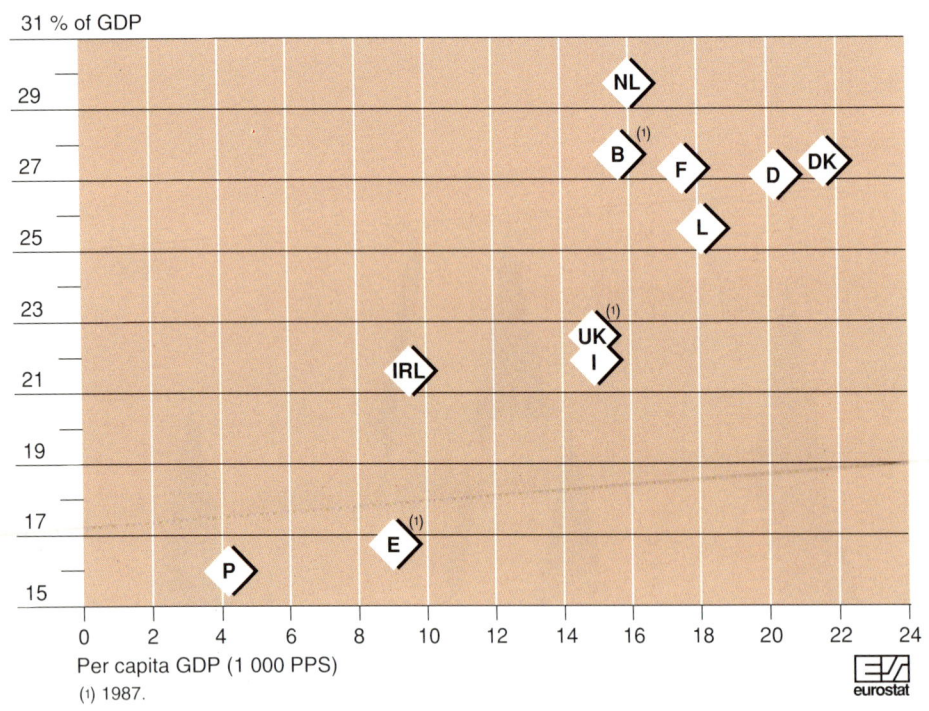

Per capita GDP (1 000 PPS)
[1] 1987.

The ratio of social protection expenditure to GDP reflects the degree of commitment to social protection. In 1988 the ratio of minimum to maximum protection in the various countries was of the order of 1:2. The proportion was highest in the Netherlands (approximately 31%). In Belgium, Denmark, France, the Federal Republic of Germany and Luxembourg it varied between 29% and 27%, while in the United Kingdom, Italy and Ireland it was approximately 23% and in Spain and Portugal approximately 17%.

The graph shows these ratios in relation to the level of per capita GDP. It can be seen that the wealthiest countries tend to devote the highest proportion of GDP to social protection, so that those benefiting from such protection in these countries enjoy a double advantage compared with their counterparts in the less well-off countries.

SOCIAL PROTECTION
PER CAPITA SOCIAL BENEFITS

The per capita amounts devoted to social protection benefits vary widely from one Community country to another. Per capita expenditure on social protection is higher than the Community average in six countries (Luxembourg, the Netherlands, the Federal Republic of Germany, France, Denmark and Belgium). However, these countries do not form a homogeneous group, since Luxembourg records 130 % and Belgium 111 % in relation to the Community average of 100 %. Percentage expenditure in the five other Community countries for which data are available (Portugal, Spain, Ireland, Italy and the United Kingdom) is lower than the Community average, varying between 30 % in Portugal and 96 % in the United Kingdom.

7.4. Per capita social protection benefits as % of the Community average (PPS consumption) — 1987

EUR [1]	3 596 PPS
EUR 12	100
B	111
DK	117
D	128
GR	:
E	53
F	119
IRL	58
I	92
L	130
NL	129
P	30
UK	96

([1]) Average excluding Greece.

7.5. Per capita social protection benefits — index 1985 = 100

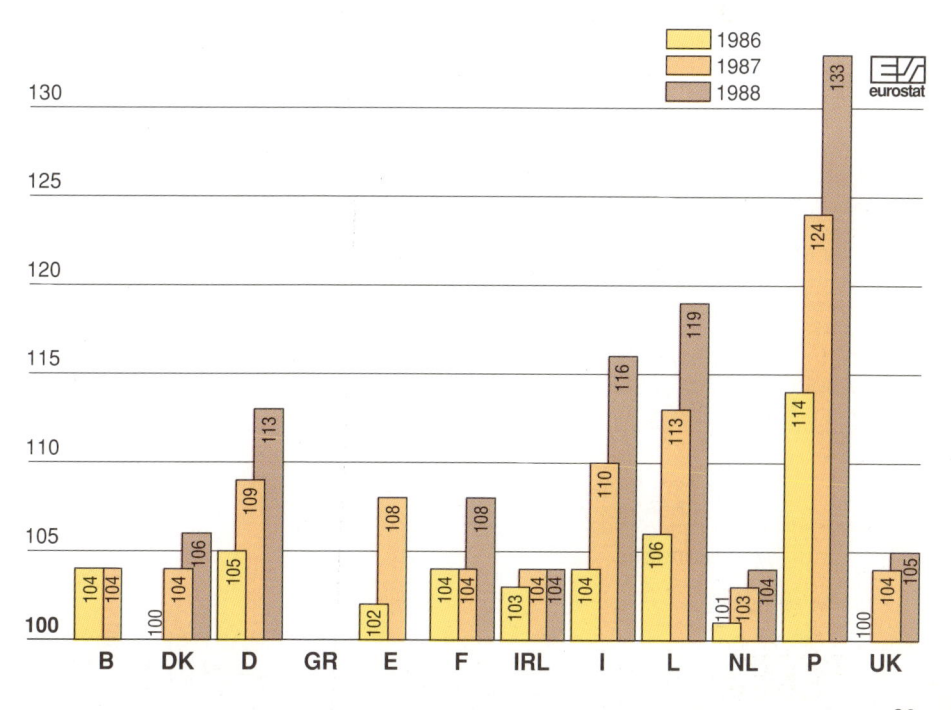

	1986	1987	1988
B	100	104	104
DK	100	104	106
D	105	109	113
GR			
E	102	108	
F	104	104	108
IRL	103	104	104
I	104	110	116
L	106	113	119
NL	101	103	104
P	114	124	133
UK	100	104	105

SOCIAL PROTECTION
SOCIAL BENEFITS BY FUNCTION

7.6. Breakdown of social protection benefits by group of functions — EUR 12 — 1987 [1]

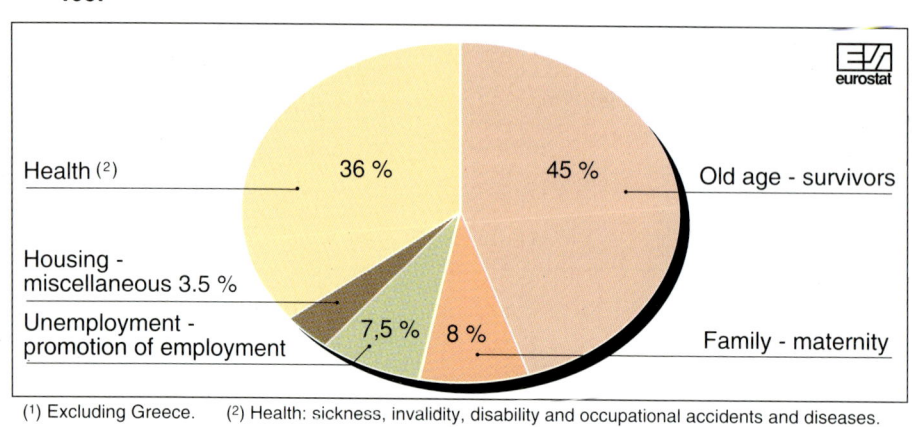

- Health [2]: 36 %
- Old age - survivors: 45 %
- Housing - miscellaneous: 3.5 %
- Unemployment - promotion of employment: 7.5 %
- Family - maternity: 8 %

[1] Excluding Greece. [2] Health: sickness, invalidity, disability and occupational accidents and diseases.

The breakdown of benefits by function reflects the priority which each country's social protection system accords to the various risks covered.

The largest share of social benefits is assigned to the sectors 'Old-age – Survivors' (45 %) and 'Health' (36 %), which alone account for over 80 % of social benefits within the Community. The proportion of benefits relating to the functions of family, maternity, unemployment and the promotion of employment and housing is much lower, varying between 8 % and 3.5 %.

National percentages are tightly bunched in the 'Old age – Survivors' function, with the exception of three countries at either end of the scale, i.e. the Netherlands (32 %) and Ireland (31 %) on the one hand and Italy (59 %) on the other.

The 'Health' function is also characterized by rates very close to the average in the majority of countries, although in Luxembourg, the Netherlands and Portugal the proportion is approximately 45 %.

In contrast, percentages for the group 'Family – Maternity' are more widely dispersed, with Spain (2 %) and Ireland (13 %) at the opposite ends of the scale.

The divergences for the functions 'Unemployment' and 'Promotion of employment' are even more marked, with percentages varying from 1 % to 17 % compared with a Community average of just over 7 %.

7.7. Breakdown of social protection benefits by function as % of overall benefits — 1987

	B	DK	D	GR	E	F	IRL	I	L	NL	P	UK
Old age - survivors	43,5	37,6	41,7		45,9	45,0	31,1	59,4	44,2	31,9	41,5	42,7
Health	34,1	31,3	40,8		34,9	34,2	34,4	33,0	44,3	45,7	45,8	30,8
Family - maternity	8,6	12,1	7,1		1,8	10,7	12,7	5,0	9,4	8,0	7,2	10,9
Unemployment - promotion of employment	12,6	12,8	6,8		16,9	6,6	16,2	2,4	1,3	11,1	3,0	8,1
Housing - miscellaneous	1,2	6,2	3,6		0,5	3,4	5,6	0,2	0,8	3,3	2,5	7,4

SOCIAL PROTECTION
RECEIPTS

Expenditure is financed from three main sources, i.e. contributions paid by the protected person, contributions paid by employers and contributions from public funds. To these can be added a fourth category of 'Other receipts', which is chiefly composed of interest on invested capital and is of importance in only a small number of countries.

There are considerable divergences in distribution between the three main categories in the period under review. For example, in 1987

(i) the share of contributions from public funds in overall receipts was approximately 78% in Denmark and 14% in the Netherlands; in the United Kingdom, Luxembourg, Italy, Belgium, Spain, the Federal Republic of Germany and Portugal it varied between 43% and 25%;

(ii) employers' contributions ranged between 53% (Italy) and 11% (Denmark), with four countries (Portugal, Spain, France and Italy) close to the maximum figure;

(iii) the share of contributions paid by protected persons varied very widely, ranging between 36% (the Netherlands) and 4% (Denmark).

The two polar positions are occupied by Denmark and Ireland on the one hand (the highest rate of contributions from public funds and the lowest rate of employers' and protected persons' contributions) and the Netherlands (where contributions paid by the protected person exceed employers' contributions and the share of contributions from public funds is lowest) on the other.

Price and income structures are influenced by the way in which financing is divided up between the budgets of general government (taxation), the social-security expenditure of enterprises and the contributions of households. It may be that the effect of structural differences between countries is especially great where wide disparities are to be observed. Here too, the scale of the problems of economic and social convergence is apparent.

7.8. Breakdown of social protection receipts by category — 1987 (%)

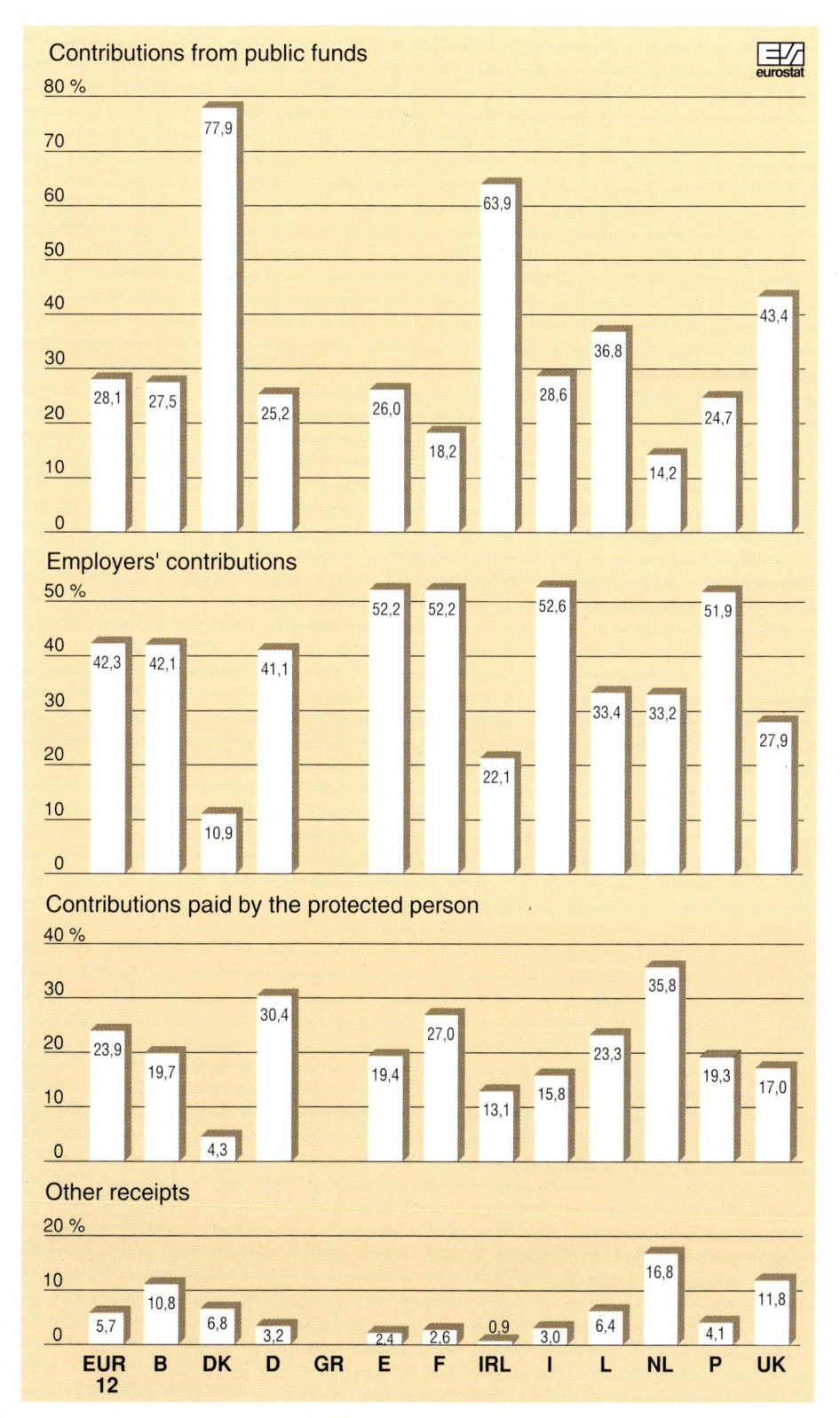

Contributions from public funds

EUR 12	B	DK	D	GR	E	F	IRL	I	L	NL	P	UK
28,1	27,5	77,9	25,2		26,0	18,2	63,9	28,6	36,8	14,2	24,7	43,4

Employers' contributions

EUR 12	B	DK	D	GR	E	F	IRL	I	L	NL	P	UK
42,3	42,1	10,9	41,1		52,2	52,2	22,1	52,6	33,4	33,2	51,9	27,9

Contributions paid by the protected person

EUR 12	B	DK	D	GR	E	F	IRL	I	L	NL	P	UK
23,9	19,7	4,3	30,4		19,4	27,0	13,1	15,8	23,3	35,8	19,3	17,0

Other receipts

EUR 12	B	DK	D	GR	E	F	IRL	I	L	NL	P	UK
5,7	10,8	6,8	3,2		2,4	2,6	0,9	3,0	6,4	16,8	4,1	11,8

SOCIAL PROTECTION
FOR FURTHER INFORMATION

References

Eurostat – Databank
– Cronos
– Esspross

HEALTH

The number of doctors per 1 000 inhabitants ranges from 1.3 in Ireland to 3.3 in Spain (8.2).

The greatest rise in health expenditure as a proportion of total household expenditure was recorded in Belgium (59 %) between 1970 and 1987 (8.4).

Denmark has the highest rate of household expenditure on alcohol and tobacco in the European Community (3.9 % in 1987) (8.9) (8.10).

Disease of the circulatory system and malignant tumours are the major causes of death in the European Community, accounting for 45 % and 24 % of deaths respectively (8.12).

AIDS strikes hardest at men between the ages of 20 and 54 in the European Community (22 940 cases), with the worst-hit groups being homosexuals (47.5 %) and drug addicts (31.1 %) (8.19) (8.22).

The death rate by suicide per 10 000 inhabitants in the European Community increases with age, rising in men from 1.1 among the 15-24 age group to 6.2 among the over-75s, and in women from 0.3 to 1.7 respectively (8.24).

In 1987, road accidents killed over 45 000 persons and injured 1 604 831 in the European Community. Nearly three-quarters of those killed were men, almost half of whom were aged between 15 and 34 (8.30) (8.32).

8.1. Standardized mortality rate by sex — 1980-84 (per 100 000 inhabitants)

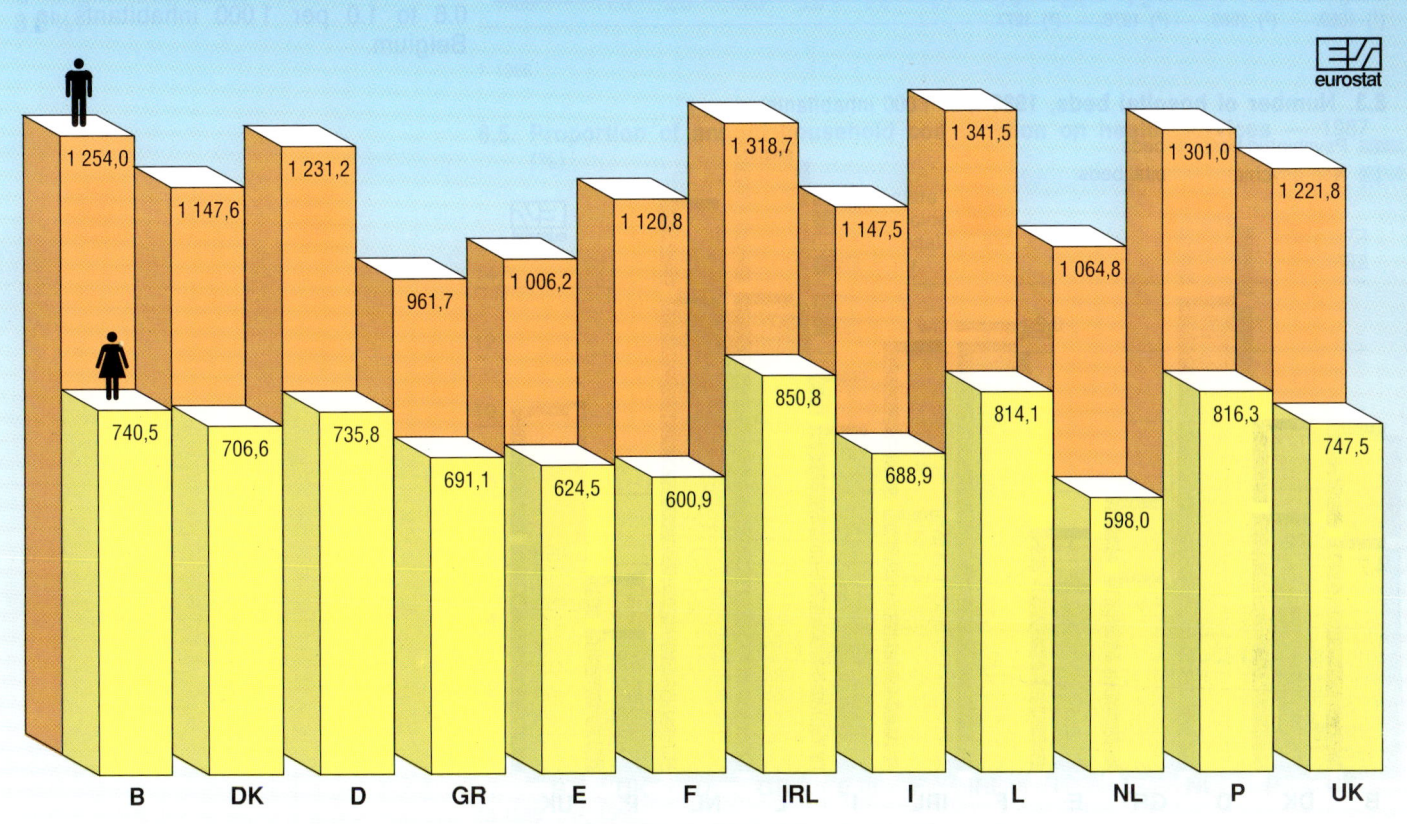

	B	DK	D	GR	E	F	IRL	I	L	NL	P	UK
Men	1 254,0	1 147,6	1 231,2	961,7	1 006,2	1 120,8	1 318,7	1 147,5	1 341,5	1 064,8	1 301,0	1 221,8
Women	740,5	706,6	735,8	691,1	624,5	600,9	850,8	688,9	814,1	598,0	816,3	747,5

Source: WHO.

HEALTH
CANCERS

8.16. Trends in the standardized mortality rate for death by cancer according to sex (per 100 000 inhabitants)

Male

	B	DK	D	GR	E	F	IRL	I	L	NL	P	UK
1960-1964	262,2	246,8	252,7	171,3	189,7	256,9	201,9	210,5	:	251,0	156,8	267,0
1970-1974	295,2	251,4	269,4	186,7	205,4	276,8	235,2	251,8	305,9	286,3	186,9	283,7
1980-1984	325,1	278,5	277,3	213,0	228,2	300,5	249,8	280,3	330,0	307,2	199,4	281,3

Female

	B	DK	D	GR	E	F	IRL	I	L	NL	P	UK
1960-1964	184,2	209,2	188,4	105,4	130,3	155,1	161,6	144,7	:	178,7	117,2	167,8
1970-1974	173,4	192,9	181,3	106,0	127,5	143,8	181,4	148,1	169,6	173,3	127,5	175,1
1980-1984	168,4	200,5	170,4	116,0	118,1	136,4	180,9	147,0	181,1	161,8	121,6	182,0

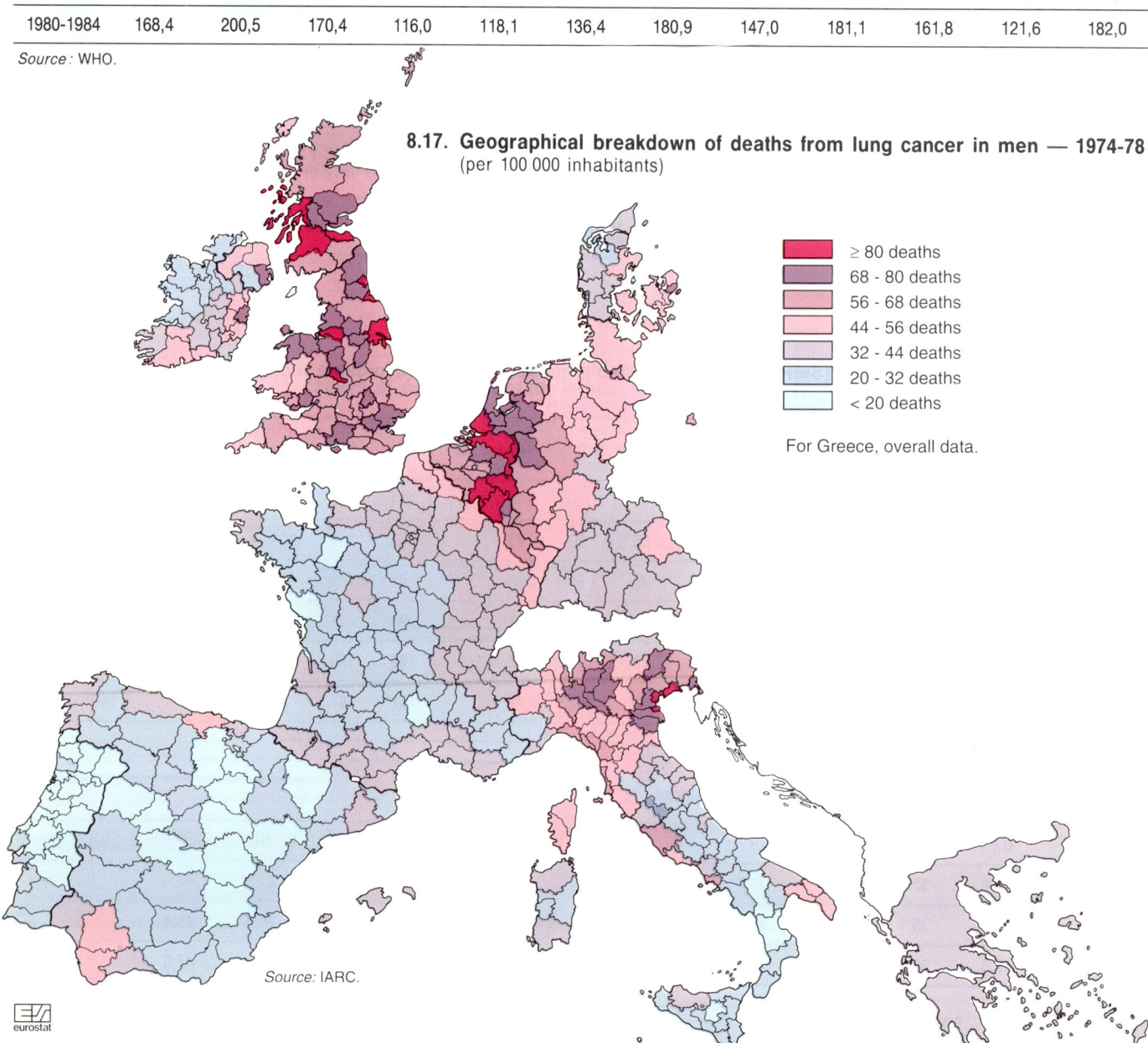

Source: WHO.

8.17. Geographical breakdown of deaths from lung cancer in men — 1974-78
(per 100 000 inhabitants)

≥ 80 deaths
68 - 80 deaths
56 - 68 deaths
44 - 56 deaths
32 - 44 deaths
20 - 32 deaths
< 20 deaths

For Greece, overall data.

Source: IARC.

HEALTH

The number of doctors per 1 000 inhabitants ranges from 1.3 in Ireland to 3.3 in Spain (8.2).

The greatest rise in health expenditure as a proportion of total household expenditure was recorded in Belgium (59%) between 1970 and 1987 (8.4).

Denmark has the highest rate of household expenditure on alcohol and tobacco in the European Community (3.9% in 1987) (8.9) (8.10).

Disease of the circulatory system and malignant tumours are the major causes of death in the European Community, accounting for 45% and 24% of deaths respectively (8.12).

AIDS strikes hardest at men between the ages of 20 and 54 in the European Community (22 940 cases), with the worst-hit groups being homosexuals (47.5%) and drug addicts (31.1%) (8.19) (8.22).

The death rate by suicide per 10 000 inhabitants in the European Community increases with age, rising in men from 1.1 among the 15-24 age group to 6.2 among the over-75s, and in women from 0.3 to 1.7 respectively (8.24).

In 1987, road accidents killed over 45 000 persons and injured 1 604 831 in the European Community. Nearly three-quarters of those killed were men, almost half of whom were aged between 15 and 34 (8.30) (8.32).

8.1. Standardized mortality rate by sex — 1980-84 (per 100 000 inhabitants)

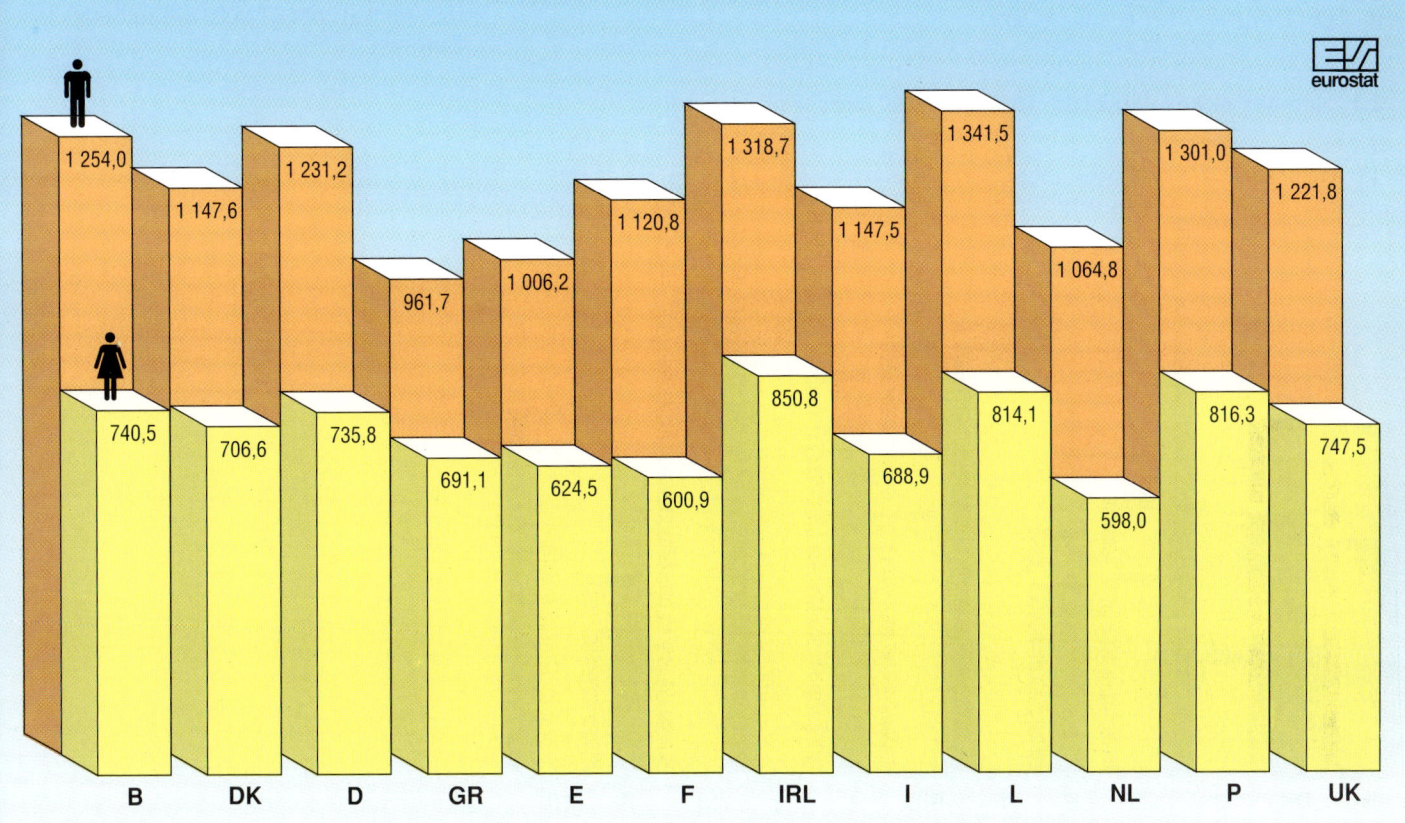

Country	Male	Female
B	1 254,0	740,5
DK	1 147,6	706,6
D	1 231,2	735,8
GR	961,7	691,1
E	1 006,2	624,5
F	1 120,8	600,9
IRL	1 318,7	850,8
I	1 147,5	688,9
L	1 341,5	814,1
NL	1 064,8	598,0
P	1 301,0	816,3
UK	1 221,8	747,5

Source: WHO.

HEALTH
INFRASTRUCTURE

8.2. Trends in the health professions (per 1 000 inhabitants)

Number of doctors per 1 000 inhabitants

	B	DK	D	GR	E	F	IRL	I(¹)	L	NL	P	UK
1960	1,3	1,2	1,4	1,3	1,2	1,0	1,1	1,6	1,0	1,1	0,8	:
1970	1,5	1,4	1,6	1,6	1,3	1,3	1,2	1,8	1,1	1,2	0,9	1,1
1980	2,3	2,2	2,3	2,4	2,3	2,0	1,3	3,1	1,5	1,9	2,0	1,4
1985	2,8	2,6	2,5	3,0	3,3	2,3	1,3	4,2	1,8	2,2	2,4	1,5

(¹) Including dentists.

Number of dentists per 1 000 inhabitants

	B	DK	D	GR	E	F	IRL	(¹) I	L	NL	P	UK
1960	0,3	:	:	0,4	0,1	0,3	0,2	1,6	0,4	0,2	:	:
1970	:	0,6	0,5	0,5	0,1	0,4	0,2	1,8	0,3	0,3	:	0,3
1980	0,4	1,0	0,5	0,8	0,1	0,6	0,3	3,1	0,4	0,4	0,1	0,3
1985	0,6	1,0	0,6	0,9	0,1	0,6	0,3	4,2	0,5	0,5	0,1	0,4

(¹) Including doctors.

Number of pharmacists per 1 000 inhabitants

	B	DK	D	GR	E	F	IRL	I	L	NL	P	UK
1960(¹)	0,6	0,3	0,3	:	:	0,4	:	0,6	0,5	0,1	0,2	0,4
1970(²)	0,7	0,4	0,3	0,3	0,5	0,5	0,6	0,7	0,5	0,1	0,7	0,3
1980	1,0	:	0,5	:	0,5(³)	:	0,6	:	0,6	0,1	:	0,4(⁴)
1985	1,0	0,3	0,5	0,6	0,8	0,4	0,6	0,8	0,7	0,1	0,5	:

(¹) 1959.   (²) 1969.   (³) 1976.   (⁴) 1977.

Since 1960, there has been a considerable increase in the number of doctors in the European Community. In Portugal, it has risen from 0.8 doctors per 1 000 inhabitants in 1986 to 2.4 in 1985; in Spain from 1.2 to 3.3; in France from 1.0 to 2.3. The upward trend has been less marked in Ireland, where 1.1 doctors were recorded per 1 000 inhabitants in 1960 and 1.3 in 1985.

There are considerably fewer dentists, but they too have increased in number. This increase has been highest in the Netherlands (from 0.2 to 0.5 per 1 000 inhabitants), Greece (from 0.4 to 0.9), France (from 0.3 to 0.6) and Belgium (from 0.3 to 0.6).

There are, on the whole, more pharmacists, but trends have varied from one country to another. Their number was constant between 1960 and 1985 in some countries—0.4 per 1 000 inhabitants in France, 0.3 in Denmark and 0.6 in Ireland—whilst it rose from 0.6 to 1.0 per 1 000 inhabitants in Belgium.

8.3. Number of hospital beds, 1986 (per 1 000 inhabitants)

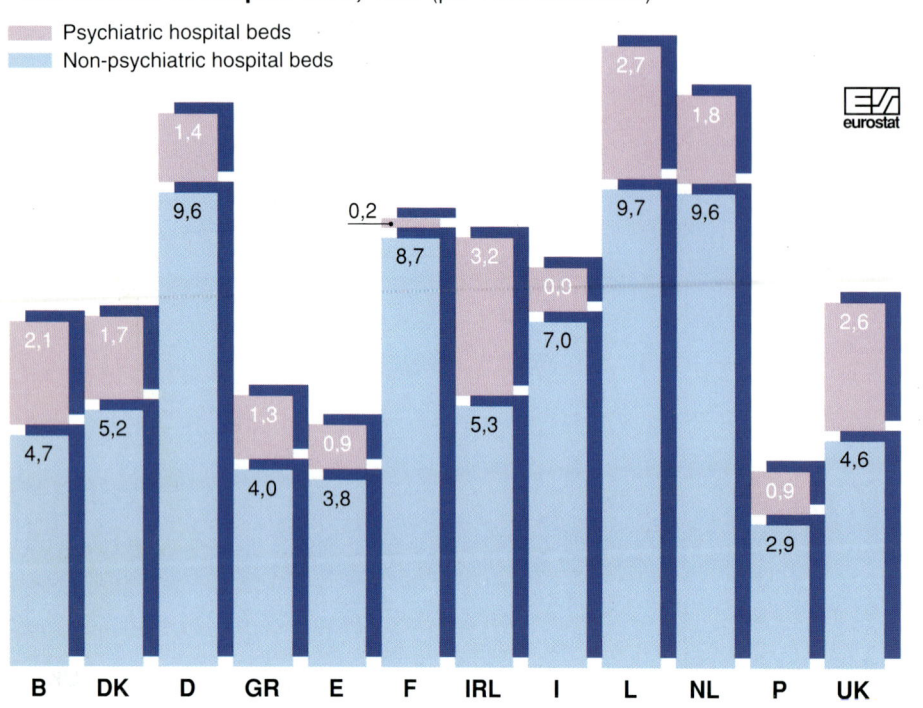

- Psychiatric hospital beds
- Non-psychiatric hospital beds

Country	Non-psychiatric	Psychiatric
B	4,7	2,1
DK	5,2	1,7
D	9,6	1,4
GR	4,0	1,3
E	3,8	0,9
F	8,7	0,2
IRL	5,3	3,2
I	7,0	0,9
L	9,7	2,7
NL	9,6	1,8
P	2,9	0,9
UK	4,6	2,6

HEALTH
EXPENDITURE

Household expenditure on health is strongly influenced by the financial organization of the social security system. In the United Kingdom, the NHS (National Health Service) is responsible for all health care. In Denmark the financial balance of the social security system is met by taxation. In other countries, households contribute directly, but to varying degrees. Valid comparisons can, therefore, only be drawn between countries if it is borne in mind that the structure of their health-care systems varies enormously. Household expenditure is highest in the Federal Republic of Germany (15.0%) and the Netherlands (12.8%), and lowest in the United Kingdom (1.3%) and Denmark (2.0%). In almost all the Member States, however, it registered an increase between 1970 and 1988 (e.g. from 9.5% to 15.0% in the Federal Republic of Germany), with the exception of Greece which recorded a slight decrease, from 4.1% to 3.6%.

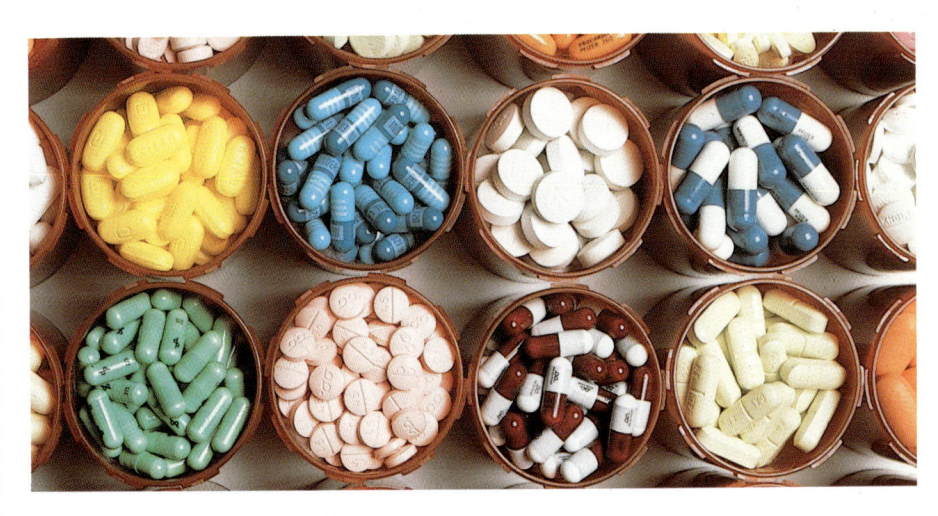

8.4. Trends in expenditure on health as a proportion of total household expenditure (%)

	B	DK	D	GR	E	F	IRL	I	L	NL	P	UK
1970	6.8	2.0	9.5	4.1	2.9	6.0	2.5	3.7	5.4	8.4	:	0.9
1975	8.9	2.0	12.9	3.9	3.4	7.0	2.2	4.2	6.3	11.2	:	0.9
1980	9.8	1.8	13.5	3.6	3.8	7.7	2.1	4.8	7.3	12.1	4.3	1.0
1985	10.4	1.8	13.9	3.6	3.6	8.6	2.6	5.5	6.7	12.6	4.6	1.3
1988	11.0	2.0	15.0	3.6	3.6	9.2	3.4	6.1	7.8	12.6	4.5[1]	1.3

[1] 1986.

8.5. Proportion of annual household consumption on health services — 1987 (%)

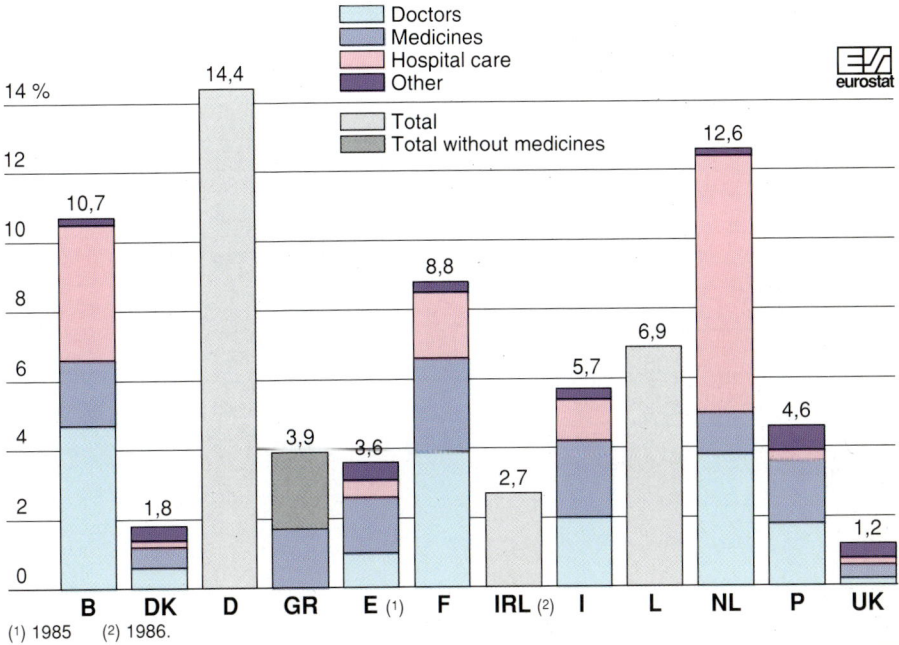

(1) 1985   (2) 1986.

HEALTH
LIFE EXPECTANCY

8.6. Life expectancy at birth by sex — 1985-88 (years)

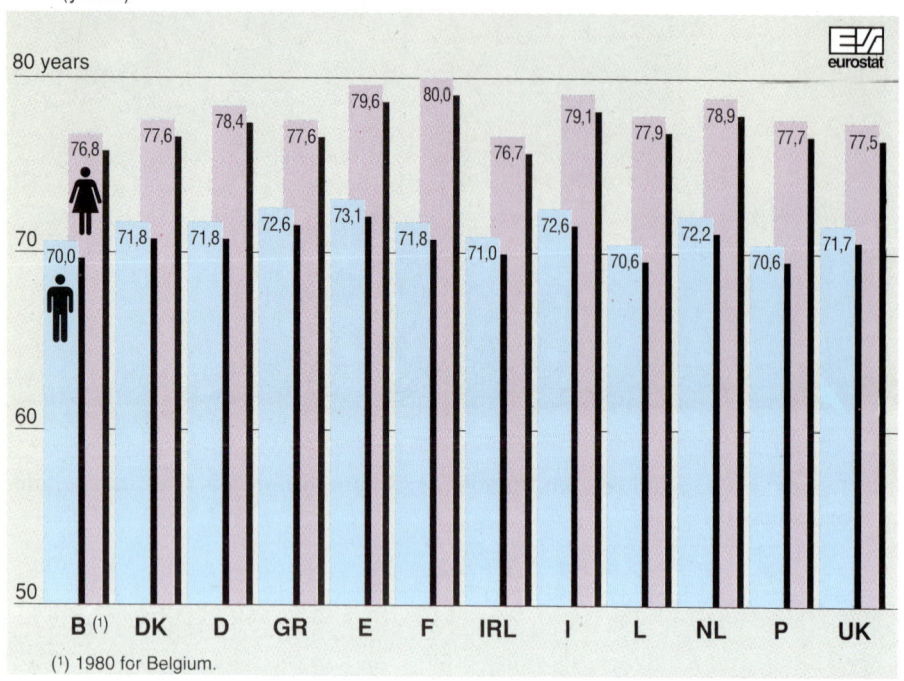

	B(¹)	DK	D	GR	E	F	IRL	I	L	NL	P	UK
Male	70.0	71.8	71.8	72.6	73.1	71.8	71.0	72.6	70.6	72.2	70.6	71.7
Female	76.8	77.6	78.4	77.6	79.6	80.0	76.7	79.1	77.9	78.9	77.7	77.5

(¹) 1980 for Belgium.

According to WHO reports, life expectancy without disability (where the human being does not suffer from problems directly related to health disorders) shows that the difference between the life expectancy of men and of women is decreasing: in France, it is 61.9 years for men and 67.2 years for women. This means, in general terms, that although women may live longer (78.9 years) they quite often spend this 'extra' period of life (after 67.2 years) disabled. It can also be deduced from these figures that disability problems appear in men after the age of 62, whilst, according to WHO calculations, their life expectancy is 70.7 years.

8.7. Life expectancy at 40 by sex — 1985-88 (years)

	B(¹)	DK	D	GR	E	F	IRL	I	L	NL	P	UK
Male	33,0	34,1	34,1	35,6	35,8	34,5	33,1	34,8	33,2	34,2	34,3	33,8
Female	38,8	39,1	39,9	39,6	41,3	41,6	38,1	40,6	39,4	40,3	39,8	39,0

(¹) 1980.

8.8. Comparison of life expectancy and life expectancy without disability in the 1960s (years)

	Male F	Male NL	Male UK	Female F	Female NL	Female UK
At birth						
Life expectancy ¹	70.7	72.8	71.8	78.9	79.5	77.7
Life expectancy without disability	61.9	58.7	58.7	67.2	60.6	61.5
At 65						
Life expectancy ¹	14.3	14.0	13.4	18.5	18.6	17.5
Life expectancy without disability	9.1	8.1	7.7	9.9	9.1	8.9

Source: WHO.
¹ WHO data.

HEALTH
RISK FACTORS

Alcohol and tobacco are risk factors for a great many diseases: cancers, cardiovascular diseases, etc. In 1987, Danish households devoted 3.4% of their expenditure to alcohol, as against 1.2% in Italy. Expenditure on alcohol decreased between 1980 and 1987 in a number of Community countries: Belgium, Denmark, France, Italy and the Netherlands. Greece (3%) and Denmark (2.9%) have the highest household expenditure on tobacco, whilst it is lowest in France (1.1%).

8.9. Trends in expenditure on alcohol as a proportion of total household expenditure (%)

	B	DK	D	GR	E	F	IRL(¹)	I	L	NL	P	UK
1980	1,8	3,8	2,2	2,3	1,3	2,3	11,3	1,6	1,8	2,0	2,6	1,8
1987	1,5	3,4	2,2	2,7	:	2,0	:	1,2	:	1,8	:	1,8

(¹) Including expenditure on alcoholic drinks in restaurants, cafés and hotels.

8.10. Trends in expenditure on tobacco as a proportion of total household expenditure (%)

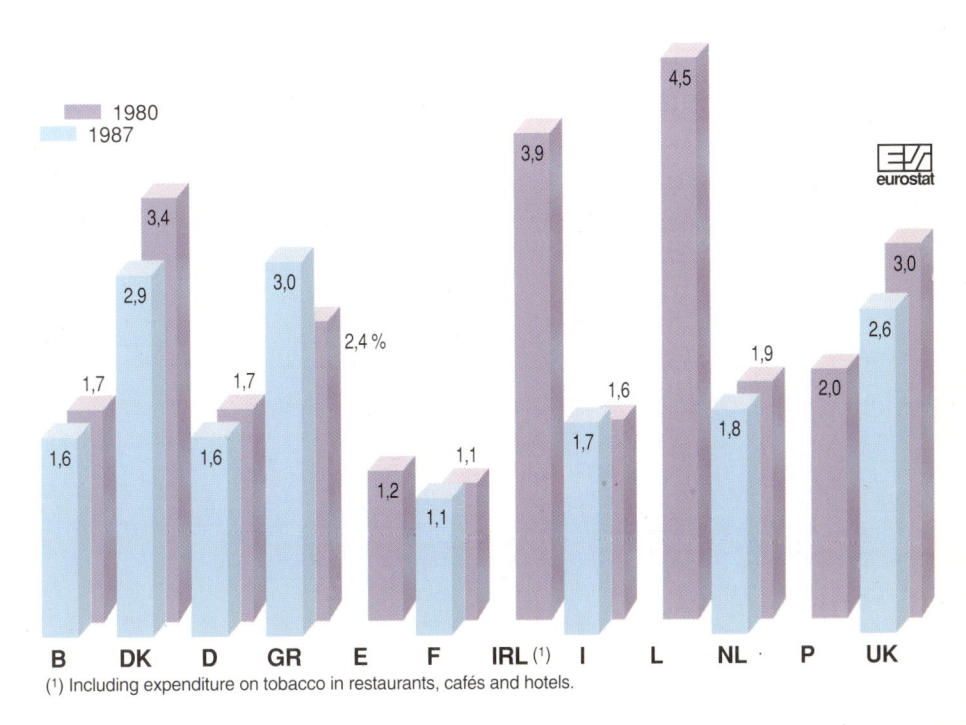

	B	DK	D	GR	E	F	IRL(¹)	I	L	NL	P	UK
1980	1,7	3,4	1,7	3,0	1,2	1,1	3,9	1,6	4,5	1,9	2,0	3,0
1987	1,6	2,9	1,6	2,4	1,1	1,1	1,7	1,6	1,8	1,8	2,0	2,6

(¹) Including expenditure on tobacco in restaurants, cafés and hotels.

HEALTH
CAUSES OF DEATH

8.11. Trends in the standardized mortality rate by sex (per 100 000 inhabitants)

Male

	B	DK	D	GR	E	F	IRL	I	L	NL	P	UK
1960-1964	1 443,5	1 197,6	1 450,0	1 107,9	1 301,5	1 441,5	1 400,6	1 347,1	:	1 123,7	1 578,7	1 471,0
1970-1974	1 419,7	1 169,6	1 436,5	1 003,9	1 195,0	1 278,6	1 410,4	1 286,8	1 516,9	1 166,6	1 613,4	1 400,9
1980-1984	1 254,0	1 147,6	1 231,2	961,7	1 006,2	1 120,8	1 318,7	1 147,5	1 341,5	1 064,8	1 301,0	1 221,8

Female

	B	DK	D	GR	E	F	IRL	I	L	NL	P	UK
1960-1964	971,0	913,1	1 006,1	871,3	960,5	884,0	1 066,8	955,7	:	824,3	1 131,1	938,9
1970-1974	894,5	776,1	921,7	747,2	816,8	724,7	992,7	829,5	933,4	747,0	1 074,1	854,8
1980-1984	740,5	706,6	735,8	691,1	624,5	600,9	850,8	688,9	814,1	598,0	816,3	747,5

Source: WHO.

8.12. Breakdown of mortality by major causes of death — EUR 12 — 1986 (%)

Infectious diseases	Malignant tumours	Circulatory system	Motor vehicle accidents	Suicides	Other	Total
0,7	23,9	44,9	1,5	1,3	27,7	100

Source: WHO.

8.13. Breakdown of mortality by causes of death according to age and sex — EUR 12 — 1986 (%)

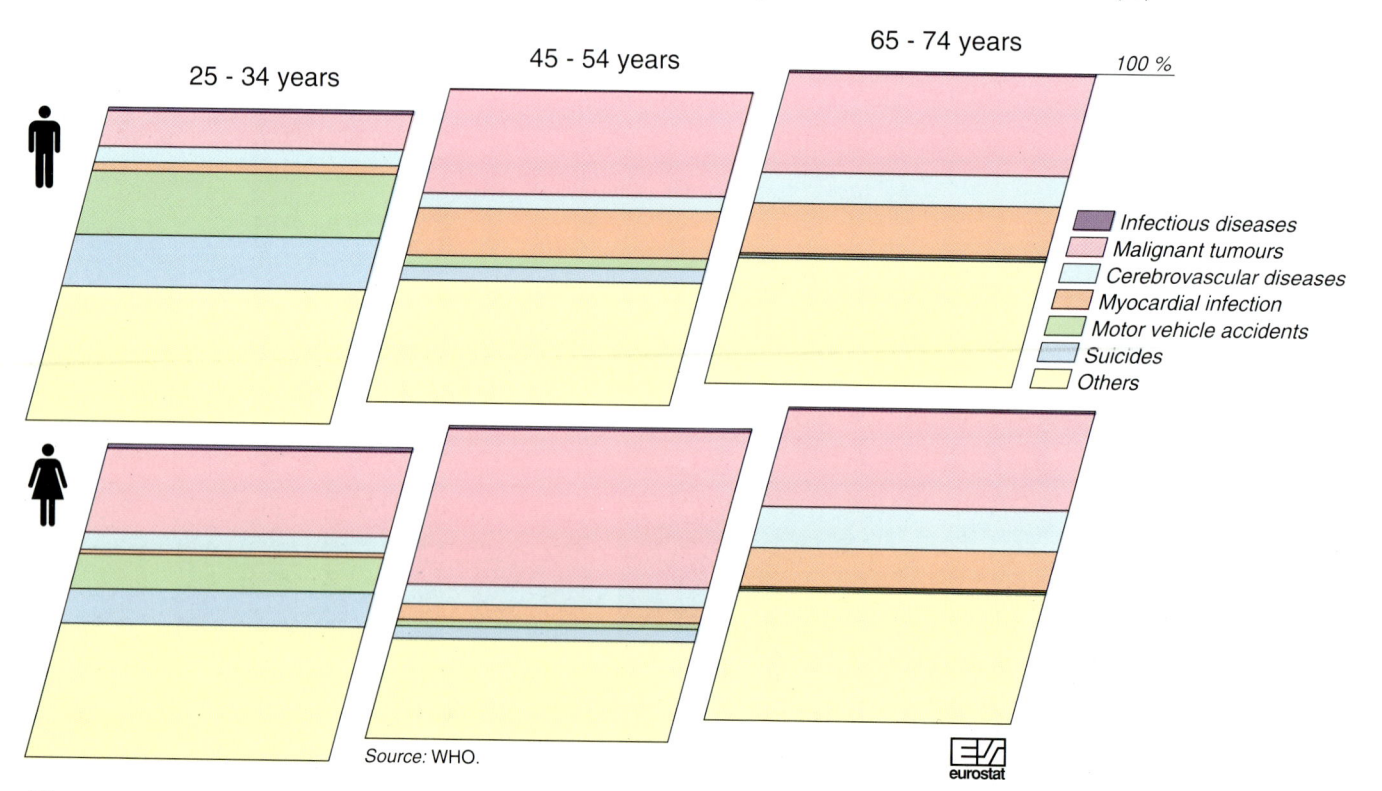

Source: WHO.

HEALTH
CAUSES OF DEATH

The standardized mortality rate allows comparisons to be made between countries by eliminating the effects of age structure.

In the Community countries, there has been a decrease in the standardized mortality rate for both males and females. The lowest rate for males was recorded in Greece (961.7 per 100 000 in 1980-84), but it is in Spain, with rates of 1 301.5 in 1980-84 and 1 006.2 in 1980-84 and France (1 441.5 and 1 120.8) that the greatest decreases can be seen. For females, the lowest rate is found in France (600.9 per 100 000 in 1980-84), with the largest reductions over 20 years being recorded in Spain (−35%) and France (−32%).

The major causes of death in the European Community are diseases of the circulatory system (45%), followed by malignant tumours (24%).

The causes of death vary with age. Between the ages of 25 and 34, malignant tumours cause 11.3% of deaths among men and 26.8% among women; between the ages of 45 and 54 they cause 33.2% of male deaths and 49.8% of female deaths; and between the ages of 65 and 74, the figures are 32.0% and 31.0% respectively. Motor-vehicle accidents are responsible for 20.4% of deaths among men aged between 25 and 34 and 11.3% of women of the same age. Between the ages of 65 and 74, these figures fall to 0.7% for men and 0.6% for women.

8.14. Standardized mortality rate (SMR) for some avoidable causes of death (avoidable mortality) — 1974-78
(per 100 000 inhabitants)

Age where death is avoidable		B	DK	D	GR	E	F	IRL	I	L	NL	P	UK[1]
5-64	Tuberculosis	91	40	106	140	:	131	165	125	59	23	:	54
35-64	Hypertension - heart disease	94	66	90	93	:	92	134	116	127	65	:	107
1-14	Diseases of the respiratory system	70	49	95	126	:	67	176	117	71	64	:	131
5-64	Appendicitis	53	59	159	37	:	98	111	98	158	66	:	69
5-44	Asthma	175	53	173	32	:	66	150	11	:	58	:	151
15-64	Cervical cancer	75	246	142	29	:	67	81	28	110	:	115	151

[1] England and Wales. *Source*: WHO.

8.15. Excess mortality rate (EMR) by sex — 1950-86 (%)

	B [3]	DK	D	GR [4]	E [2]	F [4]	IRL	I [3]	L	NL	P	UK [1] [4]
Male	51,6	37,8	41,1	17,7	25,0	32,4	64,7	37,9	:	31,3	47,0	46,6
Female	43,0	35,1	37,4	38,7	28,4	15,1	67,1	34,9	:	20,4	48,4	43,5
Total	47,3	36,5	39,1	26,9	26,6	23,5	65,8	36,5	:	25,9	47,6	45,0

Source: WHO.
[1] England and Wales.   [2] 1983.   [3] 1984.   [4] 1985.

HEALTH
CANCERS

8.16. Trends in the standardized mortality rate for death by cancer according to sex (per 100 000 inhabitants)

Male

	B	DK	D	GR	E	F	IRL	I	L	NL	P	UK
1960-1964	262,2	246,8	252,7	171,3	189,7	256,9	201,9	210,5	:	251,0	156,8	267,0
1970-1974	295,2	251,4	269,4	186,7	205,4	276,8	235,2	251,8	305,9	286,3	186,9	283,7
1980-1984	325,1	278,5	277,3	213,0	228,2	300,5	249,8	280,3	330,0	307,2	199,4	281,3

Female

	B	DK	D	GR	E	F	IRL	I	L	NL	P	UK
1960-1964	184,2	209,2	188,4	105,4	130,3	155,1	161,6	144,7	:	178,7	117,2	167,8
1970-1974	173,4	192,9	181,3	106,0	127,5	143,8	181,4	148,1	169,6	173,3	127,5	175,1
1980-1984	168,4	200,5	170,4	116,0	118,1	136,4	180,9	147,0	181,1	161,8	121,6	182,0

Source: WHO.

8.17. Geographical breakdown of deaths from lung cancer in men — 1974-78
(per 100 000 inhabitants)

- ≥ 80 deaths
- 68 - 80 deaths
- 56 - 68 deaths
- 44 - 56 deaths
- 32 - 44 deaths
- 20 - 32 deaths
- < 20 deaths

For Greece, overall data.

Source: IARC.

HEALTH
CANCERS

Whereas the general death rate in the Community fell between 1960 and 1984, the death rate from cancer increased over the same period for men in all the Member States, but decreased for women in six countries and remained stable or rose slightly in the others. In the Federal Republic of Germany, for example, the rate for men increased from 252.7 per 100 000 inhabitants in 1960-64 to 277.3 (+9.7%) in 1980-84, but dropped for women from 188.4 per 100 000 to 170.4 (−9.6%). A decrease of similar, or even slightly greater, magnitude was observed among women in Belgium (−8.6%), Spain (−9.4%), the Netherlands (−9.5%) and France (−12.1%), and a slightly lower rate (−4.2%) among Danish women.

The death rate from cancer can be analysed by type of cancer and according to sex and region. For lung cancer in men, the diagram shows high levels of mortality (over 35 per 100 000) in Scotland, England, the Benelux countries and the Milan and Venice regions. The death rate from breast cancer in women is at its highest in practically all the same regions, with the exception of Venice and eastern Belgium. On the other hand, the values recorded for Ireland and Denmark are also high.

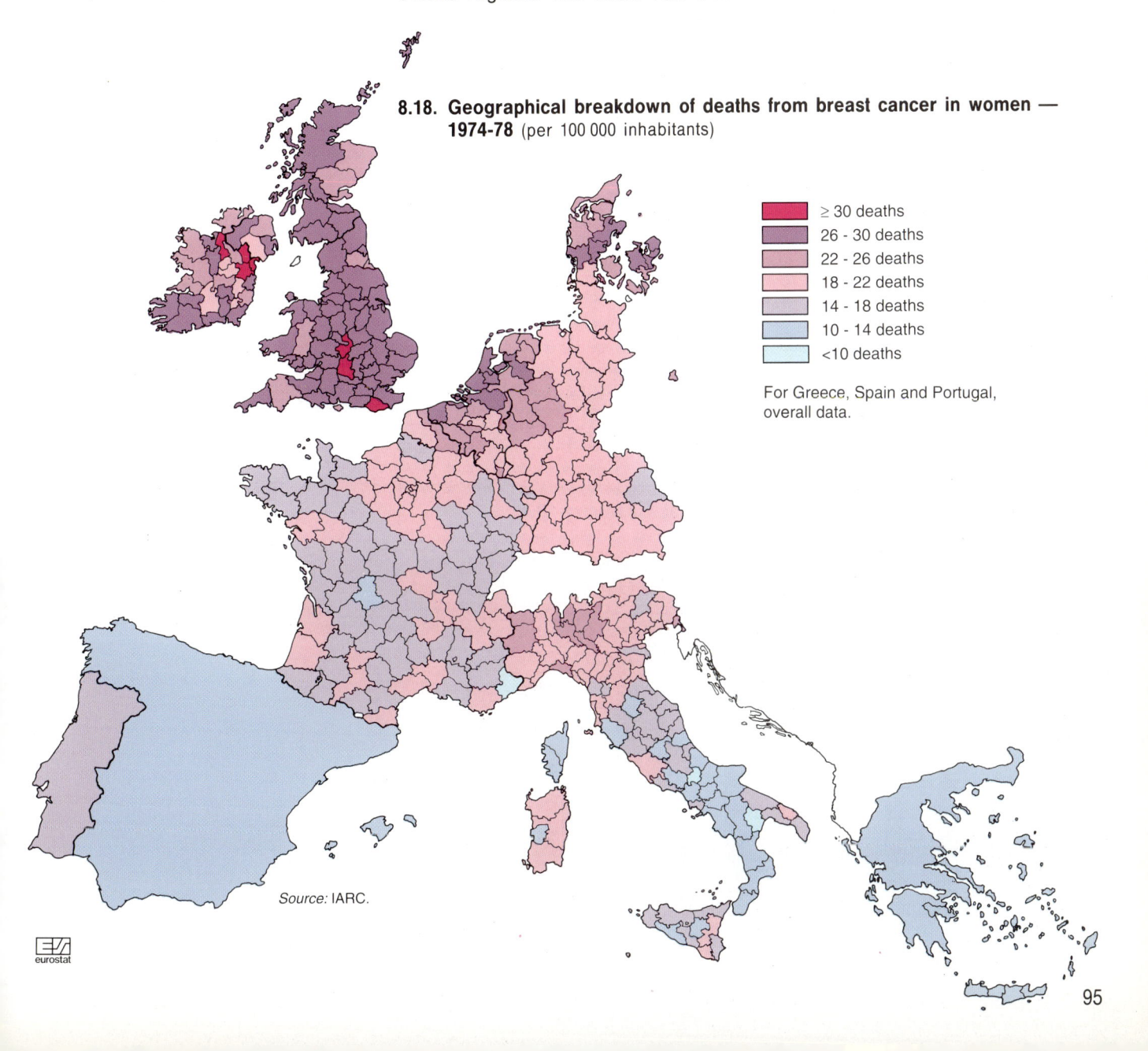

8.18. Geographical breakdown of deaths from breast cancer in women — 1974-78 (per 100 000 inhabitants)

- ≥ 30 deaths
- 26 - 30 deaths
- 22 - 26 deaths
- 18 - 22 deaths
- 14 - 18 deaths
- 10 - 14 deaths
- <10 deaths

For Greece, Spain and Portugal, overall data.

Source: IARC.

HEALTH
AIDS

8.19. Cumulative cases of AIDS by age and sex as at 1 January 1990 — EUR 12

Age group	Male	Female	Total
0 - 14	412	270	682
15 - 19	181	48	229
20 - 24	1 991	669	2 660
25 - 29	5 600	1 235	6 835
30 - 34	5 186	677	5 863
35 - 39	4 114	286	4 400
40 - 44	2 973	141	3 114
45 - 49	1 937	79	2 016
50 - 54	1 139	89	1 228
55 - 59	737	83	820
60 - 64	368	72	440
65 and over	378	129	507
Unknown	114	12	126
Total	25 130	3 790	28 920

Source: WHO — European Centre for AIDS.

It is men, particularly those between the ages of 20 and 54, who suffer most from AIDS, 87% of the 28 920 cases recorded in the Community as at 1 January 1990 being men. France has almost one-third of all recorded cases in the Community (8 883), and also the highest rate of AIDS victims per million inhabitants (158.3), followed by Spain with a rate of 118.2 and Denmark at 101.6.

This disease strikes hardest at homosexuals (47.5%), whilst drug addicts account for 31.1% of all those affected.

There are major variations in the groups at risk in the different countries; in Italy and Spain, drug addicts account for approximately two-thirds of all cases and homosexuals for around one-sixth, whilst in the United Kingdom and the Netherlands, 81% of cases are homosexuals and only 3 to 7% drug addicts. Cases of AIDS transmitted by blood transfusion are generally few (2 to 5%), although this does reach a peak of 7 to 8% in Belgium, Greece and France.

8.20. Cumulative cases of AIDS as at 1 January 1990

EUR 12	B	DK	D	GR	E	F	IRL	I	L	NL	P	UK
28 920	596	518	4 306	277	4 633	8 883	124	5 307	24	1 074	348	2 830

Source: WHO — European Centre for AIDS.

8.21. Rate of AIDS per million inhabitants as at 1 January 1990

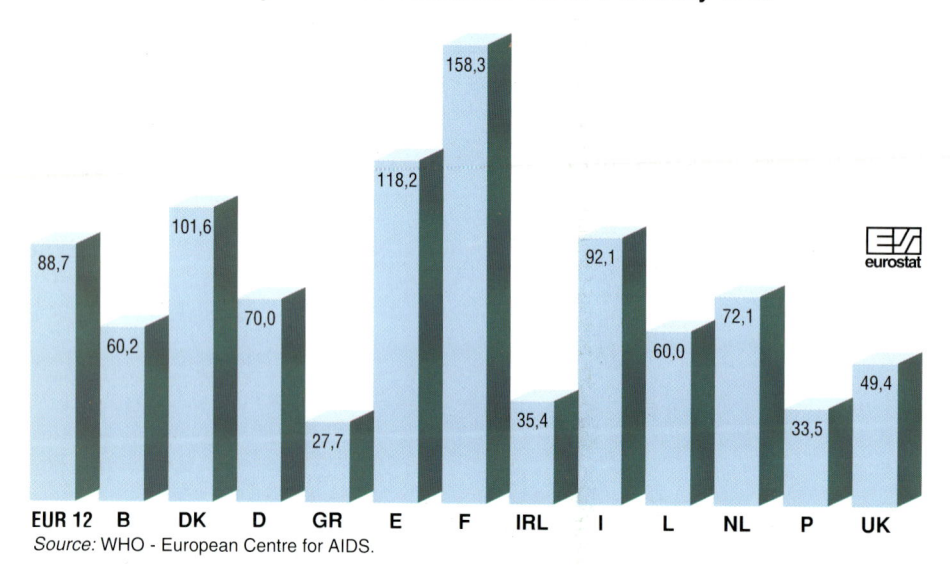

EUR 12	B	DK	D	GR	E	F	IRL	I	L	NL	P	UK
88,7	60,2	101,6	70,0	27,7	118,2	158,3	35,4	92,1	60,0	72,1	33,5	49,4

Source: WHO - European Centre for AIDS.

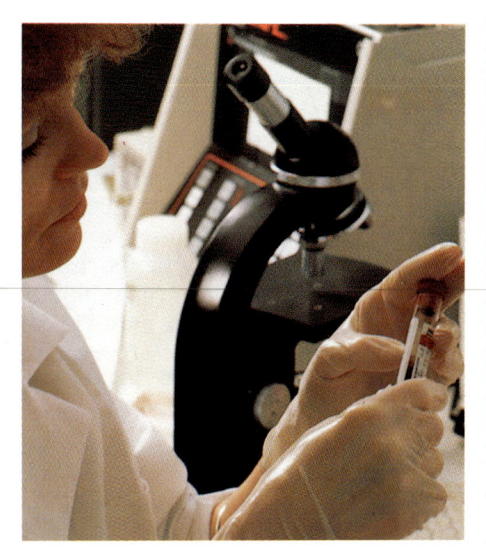

HEALTH
AIDS

8.22. AIDS by transmission group and sex as at 1 January 1990 — EUR 12 (%)
(not including paediatric cases)

Transmission group	Male	Female	Total
Homosexual/bisexual	54,3	0,1	47,5
Drug addict	27,5	56,1	31,1
Drug addicts/homosexual/bisexual	2,4	0	2,1
Haemophiliacs/coagulation disorders	3,4	0,3	3,0
Transfusion	2,1	12,4	3,4
Heterosexual	5,6	25,5	8,1
Other	0,1	0,1	0,1
Unknown	4,6	5,5	4,7
Total	100 %	100 %	100 %

Source: WHO — European Centre for AIDS.

8.23. AIDS by transmission group as at 1 January 1990 (%)

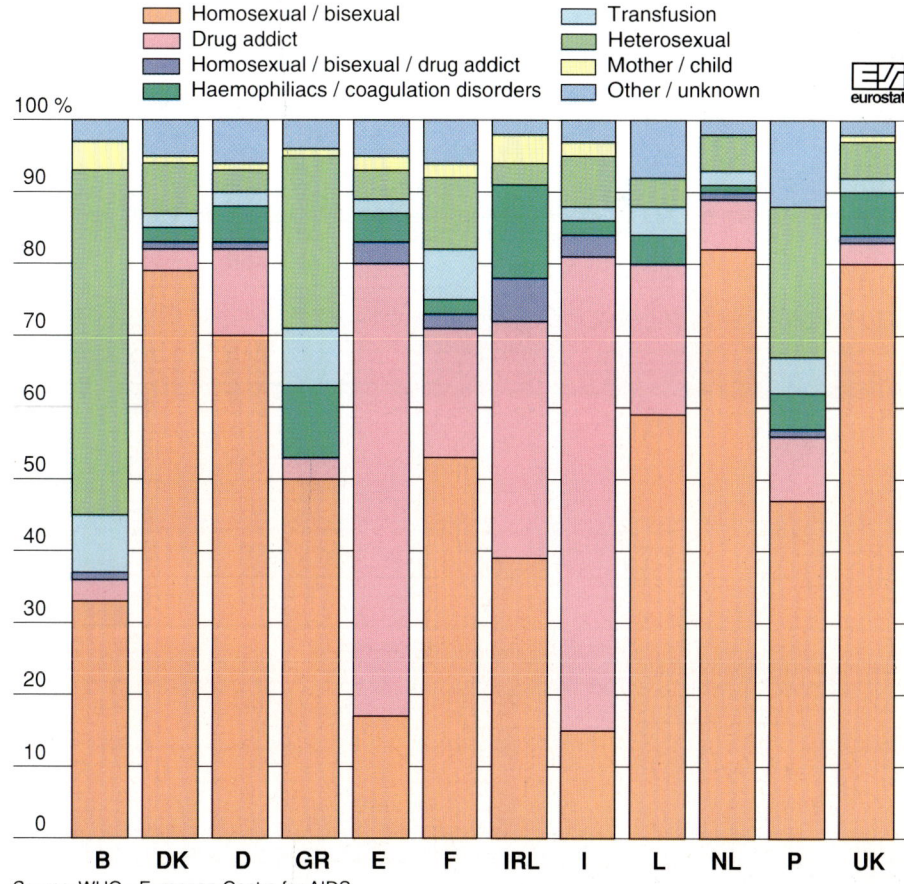

Source: WHO - European Centre for AIDS.

HEALTH
SUICIDE

8.24. Death rate by suicide according to age and sex — EUR 12 — 1986
(per 10 000 inhabitants)

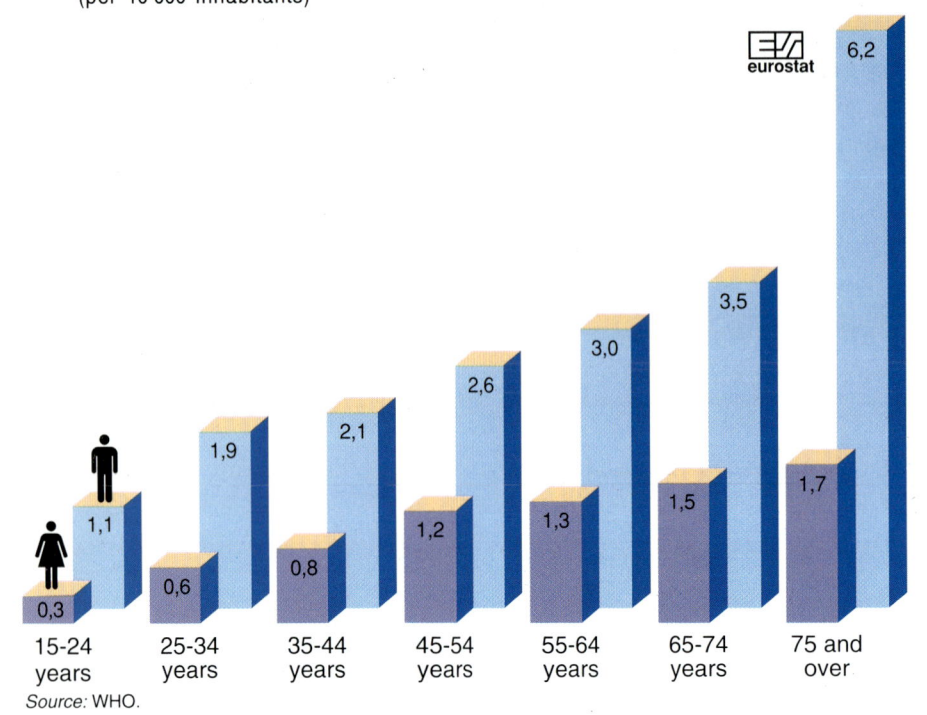

Age group	Male (♂)	Female (♀)
15-24 years	1,1	0,3
25-34 years	1,9	0,6
35-44 years	2,1	0,8
45-54 years	2,6	1,2
55-64 years	3,0	1,3
65-74 years	3,5	1,5
75 and over	6,2	1,7

Source: WHO.

The death rate by suicide is low overall, but varies according to age for both men (from 1.1 per 10 000 inhabitants between the ages of 15 and 24 to 6.2 per 10 000 among the 75 and over age group) and women (from 0.3 to 1.7 respectively). Suicide accounts for only 1.3% of the causes of death in the total population of the European Community, but this figure reaches 16.4% for men and 11.0% for women in the 25 to 34 age group; it then drops among the older age groups, becoming insignificant after the age of 65 (0.9% and 0.7% respectively), on account of the very high number of deaths due to other causes (cancers, cardiovascular diseases), which are insignificant among the younger age groups.

It can be observed that, although suicides account for only a low percentage of deaths, they did amount to no fewer than 42 710 cases in the Community as a whole in 1986, of which 29 747 (or almost 70%) were men, predominantly (64%) of working age (25 to 64 years old).

8.25. Death by suicide by age and sex — EUR 12* — 1986

Age group	Male	Female	Total
15 - 24	2 924	773	3 697
25 - 34	4 575	1 318	5 893
35 - 44	4 553	1 748	6 301
45 - 54	5 015	2 247	7 262
55 - 64	4 839	2 445	7 284
65 - 74	3 670	2 201	5 871
75 and over	4 171	2 231	6 402
Total	29 747	12 963	42 710

Source: WHO.

HEALTH
SUICIDE

8.26. Proportion of suicides in the total deaths for each age group — EUR 12* — 1986 (%)

Age group	Male	Female
15 - 24	11.4	8.7
25 - 34	16.4	11.0
35 - 44	9.9	7.3
45 - 54	4.5	4.0
55 - 64	1.7	1.8
65 - 74	0.9	0.7
75 and over	0.6	0.0

The death rate by suicide is subject to major differences between the Member States, both for men (1.9 per 10 000 in the Europe of Twelve) and for women (0.8). The highest rates are recorded in Denmark (men: 3.6 per 10 000; women: 2.0) and the lowest rates in Greece (men: 0.6; women: 0.2). It is, however, a known fact that not all suicides are recorded as such on death certificates.

8.27. Death rate by suicide in men — 1986
(per 10 000)

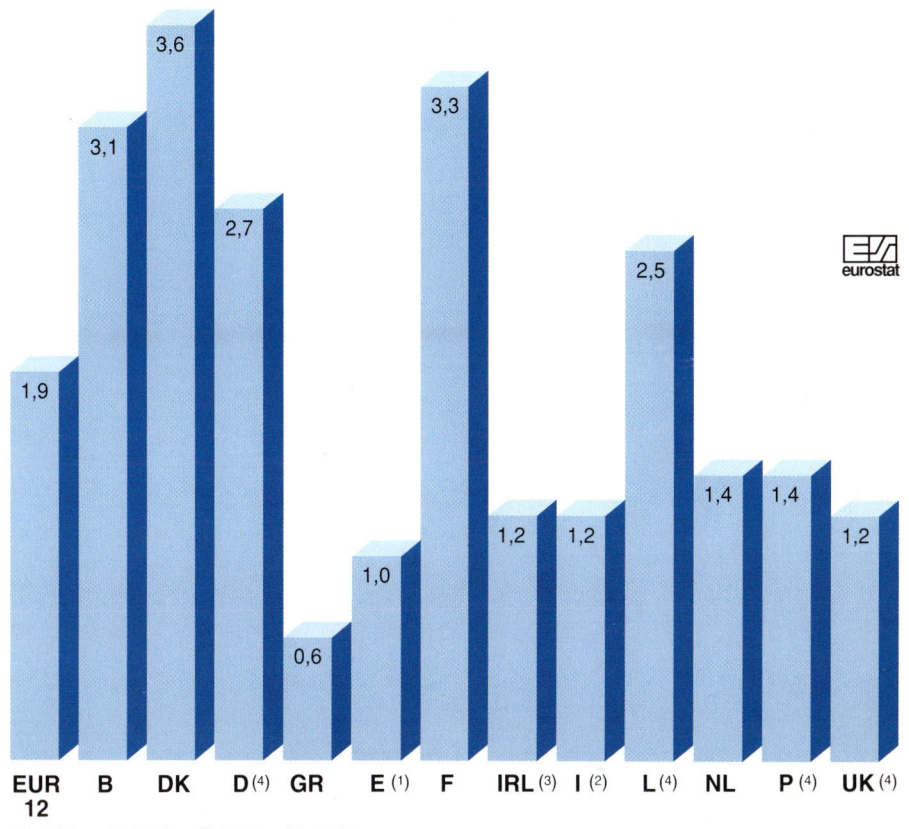

EUR 12	B	DK	D[4]	GR	E[1]	F	IRL[3]	I[2]	L[4]	NL	P[4]	UK[4]
1,9	3,1	3,6	2,7	0,6	1,0	3,3	1,2	1,2	2,5	1,4	1,4	1,2

[1] 1982. [2] 1984. [3] 1985. [4] 1987.
Source: WHO.

8.28. Death rate by suicide in women — 1986
(per 10 000)

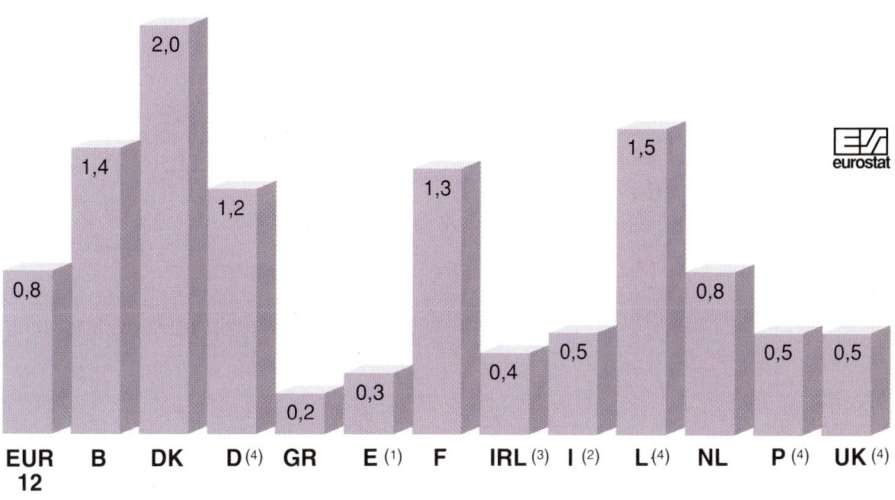

EUR 12	B	DK	D[4]	GR	E[1]	F	IRL[3]	I[2]	L[4]	NL	P[4]	UK[4]
0,8	1,4	2,0	1,2	0,2	0,3	1,3	0,4	0,5	1,5	0,8	0,5	0,5

[1] 1982. [2] 1984. [3] 1985. [4] 1987.
Source: WHO.

HEALTH
ACCIDENTS

8.29. Death rate by motor-vehicle accident according to age and sex — EUR 12* — 1986 (per 10 000)

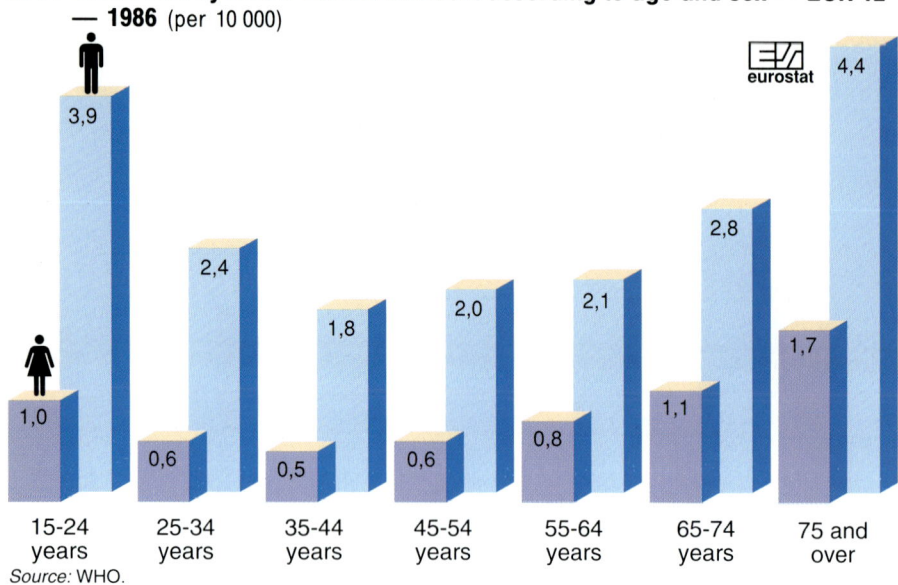

Age group	Male	Female
15-24 years	3,9	1,0
25-34 years	2,4	0,6
35-44 years	1,8	0,5
45-54 years	2,0	0,6
55-64 years	2,1	0,8
65-74 years	2,8	1,1
75 and over	4,4	1,7

Source: WHO.

Road accidents have become a major cause for concern, particularly among young people aged between 15 and 34. In 1986, 44 681 deaths were recorded in the European Community as a result of motor-vehicle accidents, of which 33 098 were men (almost three-quarters) and 11 585 women. Amongst 15 to 24-year-olds alone, motor-vehicle accidents accounted for 40.7% of male deaths and 29.1% of female deaths in this age group. The percentage figures fall for the older age groups, dropping to 0.4% and 0.2% respectively of causes of death among persons aged 75 and over.

The figures for road accident victims, covering both injured and killed, are frightening: 1 650 173 in 1987 for the Community as a whole, of which 432 589 were recorded in the Federal Republic of Germany and 321 409 in the United Kingdom. 45 342 people were killed (all types of vehicle), of whom 10 961 were in France (1986) and 7 967 in the Federal Republic of Germany.

Accidents in the home are the other major category of accident. Almost 45% of accidents in the home are falls. Children (between 0 and 14 years) are amongst the main victims of these accidents, accounting for 40% of male victims and 34% of female victims.

8.30. Deaths by motor-vehicle accident according to age and sex — EUR 12* — 1986

Age group	Male	Female	Total
15 - 24	10 404	2 602	13 006
25 - 34	5 688	1 352	7 040
35 - 44	3 848	1 106	4 954
45 - 54	3 747	1 118	4 865
55 - 64	3 491	1 449	4 940
65 - 74	2 936	1 722	4 658
75 and over	2 982	2 236	5 218
Total	33 096	11 585	44 681

Source: WHO.

8.31. Proportion of motor-vehicle accidents in the total deaths for each age group — EUR 12* — 1986 (%)

Age group	Male	Female
15 - 24	40,7	29,1
25 - 34	20,4	11,3
35 - 44	8,4	4,6
45 - 54	3,4	2,0
55 - 64	1,3	1,1
65 - 74	0,7	0,6
75 and over	0,4	0,2

Source: WHO.

HEALTH
ACCIDENTS

8.32. Number of injured and killed in road accidents

	EUR 12	B	DK	D	GR	E	F	IRL	I	L	NL	P	UK
Victims													
1970	:	107 777	26 656	550 988	25 719	:	336 590	9 809	238 444	2 499	71 406	:	371 542
1980	1 780 618	84 700	15 751	513 504	26 668	112 692	348 326	9 068	231 410	2 381	58 620	43 502	333 996
1987	1 650 173 *	83 856	12 714	432 589	27 980	159 246	269 976 (¹)	8 871	224 295	1 750	50 674	56 813	321 409
Killed													
1970	:	1 544	1 208	19 193	931	:	15 034	540	10 208	132	3 181	:	7 771
1980	54 585	2 396	690	13 041	1 225	5 017	12 510	564	8 537	98	1 997	2 328	6 182
1987	45 342 *	1 922	698	7 967	1 502	5 858	10 961 (¹)	462	6 784	68	1 485	2 296	5 339
Injured													
1970	:	106 233	25 448	531 795	24 788	:	321 556	9 269	228 236	2 367	68 225	:	363 771
1980	1 726 033	82 304	15 061	500 463	25 443	107 675	335 816	8 504	222 873	2 283	56 623	41 174	327 814
1987	1 604 831 *	81 934	12 016	424 622	26 478	153 388	259 015 (¹)	8 409	217 511	1 682	49 189	54 517	316 070

(¹) 1986.

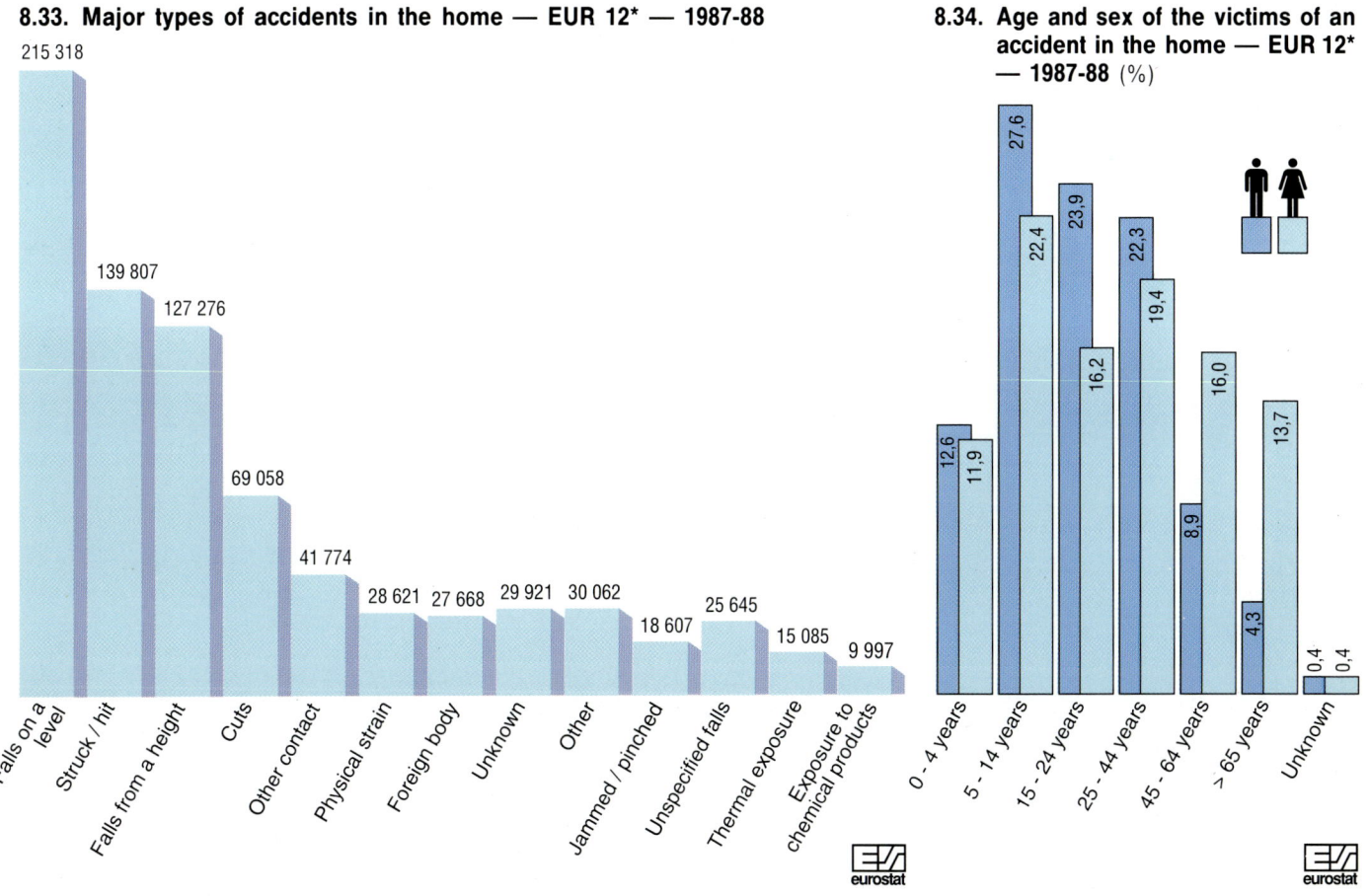

8.33. Major types of accidents in the home — EUR 12* — 1987-88

Falls on a level	215 318
Struck / hit	139 807
Falls from a height	127 276
Cuts	69 058
Other contact	41 774
Physical strain	28 621
Foreign body	27 668
Unknown	29 921
Other	30 062
Jammed / pinched	18 607
Unspecified falls	25 645
Thermal exposure	15 085
Exposure to chemical products	9 997

8.34. Age and sex of the victims of an accident in the home — EUR 12* — 1987-88 (%)

Age	Male	Female
0 - 4 years	12,6	11,9
5 - 14 years	27,6	22,4
15 - 24 years	23,9	16,2
25 - 44 years	22,3	19,4
45 - 64 years	8,9	16,0
> 65 years	4,3	13,7
Unknown	0,4	0,4

eurostat

HEALTH
FOR FURTHER INFORMATION

Definitions

Life expectancy at age X: the average length of the life of individuals at age X on the basis of the death rate from a table of deaths.

Life expectancy without disability: this is an indicator of the average length of life lived in good health, based on data on both the death rate and disability.

Death rate: the ratio of deaths in one year to the average population for that year.

Standardized mortality rate (SMR): the ratio between the expected and observed number of deaths.

Observed number of deaths: this is the total number of deaths in a population.

Expected number of deaths: this is the total number of deaths that can be expected in the population if the age-specific death rates (e.g. rates in the WHO Europe region) are applied to the age pyramid of a Member State.

Excess mortality rate (EMR): to calculate the excess mortality rate, the lowest mortality rates are, first of all, applied to the breakdown by age group and sex of the population in a given country for a given calendar year, in order to obtain the number of deaths which could have been expected with the lowest death rate system; this expected number is then deducted from the actual number of deaths recorded in the country during the calendar year in order to obtain the 'excess'. The indicator is then calculated by taking the ratio of this 'excess' to the expected minimum.

Avoidable death rate: the avoidable death rate is a subset of causes of death, where the unexpected cause is closely related to the working of the health care system.

References

Eurostat

- National accounts ESA, 1989
- Regions Statistical yearbook, 1988
- Demographic statistics 1989, 1990
- Ehlass (European home and leisure accident surveillance system) — 1987/88 report

WHO

- World health statistics, quarterly reports, Volume 42 — 1989
- World health statistic annual — 1988, 1989

Other

- Centre européen pour le sida (European Centre for AIDS) — Claude Bernard Hospital, Paris, France

Eurostat databank

- Cronos
- Regio

THE ENVIRONMENT

Forests cover 24.2 % of the Community's surface area of 2 258 000 km^2 (9.2).

In 1987 almost 5 % of Community citizens professed adherence to a nature-conservation, wildlife-protection or other ecological movement. National proportions varied between 0.8 % in Portugal and 19.7 % in Denmark, and were below the Community average in five countries other than Portugal (Greece, Spain, France, Italy and the Federal Republic of Germany) (9.8).

Per capita energy consumption rose in the Community by 14 % between 1981 (2.9 toe) and 1988 (3.3 toe) (9.11).

The number of motor vehicles per 1 000 inhabitants continues to increase in all the countries of the Community. It rose from 301 in 1980 to 343 in 1985 (9.1).

In 1985 the Community's road network exceeded 2.5 million km, compared with its railway network of 125 600 km (9.14) (9.17).

The cumulative production of chlorofluorocarbons (CFC 11 and CFC 12) rose dramatically from 217 000 tonnes in 1950 to 14.5 million tonnes in 1983. CFCs, which are present in aerosols, industrial foaming agents and coolants, are thought to contribute to depletion of the ozone layer in the stratosphere (9.20).

9.1. Number of motor vehicles per 1 000 inhabitants

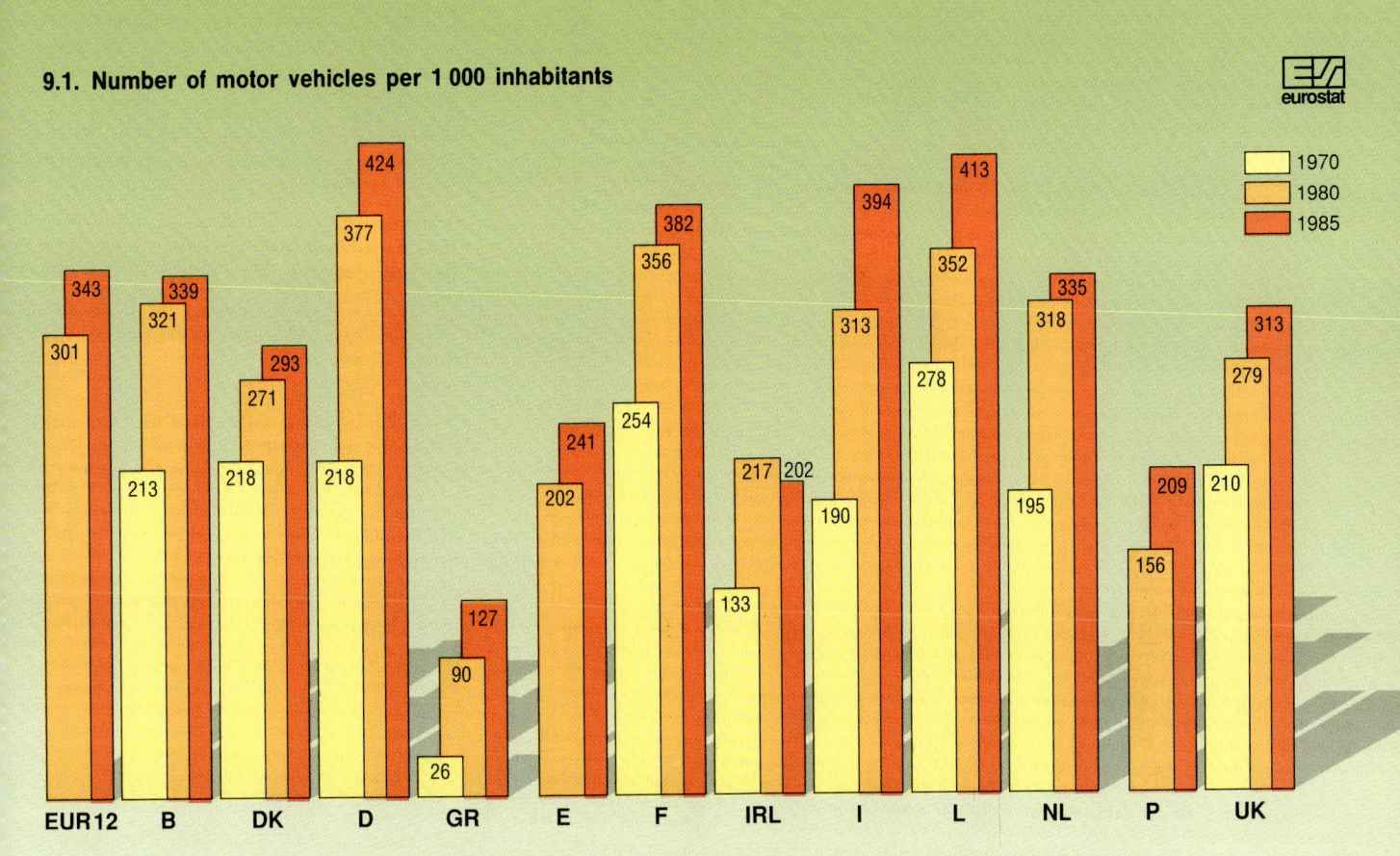

THE ENVIRONMENT
LAND USE

9.2. Land use — EUR 12 — 1987

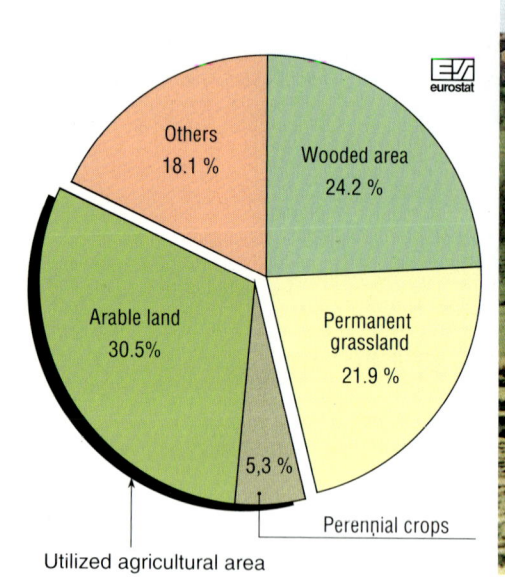

- Others 18.1 %
- Wooded area 24.2 %
- Arable land 30.5 %
- Permanent grassland 21.9 %
- Perennial crops 5,3 %
- Utilized agricultural area

9.3. Wooded area as % of total surface area — 1987

EUR 12	B	DK	D	GR	E	F	IRL	I	L	NL	P	UK
24,2	20,4	11,6	30,1	44,6	25,1	27,1	4,7	21,8	34,4	9,1	32,4	9,5

9.4. Total volume of wood removed — 1984 (1 000 m³)

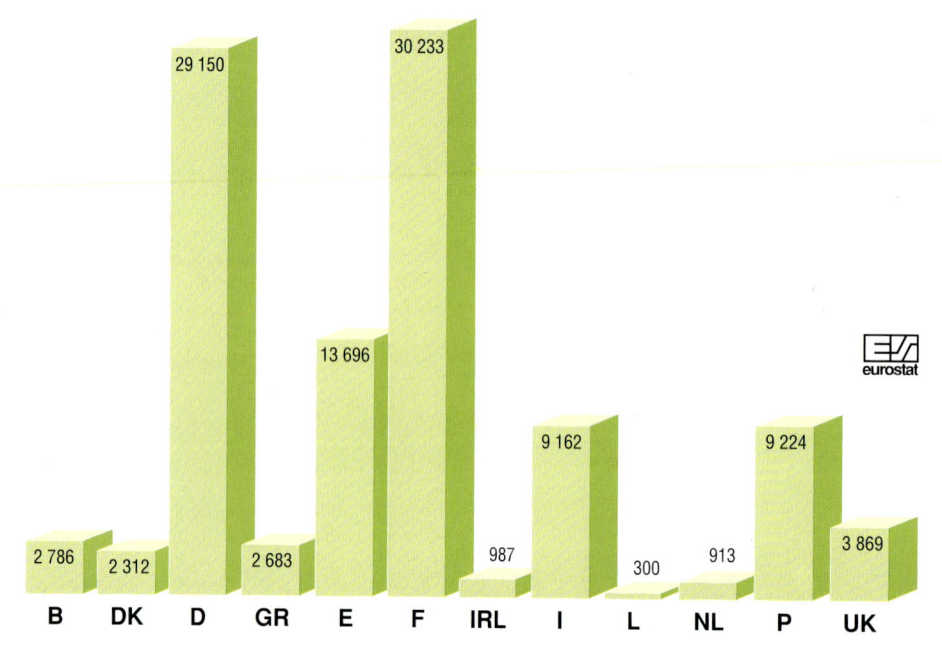

B	DK	D	GR	E	F	IRL	I	L	NL	P	UK
2 786	2 312	29 150	2 683	13 696	30 233	987	9 162	300	913	9 224	3 869

The territory of the European Community (2 258 269 km²) is made up of a wide variety of land of varying quality, almost a third of which is arable (30.5 %), approximately a quarter wooded (24.2 %) and a substantial proportion grassland (21.9 %). Forests—which are valuable in both environmental and economic terms—are unevenly distributed, and the proportion of territory they occupy varies from one country to another. Greece has the highest proportion of forest cover (44.6 %), while in Luxembourg the proportion is 34.4 %, in Portugal 32.4 % and in the Federal Republic of Germany 30.1 %. In Ireland (4.7 %), the Netherlands (9.1 %) and the United Kingdom (9.5 %) the proportions are well below the Community average of 24.2 %.

French and German forests yield the most timber (30 million m³ and 29 million m³ respectively).

THE ENVIRONMENT
CLIMATE

The European Community, which stretches between 35°N and 60°N and borders on the North Sea, the Atlantic Ocean and the Mediterranean, is situated within the temperate climate zone which is largely dominated by maritime influences. Its numerous minor variations in climate can be grouped together into the four major climatic areas described below.

The maritime climate, with its mild winters, cool summers and stable humidity, is conducive to a cover of hardwood and coniferous forests, grasslands and—in upland areas—heather, broom and gorse. This climate prevails along the whole western face of the continent of Europe, shading off gradually into the continental climate of the European interior. This continental climate, which prevails along the eastern edges of the Community and is well-suited to coniferous forests and grasslands, is characterized by cold, dry winters and hot, sultry summers.

The Mediterranean climate, which is characterized by mild, rainy winters, hot, dry summers and sparse but often torrential precipitation, prevails along the coastal regions of the Mediterranean. Its characteristic vegetation (chiefly shrubs and other plants able to withstand the summer droughts) includes few forests but large areas of scrub.

The mountain areas (the Alps, Pyrenees, Cantabrian Mountains, Sierra Nevada etc.) have their own particular type of climate determined by the altitude and exposure to the sun and winds. The greater the altitude, the sparser their vegetation becomes.

9.5. Climatic zones of the European Community — 1987

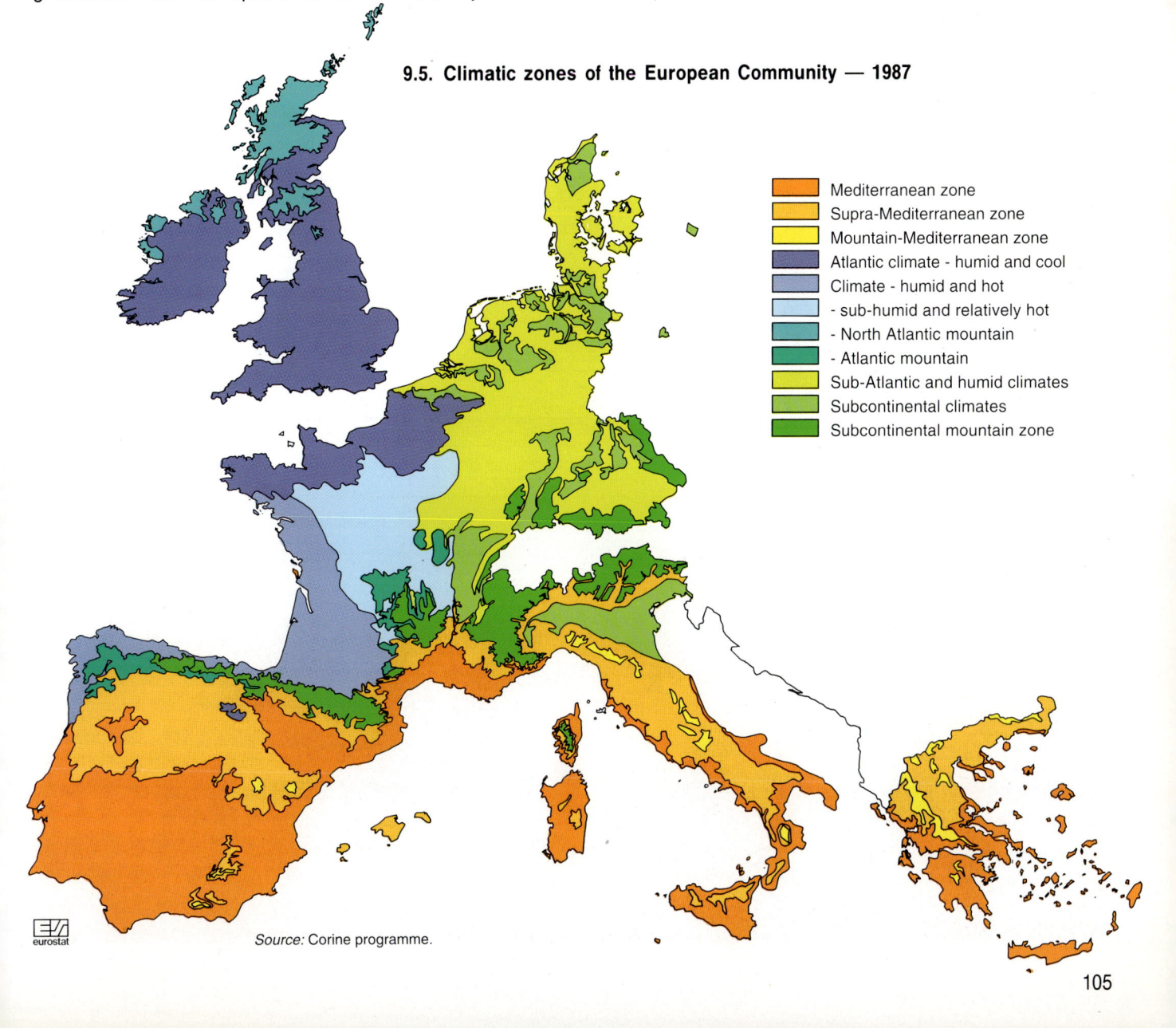

- Mediterranean zone
- Supra-Mediterranean zone
- Mountain-Mediterranean zone
- Atlantic climate - humid and cool
- Climate - humid and hot
- - sub-humid and relatively hot
- - North Atlantic mountain
- - Atlantic mountain
- Sub-Atlantic and humid climates
- Subcontinental climates
- Subcontinental mountain zone

Source: Corine programme.

THE ENVIRONMENT
OPINIONS

9.6. Public perception of the environment — EUR 12 — 1988 (%)
Question: Where you live now, do you have cause to complain about the following?

	A great deal	A fair amount	Not very much	Not at all	No reply	Total
The quality of the drinking water	10	14	17	57	2	100
Noise	10	14	22	53	1	100
Air pollution	11	17	23	48	1	100
Methods of waste disposal	10	13	19	56	2	100
Lack of access to open spaces and countryside	7	11	14	67	1	100
Loss of good farmland	8	14	17	54	7	100
Damage done to the landscape	14	18	18	47	3	100

Source: Eurobarometer.

Although the opinion polls reflect a degree of awareness of environmental problems, the majority of Community citizens (almost three-quarters of those polled in 1988) perceive few if any direct threats to their immediate environment. The areas in which threats to the environment are most keenly felt (i.e. in which respondents feel that they have some or every cause to complain) are damage to the landscape (32%), air pollution (28%), the quality of drinking water (24%) and noise (24%).

9.7. Index of dissatisfaction (0-3) with the immediate environment — 1988
Question: Where you live now, do you have cause to complain about the following?

	EUR 12	B	DK	D	GR	E	F	IRL	I	L	NL	P	UK
The quality of the water	.78	.58	.24	.87	.95	.95	.64	.56	1.22	.51	.39	.84	.42
Noise	.80	.76	.37	1.11	1.15	1.00	.56	.41	.93	.75	.54	.96	.49
Air pollution	.91	.91	.51	1.20	1.24	1.00	.71	.55	1.17	1.03	.64	.97	.51
Methods of waste disposal	.76	.53	.20	.67	1.42	.79	.49	.88	1.13	.65	.76	1.13	.66
Lack of access to open spaces and countryside	.57	.48	.15	.63	1.07	.91	.41	.26	.76	.20	.31	.79	.26
Loss of good farmland	.74	.69	.22	.70	1.00	.91	.73	.26	.98	.56	.70	.89	.48
Damage done to the landscape	.98	.87	.43	.98	1.43	1.12	.82	.50	1.26	.98	1.02	.95	.80

0: not at all
1: not very much
2: a fair amount
3: a great deal
Source: Eurobarometer.

THE ENVIRONMENT
OPINIONS

9.8. Adherence to nature-conservation, wildlife-protection or other ecological movements — 1987

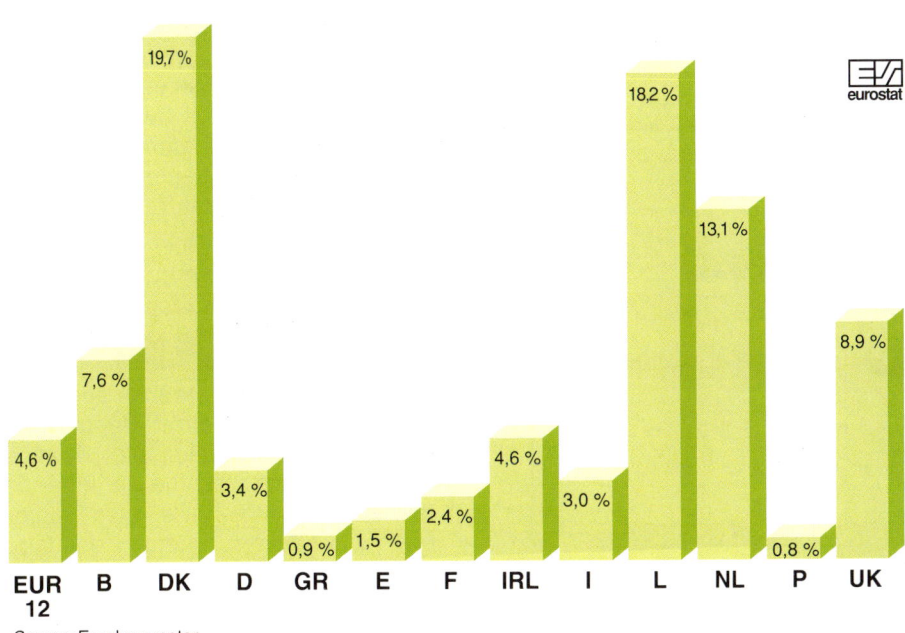

EUR 12	B	DK	D	GR	E	F	IRL	I	L	NL	P	UK
4,6 %	7,6 %	19,7 %	3,4 %	0,9 %	1,5 %	2,4 %	4,6 %	3,0 %	18,2 %	13,1 %	0,8 %	8,9 %

Source: Eurobarometer.

9.9. Index of environmental awareness — EUR 12 — 1988

Question: *Concerning your country as a whole, I would like to know how worried or concerned you are about the following problems.*

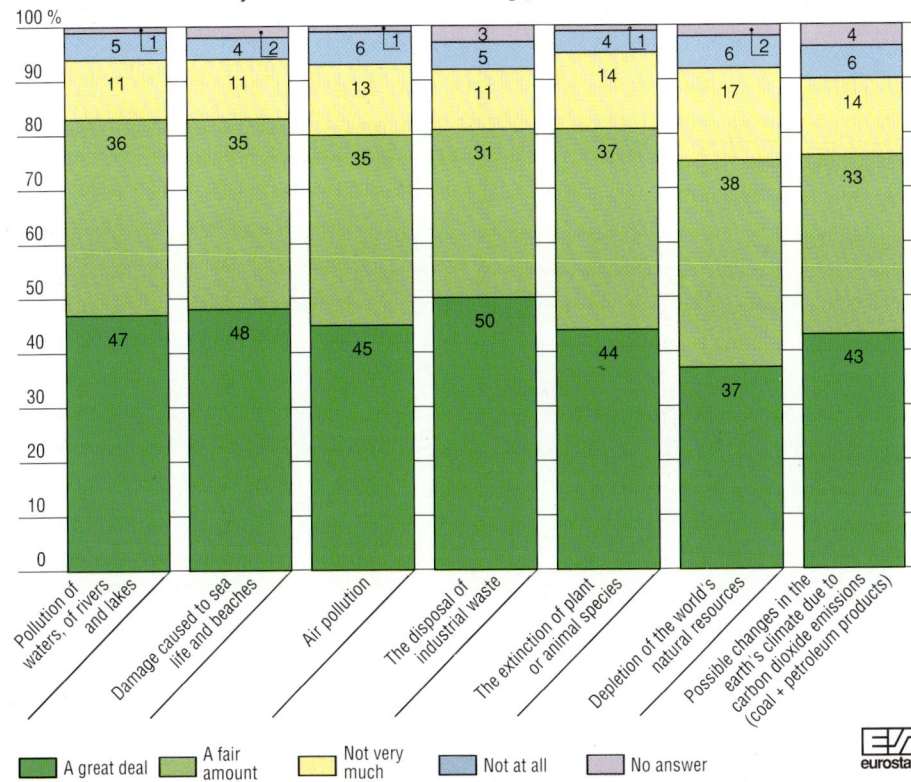

Problem	A great deal	A fair amount	Not very much	Not at all	No answer
Pollution of waters, of rivers and lakes	47	36	11	5	1
Damage caused to sea life and beaches	48	35	11	4	2
Air pollution	45	35	13	6	1
The disposal of industrial waste	50	31	11	3	5
The extinction of plant or animal species	44	37	14	4	1
Depletion of the world's natural resources	37	38	17	6	2
Possible changes in the earth's climate due to carbon dioxide emissions (coal + petroleum products)	43	33	14	4	6

Source: Eurobarometer.

Dissatisfaction concerning almost all aspects of the environment is most widespread in Greece, the one exception being water quality, for which Italy tops the list of complainants. Noise pollution is a particular source of grievance in the Federal Republic of Germany as well as in Greece, while complaints about air pollution are especially widespread in Greece, the Federal Republic of Germany, Italy and Luxembourg. Waste and waste disposal are seen as a threat to the environment chiefly in Greece, Italy and Portugal. Although Community citizens would appear to be less concerned about lack of access to open spaces and the loss of good farmland, damage to the landscape arouses stronger feelings in Greece, Italy, Spain, the Netherlands and the Federal Republic of Germany than in the other Community countries.

In 1987 relatively few Community citizens professed adherence to an ecological or nature-conservation movement (4.6 % for the Community as a whole). Adharance to such movements is most widespread in the Community's northern countries (19.7 % in Denmark, 18.2 % in Luxembourg, 13.1 % in the Netherlands and 8.9 % in the United Kingdom). The figures for the southern countries are markedly lower (0.8 % in Portugal, 0.9 % in Greece and 1.5 % in Spain).

As the index of environmental awareness shows, Community citizens are most concerned about the risks associated with the disposal of industrial waste (50 % of those polled being highly concerned), damage to marine life and beaches (48 %), the pollution of rivers (47 %) and air pollution (45 %). Depletion of the earth's natural resources gives rise to the least concern (37 %).

THE ENVIRONMENT
ENERGY

9.10. Production and consumption of energy — 1988 (million toe)

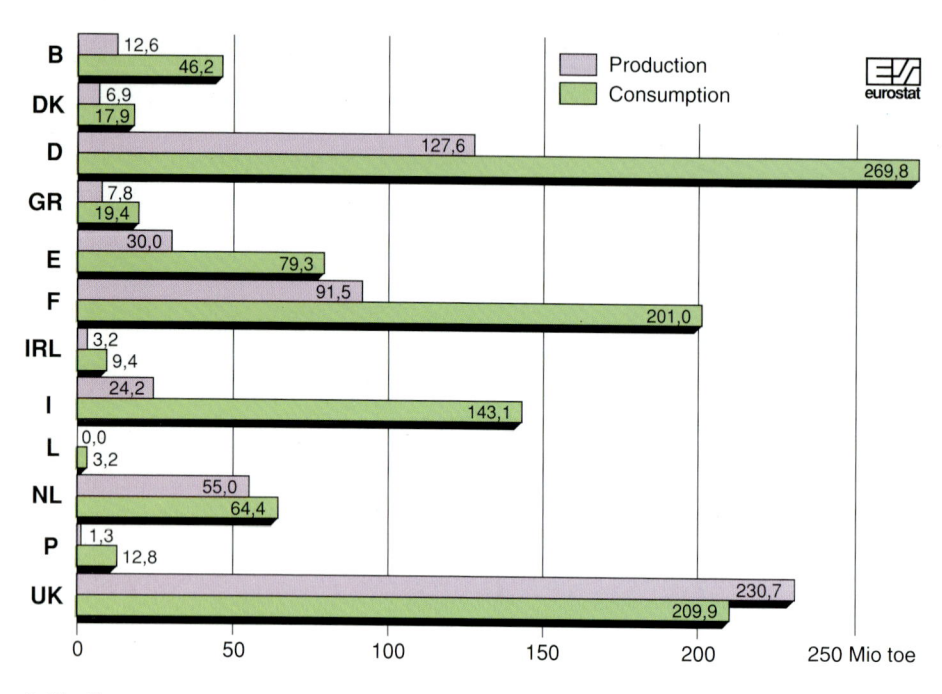

Country	Production	Consumption
B	12,6	46,2
DK	6,9	17,9
D	127,6	269,8
GR	7,8	19,4
E	30,0	79,3
F	91,5	201,0
IRL	3,2	9,4
I	24,2	143,1
L	0,0	3,2
NL	55,0	64,4
P	1,3	12,8
UK	230,7	209,9

9.11. Energy consumption — EUR 12 (in toe per capita)

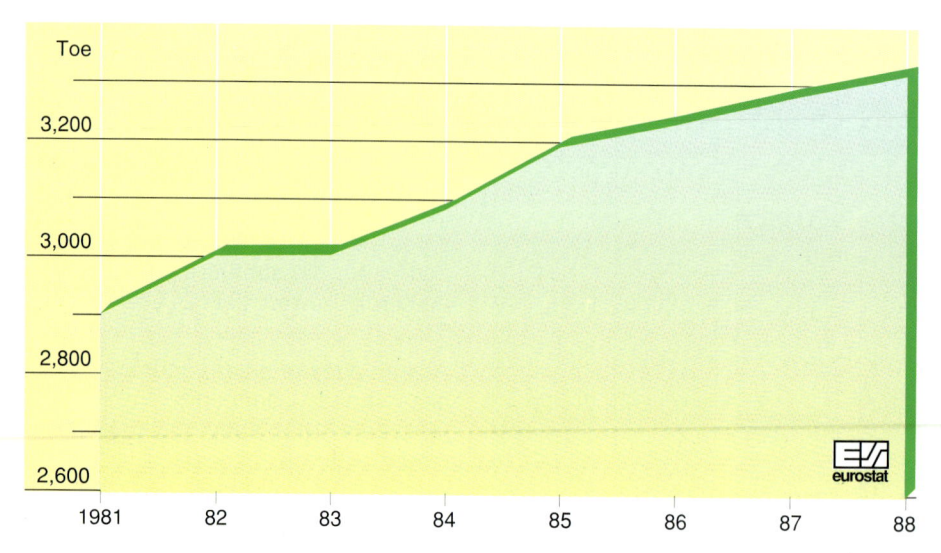

While energy is vital to economic life, its production and consumption have an impact on the environment. For example, human choices as regards energy have a direct bearing on air or water pollution, damage to the landscape and the depletion of fossil fuel reserves (oil, natural gas, coal).

In 1988 all the Member States consumed more energy than they produced, with the exception of the United Kingdom (production of 230.7 million toe), whose North Sea oil deposits allow it to produce and even export oil. The Federal Republic of Germany (127.6 million toe), France (91.5 million toe) and the Netherlands (55.0 million toe) are also major energy producers. Energy consumption is highest in the Federal Republic of Germany (269.8 million toe), the United Kingdom (209.9 million toe) and France (201.0 million toe).

Per capita energy consumption has increased steadily in the past few years, rising in the Community from 2.9 toe in 1981 to 3.3 toe in 1988.

Oil and petroleum products play an important part in energy consumption, and are used in transport, industry and for domestic purposes. In 1988 each inhabitant of the Community consumed an average of 1 491 kgoe crude oil and petroleum products. Per capita oil consumption was highest in Luxembourg (3 614 kgoe) and lowest in Portugal (901 kgoe).

THE ENVIRONMENT
ENERGY

Community households consume an average of 847 kgoe per capita for heating and other domestic purposes. Per capita consumption for these purposes is very high in Luxembourg (1 610 kgoe) and low in Portugal (194 kgoe). Households in the Community's northern countries consume more for these purposes than those in the southern countries, whose consumption is in all cases below the Community average. This divergence can be explained by the contrasting climate and way of life in these countries. Community households use several types of fuel for heating, an average of 5.5% burning solid fuels (coal, lignite), 36.3% burning liquid fuels (oil, diesel, heating oil), 34.2% using gas (natural gas, petroleum gas) and 23.8% using electricity. The most commonly used fuels in most Community households are oil and petroleum products, although gas predominates in the Netherlands (955 kgoe per capita) and solid fuels in Ireland (433 kgoe per capita).

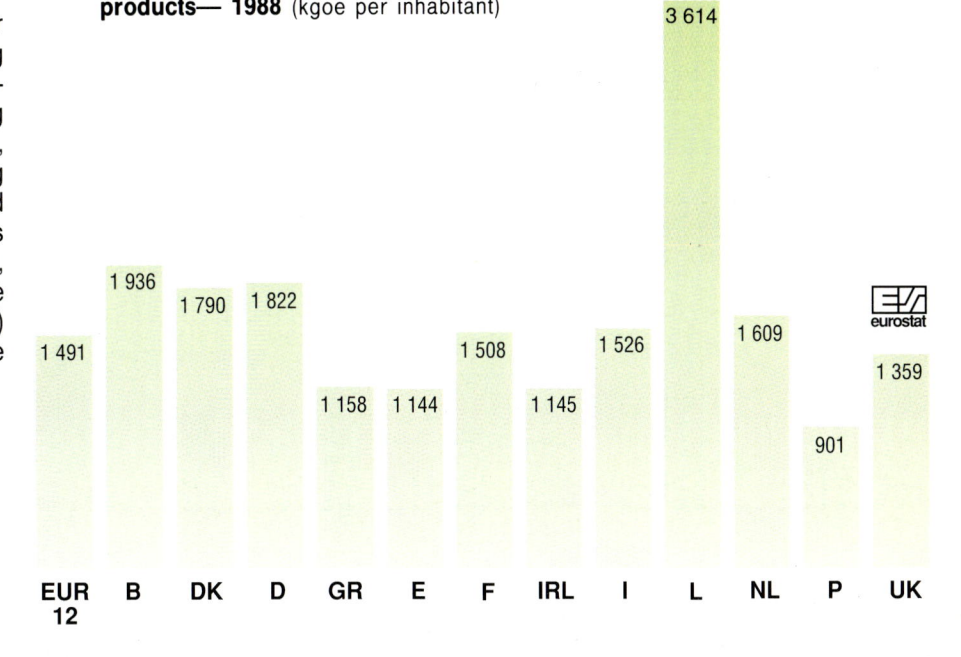

9.12. Per capita gross domestic consumption of crude oil and petroleum products — 1988 (kgoe per inhabitant)

	EUR 12	B	DK	D	GR	E	F	IRL	I	L	NL	P	UK
	1 491	1 936	1 790	1 822	1 158	1 144	1 508	1 145	1 526	3 614	1 609	901	1 359

9.13. Per capita household consumption of energy by type of fuel — 1988 (kgoe/per habitant)

	EUR 12	B	DK	D	GR	E	F	IRL	I	L	NL	P	UK
Solid fuels	47	69	61	45	5	10	36	433	2	30	1	0	127
Liquid fuels	308	574	575	584	235	161	358	223	267	809	125	108	133
Gas	290	380	170	301	1	18	224	35	234	459	955	5	529
Electricity	202	210	326	254	130	112	251	162	132	312	210	81	249
Total	847	1 233	1 132	1 184	371	301	869	853	635	1 610	1 291	194	1 038

THE ENVIRONMENT
TRANSPORT

9.14. Road-network length (all roads) (km)

	B	DK	D	GR	E	F	IRL	I	L	NL	P	UK
1970	94 218	62 678	440 322	35 257	:	783 000	86 695	280 325	4 949	:	:	344 057
1975	122 370	65 792	462 803	36 482	:	774 788	:	285 540	4 963	:	:	351 457
1980	121 750	68 405	477 854	37 367	:	797 000	92 294	288 562	5 094	93 430 (¹)	18 634	360 292
1985	131 810	69 554	485 890	40 359	168 470	796 355	92 294	293 754	5 157	94 233 (²)	18 582	369 076
1986	:	69 597	487 041	40 395	168 469	796 257	92 294	294 295	5 208	:	18 638	371 058

(¹) 1982. (²) 1984.

9.15. Road-network length (motorways) (km)

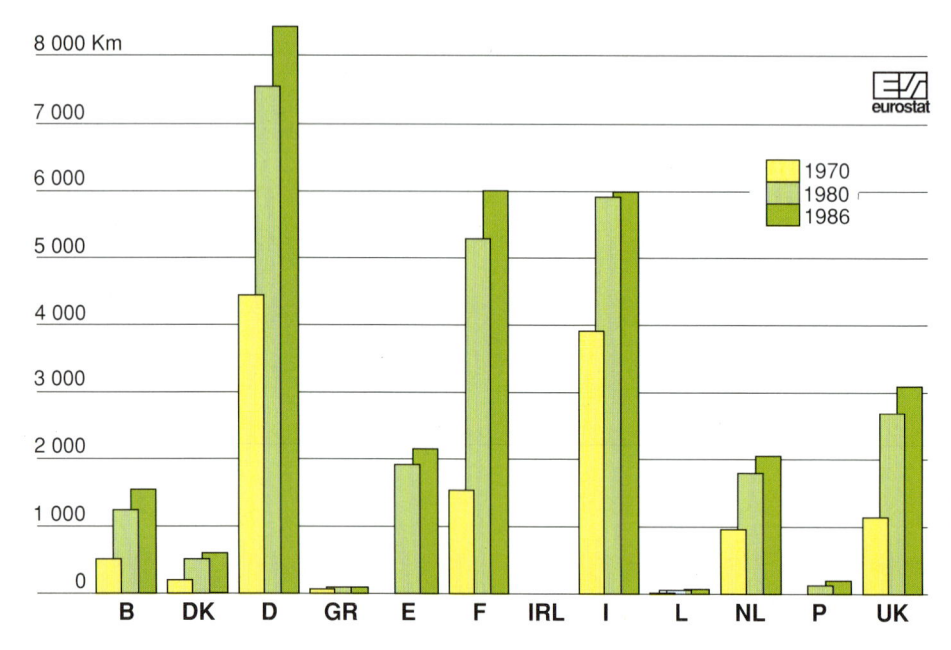

The substantial progress achieved in the fields of transport and communications places a major burden on the environment, i.e. through air pollution from vehicle exhaust fumes, pollution of the sea by oil spillages, the accumulation of cars for scrapping, the destruction of open spaces and farmland to enable the construction of motorways, railways and airports, the noise produced by aircraft, lorries, railways, etc.

The longest national road networks are in France (796 000 km in 1986), the Federal Republic of Germany (487 000 km) and the United Kingdom (371 000 km).

9.16. Road-vehicle stocks (passenger cars) (1 000)

	EUR 12	B	DK	D	GR	E	F	IRL	I	L	NL	P	UK
1970	:	2 060	1 077	13 941	227	:	12 470	393	10 181	85	2 564	:	11 669
1975	:	2 614	1 295	17 898	439	:	15 520	516	15 060	128	3 495	:	13 949
1980	95 649	3 159	1 390	23 192	863	7 557	19 130	738	17 686	129	4 550	1 546	15 712
1984	106 592	3 300	1 440	25 218	1 155	8 874	20 800	717	20 888	146	4 841	2 000	17 213
1985	110 386	3 343	1 501	25 845	1 263	9 274	21 090	715	22 495	152	4 852	2 119	17 737
1986	:	3 409	:	26 917	1 359	9 643	21 500	717	:	156	4 921	2 257	18 355

THE ENVIRONMENT
TRANSPORT

9.17. Rail-network length (km)

	EUR 12	B	DK	D	GR	E	F	IRL	I	L	NL	P	UK
1970	:	4 332	2 352	29 527	2 571	:	36 117	2 189	16 069	271	3 148	:	19 229
1975	:	3 992	2 445	28 813	2 476	:	34 255	2 006	16 077	275	2 825	:	18 456
1980	128 227	3 978	2 461	28 517	2 461	13 542	34 382	1 987	16 133	270	2 880	3 588	18 028
1985	125 616	3 712	2 471	27 634	2 461	12 710	34 678	1 944	16 183	270	2 824	3 607	17 122
1986	:	3 691	2 471	27 490	2 461	12 721	34 665	1 944	:	270	2 817	3 607	17 038

9.18. Rail and air passenger traffic in 1986 (million passengers)

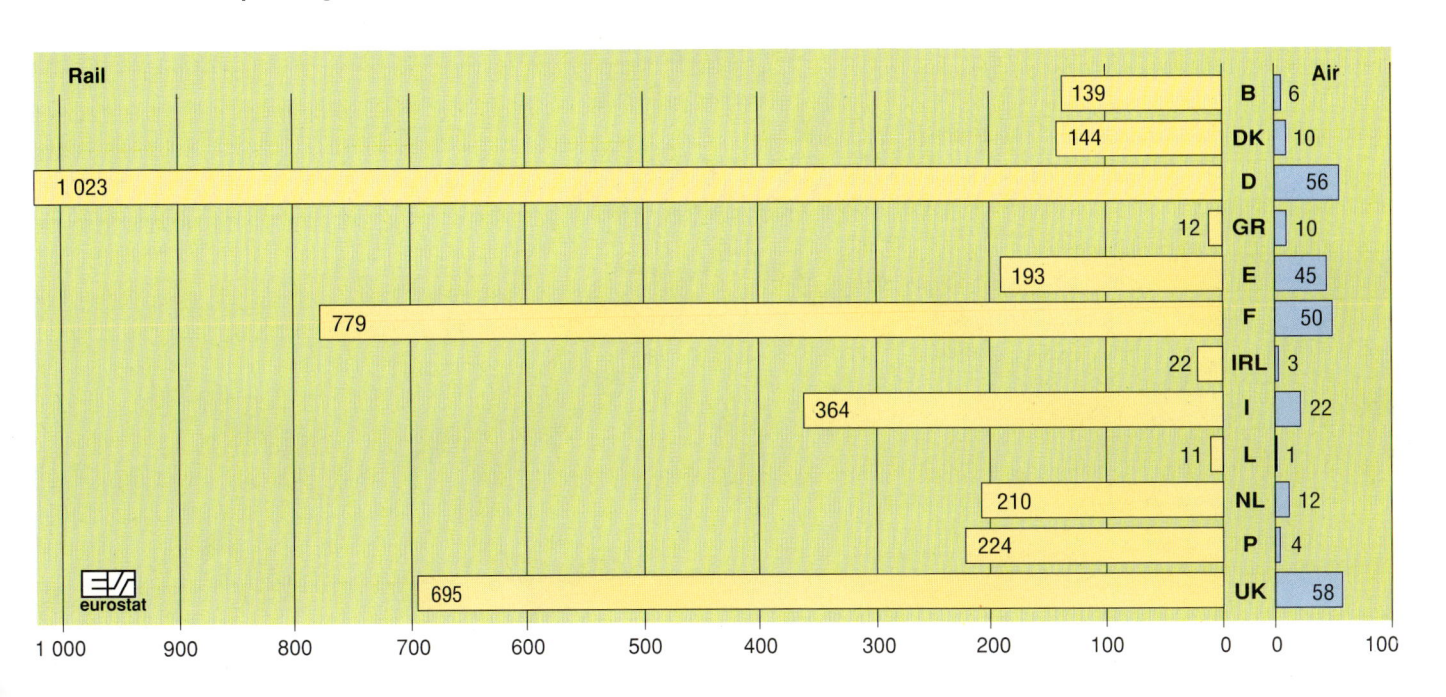

Country	Rail	Air
B	139	6
DK	144	10
D	1 023	56
GR	12	10
E	193	45
F	779	50
IRL	22	3
I	364	22
L	11	1
NL	210	12
P	224	4
UK	695	58

The Federal Republic of Germany has the longest motorway network (over 8 400 km in 1988), followed by France and Italy (6 000 km). Ireland has no motorways.

The number of vehicles on these roads is rising steadily. In 1985 the Community's stock of passenger vehicles exceeded 110 million, of which nearly 26 million (double the 1970 figure) were registered in the Federal Republic of Germany.

The rail network, which covered over 125 000 km in the Community as a whole in 1985, is steadily shrinking due to the closure of lines no longer economically viable against a background of rural depopulation and competition from the motor car. In Belgium, for example, the rail network shrank from 4 332 km in 1970 to 3 691 km in 1986. Denmark, Italy and Portugal, on the other hand, have maintained and even extended their rail network.

In 1986 the rail network carrying the most passengers in the Community (1 023 million) was the Federal Republic of Germany's Bundesbahn. France's SNCF carried 779 million passengers and the United Kingdom's British Rail 695 million.

The volume of passenger air traffic is substantially lower than rail traffic in all the Community countries. In 1986 it totalled 58 million passengers in the United Kingdom, 56 million in the Federal Republic of Germany and 50 million in France.

THE ENVIRONMENT
POLLUTION

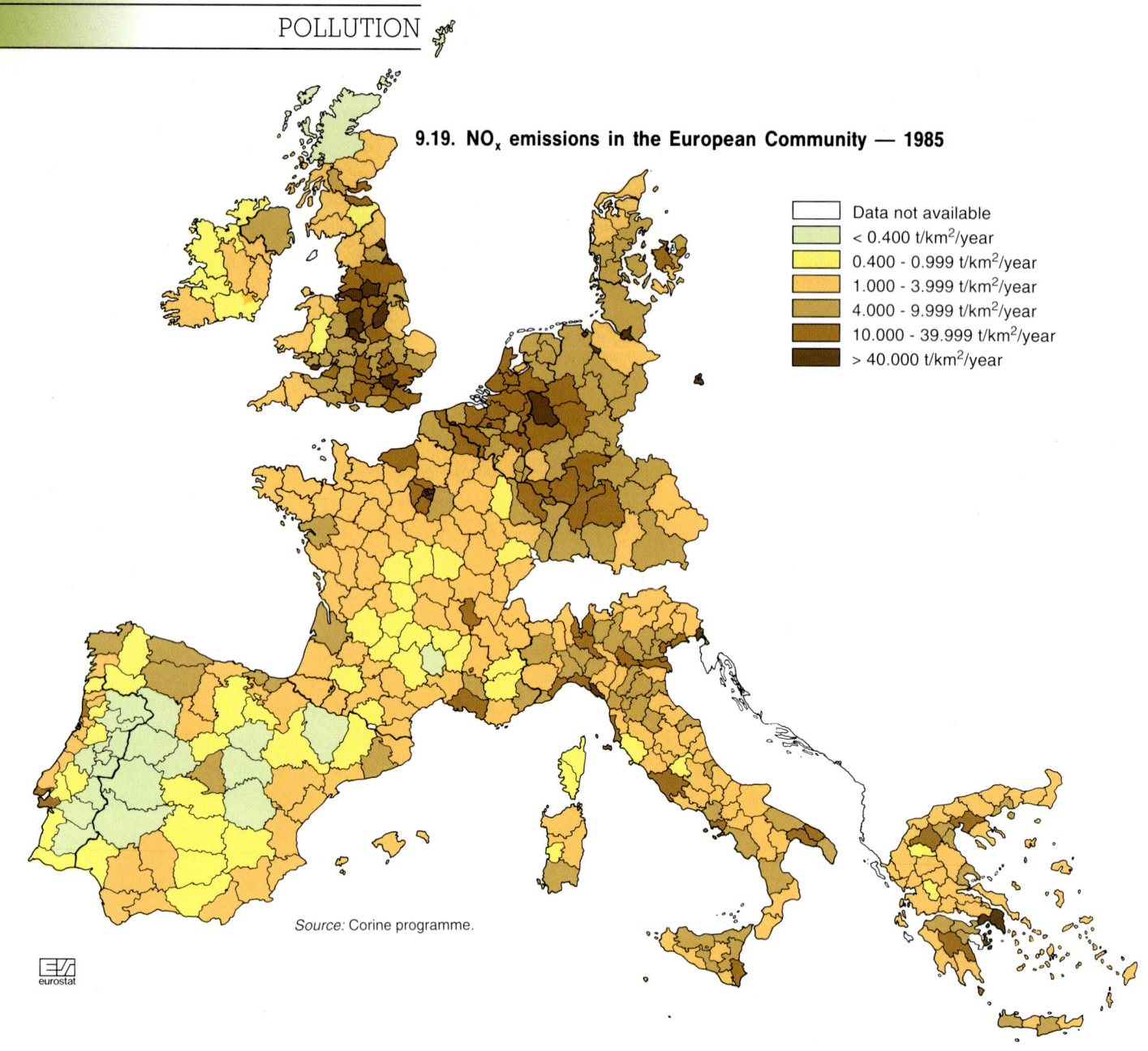

9.19. NO$_x$ emissions in the European Community — 1985

☐	Data not available
	< 0.400 t/km²/year
	0.400 - 0.999 t/km²/year
	1.000 - 3.999 t/km²/year
	4.000 - 9.999 t/km²/year
	10.000 - 39.999 t/km²/year
	> 40.000 t/km²/year

Source: Corine programme.

9.20. Cumulative production and release into the atmosphere of CFC 11 and CFC 12 since 1931 (2 000 t)

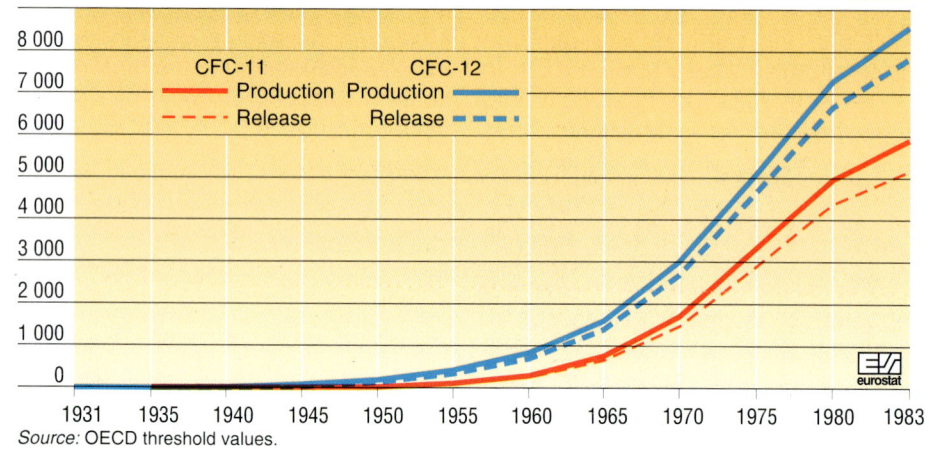

CFC-11 Production / Release
CFC-12 Production / Release

Source: OECD threshold values.

9.21. CO$_2$ emissions in 1987
(tC per inhabitant)

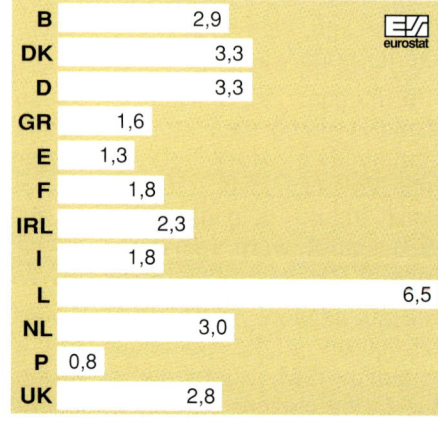

B	2,9
DK	3,3
D	3,3
GR	1,6
E	1,3
F	1,8
IRL	2,3
I	1,8
L	6,5
NL	3,0
P	0,8
UK	2,8

THE ENVIRONMENT
POLLUTION

Pollution by humanly produced solid, liquid or gaseous waste affects the three primary elements of our planet, i.e. the air, the water and the earth.

Air pollution, which is caused chiefly by the emission of industrial gases and traffic fumes, is highest in the densely populated industrial regions, particularly in the north of the Community. Rural regions, such as the Spanish Meseta, the French Massif Central or Ireland, have markedly lower levels of pollution. However, since pollution is carried across frontiers by winds, the problem extends beyond the confines of the Community to the international arena.

Among the most powerful air pollutants are nitrogen oxides (NO_x), carbon dioxide (CO_2) and chlorofluorocarbons (CFCs), which some researchers see as contributing to the 'greenhouse effect'.

The production of CFC 11 and 12 has increased steadily to reach spectacular proportions, rising from 217 000 tonnes in 1950 to 14.5 million tonnes in 1983, and this has been matched by a parallel increase in the use of these products and their release into the atmosphere, annual releases having risen over the same period from 163 000 tonnes to 13 million tonnes.

The problem as regards water is one of both quantity and quality. Water requirements, particularly in industry and for irrigation purposes, are increasing continuously. The Mediterranean countries are major users of water. In Spain, for example, annual per capita consumption is 1 175 m^3, in Portugal 1 075 m^3 and in Italy 996 m^3.

Pollution in rivers is less pronounced the greater the quantity of oxygen dissolved and the higher the biochemical oxygen demand. In France these values are high for the Loire (12.1 and 7.8 mgr/l), making it a relatively unpolluted river, but much lower for the Seine (5.2 and 3.2), which flows through more populated and industrialized regions, in particular Paris.

9.22. Per capita water withdrawal — 1985 (m^3 per capita)

B ([1])	DK	D	GR ([1])	E	F	IRL ([1])	I ([1])	L	NL	P ([1])	UK
917	286	675	720	1 175	725	233	996	182	999	1 075	231

([1]) 1980.

9.23. Water-quality indicators — selected rivers — 1985 (mg/l)

	Selected rivers	Dissolved oxygen	Biological oxygen demand
Belgium	Meuse, Heer/Agimont	10,4	8,0
	Meuse - Lanage	8,1	4,3
	Escaut - Doel	3,3	3,0
Denmark	Gudenaa	10,7	4,5
	Skjernaa	10,4	8,0
	Susaa	8,7	2,0
Federal Republic of Germany	Rhin - Kleve - Bimmen	9,3	3,8
	Elbe	8,1	8,6
	Weser	8,7	4,4
	Donau - Jochenstein	10,5	3,2
Spain	Guadalquivir	5,7	8,8
	Duero	7,3	2,7
	Tajo	7,6	3,0
	Ebro	9,4	4,6
France	Loire	12,1	7,8
	Seine	5,2	3,2
	Garonne	9,3	2,2
	Rhône	8,6	5,0

	Selected rivers	Dissolved oxygen	Biological oxygen demand
Italy	Pô	8,6	5,0
	Tevere	8,8	2,0
Netherlands	Meuse - Keizersveer	9,7	1,6
	Meuse - Eijsden	8,1	2,9
	Nieuwe - Waterweg /Scheur Maasl.	9,3	1,5
	IJssel - Kampen	8,2	2,3
	Rhire - Lobit	8,0	2,3
Portugal	Tejo	7,8	1,7
	Minho	10,1	2,9
United Kingdom	Thames	10,0	2,4
	Severn	10,8	1,7
	Clyde	9,1	3,2
	Mersey	6,2	5,0

THE ENVIRONMENT
NATURE CONSERVATION

The map shows, for each region, the percentage of land which is of special scientific interest in terms of nature conservation. As can be seen, large areas fall into this category in the southern regions of the Community, particularly in Spain, Italy and Greece, and in the Alps and the Pyrenees. Regions with a high percentage of such land are far more widely dispersed in the north of the Community.

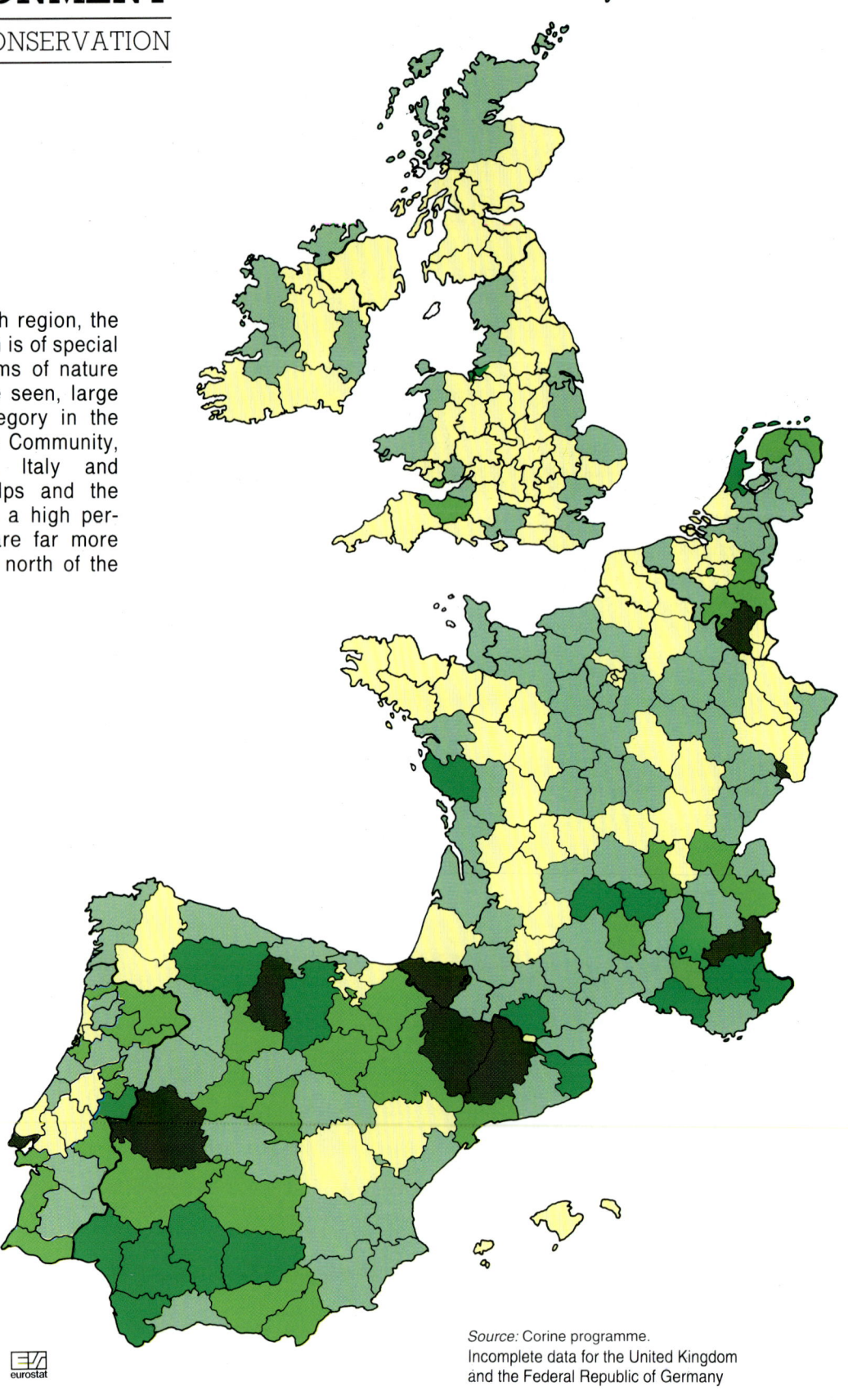

Source: Corine programme.
Incomplete data for the United Kingdom and the Federal Republic of Germany

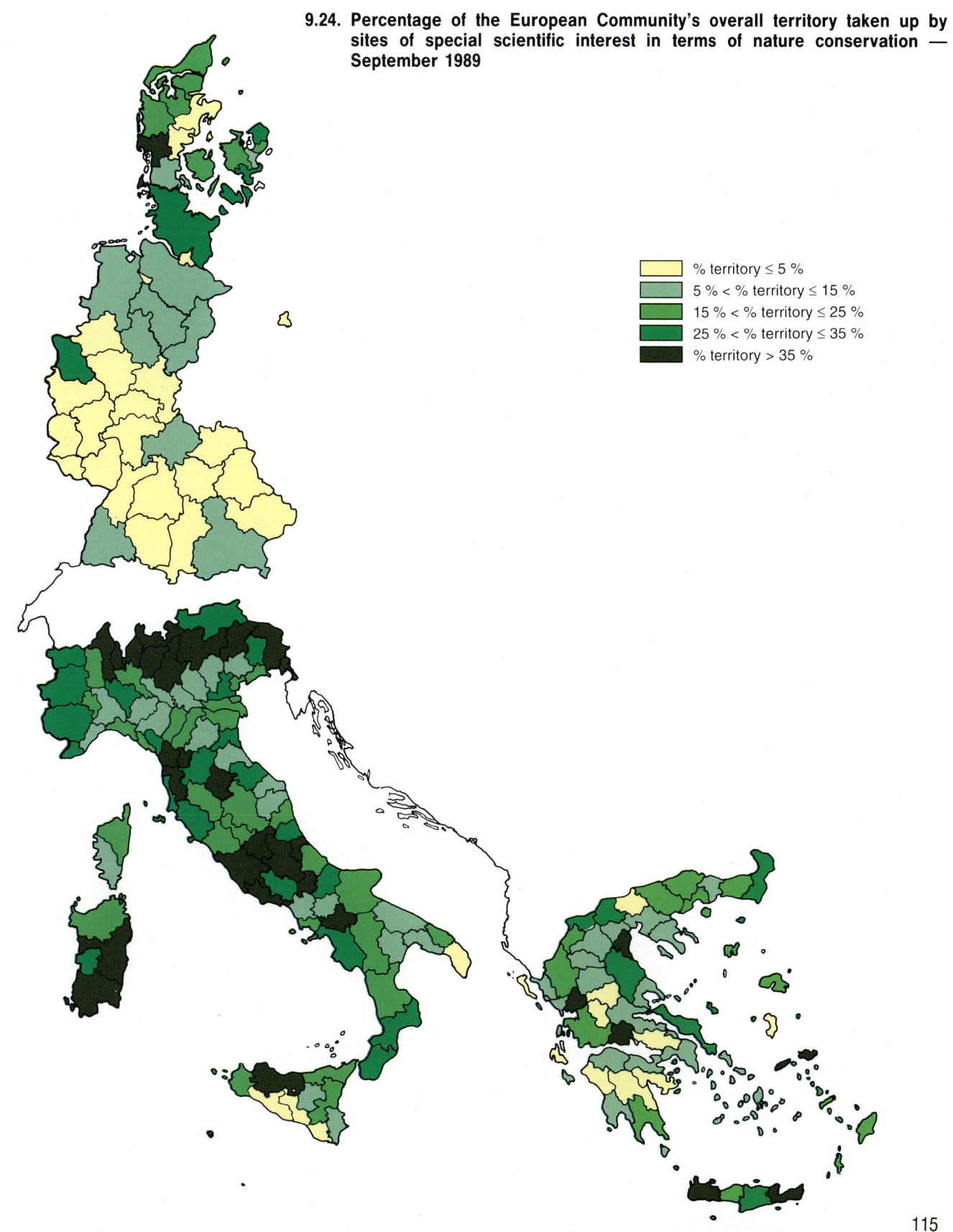

THE ENVIRONMENT
NATURE CONSERVATION

9.24. Percentage of the European Community's overall territory taken up by sites of special scientific interest in terms of nature conservation — September 1989

% territory ≤ 5 %
5 % < % territory ≤ 15 %
15 % < % territory ≤ 25 %
25 % < % territory ≤ 35 %
% territory > 35 %

THE ENVIRONMENT
FOR FURTHER INFORMATION

Definitions

NO$_x$ emissions: nitrogen oxides are produced mainly through the burning of fossil fuels at high temperatures, and are a source of concern due to their harmful effects on health and the environment.

CFC 11 and 12: chlorofluorocarbons are intermediary chemical products used as aerosol propellants, foaming agents in the manufacture of foan plastics and coolants in refrigeration and air-conditioning systems. CFCs are thought to contribute to depletion of the ozone layer in the stratosphere, thus posing a threat to human health.

Dissolved oxygen concentration and biological oxygen demand: these are a measure of water quality and provide information on the degree of pollution by organic matter and nutrients.

Site of special scientific interest in terms of nature conservation: these are sites whose protection is justified by their importance to scientific research.

References

Eurostat
– Environmental statistics, 1989
– Transport and communications, 1970-1986
– Agriculture, 1989
– Energy, 1987

Eurobarometer
– Europeans and the environment in 1988

OECD
– OECD environmental data, 1985

Eurostat databank
– Cronos
– Regio

DG XI databank
– Corine

HOUSING

In Ireland, Spain and Greece over 70% of dwellings are owner-occupied; the figure is approximately 40% in the Federal Republic of Germany and the Netherlands and just over 50% in the Community as a whole (10.3).

The 1981-82 censuses showed that nearly a quarter of all dwellings in the Community were built after 1970 and one-third before 1945, particularly in the United Kingdom (50.4%), Belgium (48.4%) and Denmark (45.5%) (10.7).

These same censuses recorded an average of 0.6 persons per room for dwellings in the Community (10.9).

The vast majority of dwellings in the Community are equipped with a bathroom and/or shower on the premises, as well as an internal WC (10.10).

The most widespread item of household equipment is the refrigerator (present in over 90% of households in the majority of Community countries), followed by the washing machine (10.11).

Rents rose most significantly between 1980 and 1986 in Greece and Italy (from base 100 to 282 in the former and 226 in the latter), while in the Federal Republic of Germany and the Netherlands they rose only slightly (from base 100 to 126 and 136 respectively) (10.15).

10.1. Percentage of dwellings with bathroom

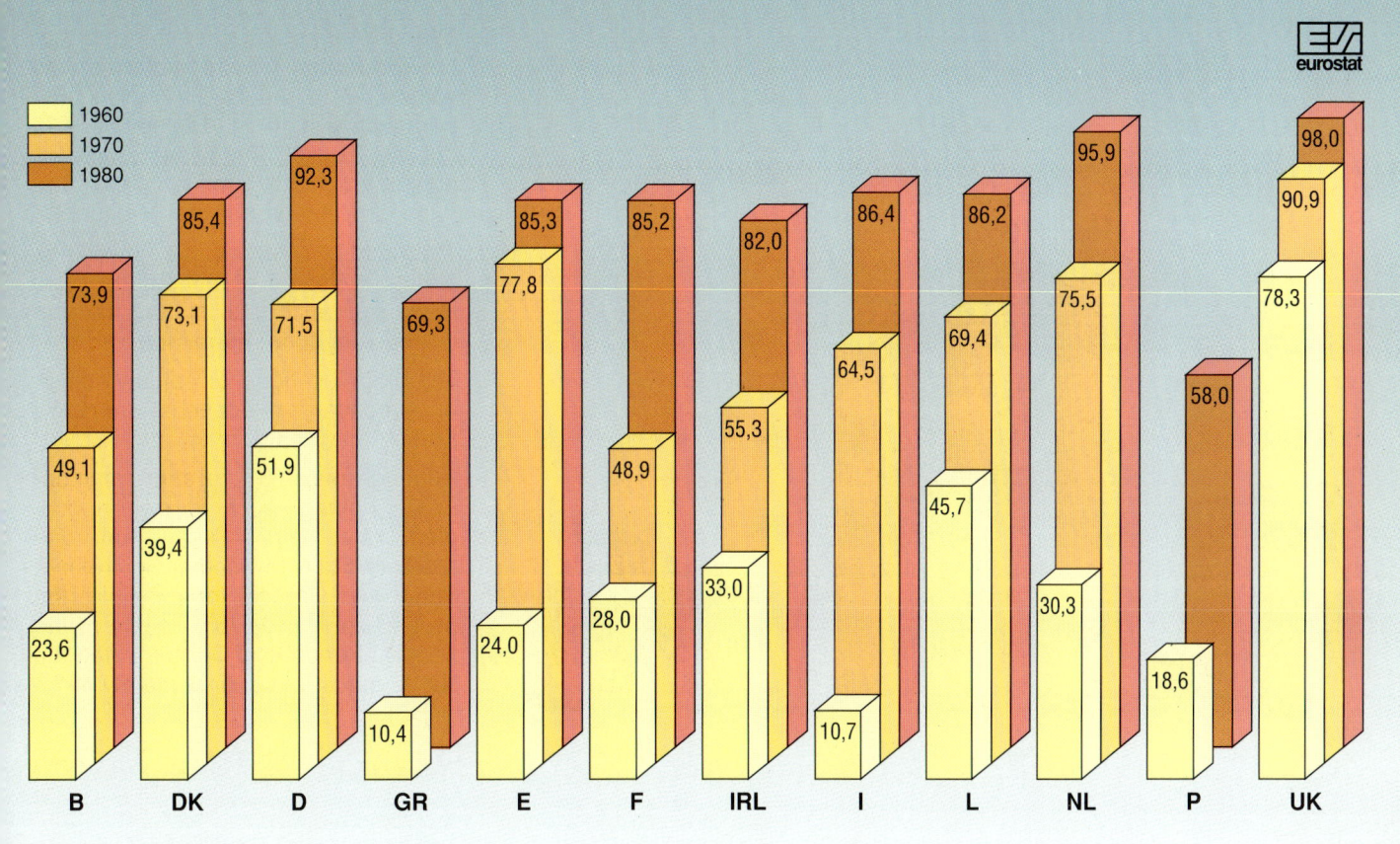

Country	1960	1970	1980
B	23,6	49,1	73,9
DK	39,4	73,1	85,4
D	51,9	71,5	92,3
GR	10,4	—	69,3
E	24,0	77,8	85,3
F	28,0	48,9	85,2
IRL	33,0	55,3	82,0
I	10,7	64,5	86,4
L	45,7	69,4	86,2
NL	30,3	75,5	95,9
P	18,6	—	58,0
UK	78,3	90,9	98,0

eurostat

HOUSING
DWELLING STOCK

10.2. Types of housing unit in the Community — 1981-82 censuses (1 000)

	B	DK	D	GR	E	F	IRL	I	L	NL	P	UK
Main residences	3 660	2 029	23 797	2 896	10 470	19 438	876	17 542	124	4 941	2 769	19 635
• one-family houses	2 512	1 175	11 394 [1]	2 896	3 835	10 291	835	5 484	79	3 372	1 788	19 635
• blocks of flats	1 148	853	12 403		6 635	9 147	40	12 058	45	1 569	981	
Unoccupied dwellings	152	120	:	1 084	2 396	1 854	:	2 032	:	113	430	1 583
Holiday homes and secondary residences	135	186	250		1 861	2 265	:	2 364	:	17	184	236

[1] One-family houses + two-family houses.

10.3. Percentage of owner-occupied dwellings — 1981-82 censuses

	EUR 12	B	DK	D	GR	E	F	IRL	I	L	NL	P	UK
1981 - 82	53.8	59.3	54.9	40.5	70.1	73.1	51.0	74.4	58.9	60.2	41.8	56.6	55.7

10.4. Geographical distribution of rented dwellings — 1986

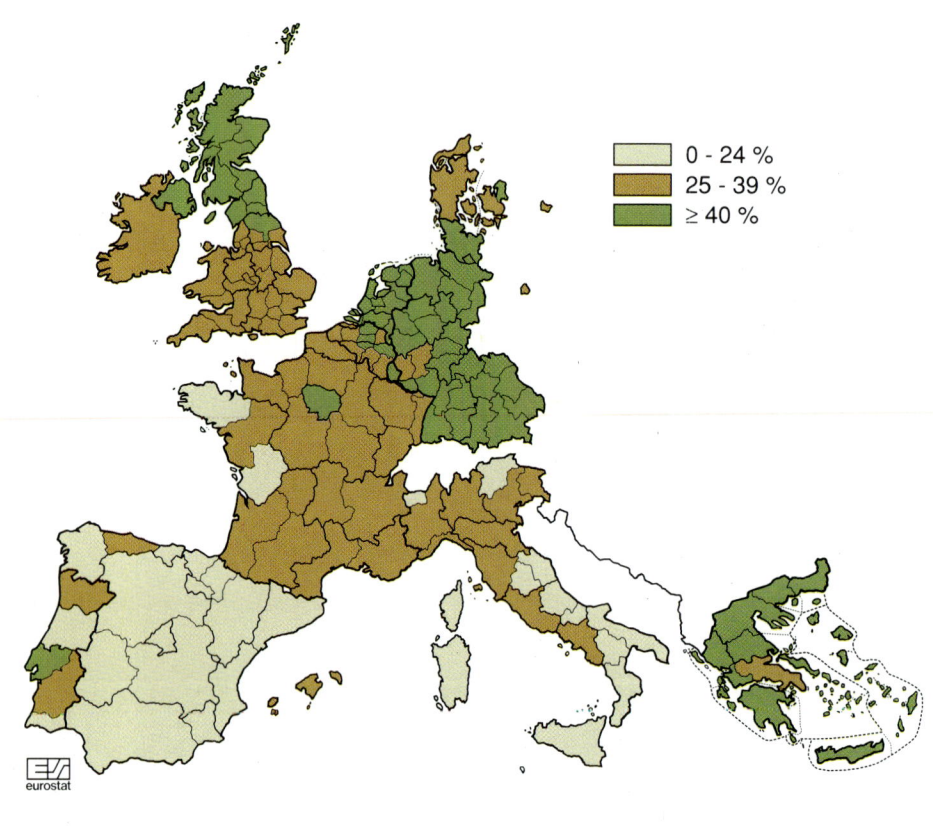

0 - 24 %
25 - 39 %
≥ 40 %

The 1981-82 censuses showed that the proportion of one-family houses within the overall dwelling stock was particularly high in Ireland (835 000 out of 876 000), the Netherlands (3.4 million out of 4.9 million) and Belgium (2.5 million out of 3.7 million).

The number of unoccupied dwellings is high in Spain (2.4 million), Italy (2.0 million), France (1.9 million) and the United Kingdom (1.6 million).

The main locations for holiday homes or secondary residences are Italy, France and Spain.

Although over 50 % of the Community's dwelling stock is owner-occupied, rates vary greatly from one Member State to another. In Ireland, Spain and Greece, for example, the proportion is over 70 %, while in the Federal Republic of Germany and the Netherlands it is approximately 40 %.

HOUSING
DWELLING STOCK

10.5. Geographical distribution of the dwelling stock per thousand inhabitants in 1986

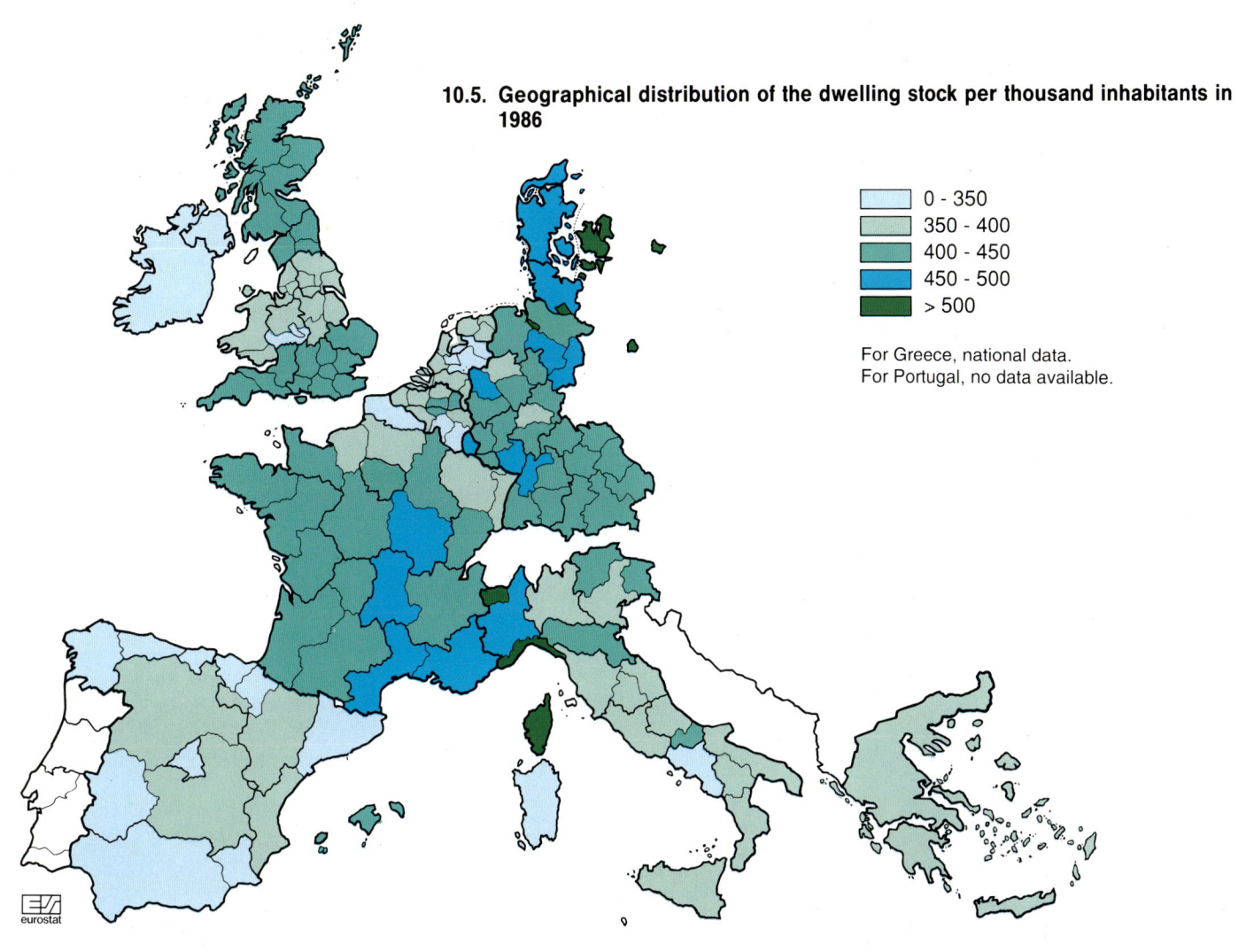

- 0 - 350
- 350 - 400
- 400 - 450
- 450 - 500
- > 500

For Greece, national data.
For Portugal, no data available.

10.6. New dwellings per 1 000 inhabitants in 1970, 1978 and 1988

The regional distribution of dwellings is far from uniform. Urban regions have a higher number of dwellings per 1 000 inhabitants (over 500 in Bremen or Hamburg in the Federal Republic of Germany), while certain rural areas have lower rates.

Comparing 1978 with 1970, the construction of new dwellings showed an upward trend in Belgium, Greece, Ireland and Luxembourg, while the other eight Community countries recorded a general decline. However, comparison of 1988 with 1978 reveals an overall decline, except in Italy, the Netherlands and Portugal.

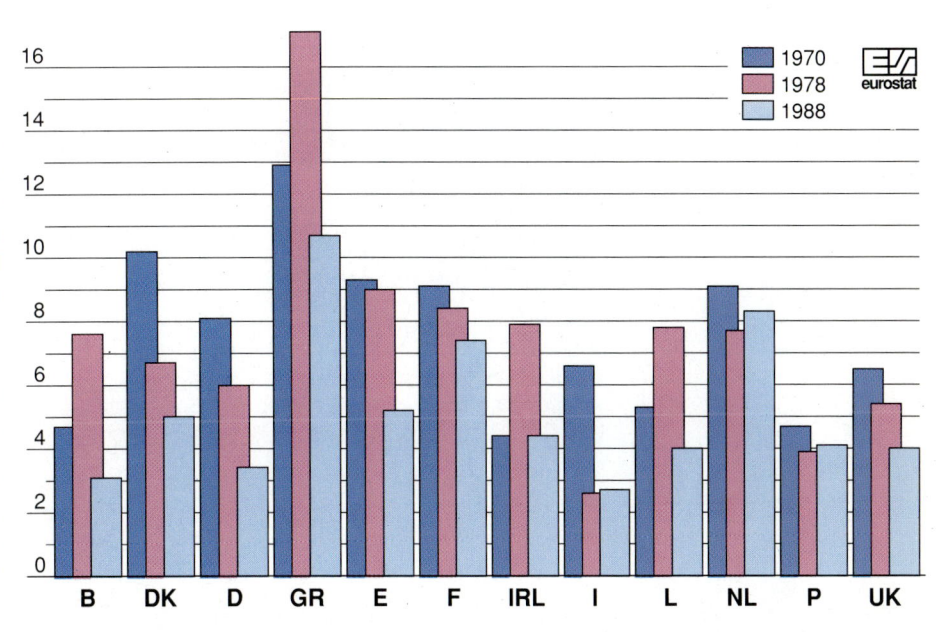

119

HOUSING
AGE OF DWELLINGS

10.7. Percentage breakdown of dwellings by period of construction. 1981-82 censuses

	Pre-1945	1945-1970	Post-1970
B	48.4	32.1	19.5
DK	45.5	35.7	18.8
D	33.1 [1]	48.8	18.1
GR	21.8	49.1	29.1
E	27.8	45.6	26.6
F	43.8 [1]	30.6	25.6
IRL	45.3	28.4	26.3
I	29.9	49.2	20.9
L	41.8	35.8	22.4
NL	27.9	35.0	37.1
P	38.7	35.5	25.8
UK	50.4	34.7	14.9

[1] Pre-1948.

The 1981-82 censuses show that almost a quarter of dwellings in the Community were built after 1970. This proportion is lower (one-sixth) in the United Kingdom but higher (over one-third) in the Netherlands.

Over one-third of dwellings in the Community were built before 1945, the proportions in the United Kingdom (50.4%) and Belgium (48.4%) being particularly high.

At regional level, a high proportion of dwellings in the traditionally industrial areas of the United Kingdom, Belgium and France were built before 1945/50. This is not the case in the traditionally industrial areas of the Federal Republic of Germany, which have a lower proportion of older dwellings due to the damage suffered during the Second World War. Madrid, Rome and Sardinia stand out clearly as having a housing stock of more recent origin.

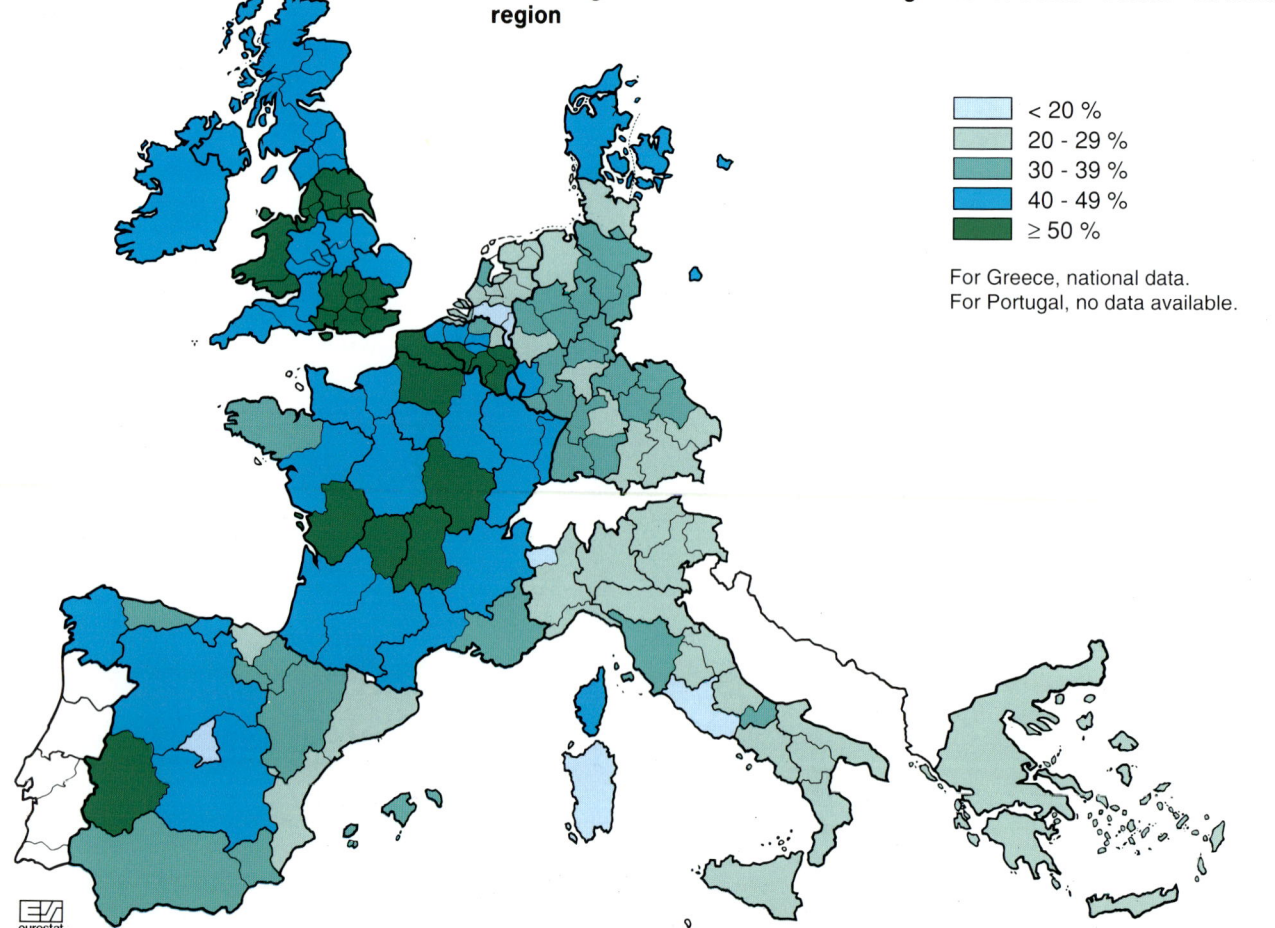

10.8. Percentage breakdown of dwellings constructed before 1945/50 by region

- < 20 %
- 20 - 29 %
- 30 - 39 %
- 40 - 49 %
- ≥ 50 %

For Greece, national data.
For Portugal, no data available.

HOUSING
AMENITIES

10.9. Number of persons per room — 1981-82 censuses

	EUR 12	B	DK	D	GR	E	F	IRL	I	L	NL	P	UK
1960 - 1962	:	0,6	0,7	0,9	1,5	0,9	1,0	:	1,1	0,6	0,8	1,1	0,7
1968 - 1971	:	0,6	0,8	0,7	:	:	0,9	0,9	0,9	0,6	0,7	:	0,6
1981 - 1982	0,6	0,6	0,5	0,6	0,8	0,8	0,6	0,8	0,8	0,5	0,6	0,9	0,6

10.10. Basic amenities (%) — 1981-82 censuses

	Bathroom or shower on the premises	Internal WC	Central heating on the premises
B	73,9	79,0	:
DK	85,1	95,8	54,6
D	92,3	96,0	70,0
GR	69,3	70,9	:
E	85,3	:	22,5
F	85,2	85,4	67,6
IRL	82,0	84,5	39,2
I	86,4	87,7	56,5
L	86,2	97,3	73,9
NL	95,9	:	66,1
P	58,0	58,7	:
UK	98,0	97,3	:

The 1981-82 censuses show an average of 0.6 persons per room for the Community as a whole. The results by country are relatively uniform: Portugal, with 0.9, is the only country well above the average, while Denmark and Luxembourg, with 0.5, lie slightly below. With the exception of Belgium, which already recorded 0.6 persons per room in 1960, all the countries showed improvements during the period 1960-62 to 1981-82.

The vast majority of dwellings in the United Kingdom (98.0%), the Netherlands (95.9%) and the Federal Republic of Germany (92.3%) are equipped with a bathroom and/or shower on the premises. The figures for the other countries lie between 82.0% (Ireland) and 86.4% (Italy), with the exception of Belgium (73.9%), Greece (69.3%) and Portugal (58.0%).

The relative positions are similar as regards an internal WC, the corresponding percentages being even higher.

The percentage of dwellings equipped with a central heating system is particularly high in Luxembourg (73.9%) and the Federal Republic of Germany (70.0%).

HOUSING
CONSUMER DURABLES

10.11. Percentage of households equipped with household appliances in 1980 and 1985

	Refrigerators ± 1980	1985	Freezers ± 1980	1985	Dishwashers ± 1980	1985	Washing machines ± 1980	1985
B	94.0	:	51.1	:	15.5	:	80.4	:
DK	98.0	:	65.0	:	17.0	:	58.0	:
D	96.1	96.0	56.8	48.8	15.4	23.5	81.0	82.5
GR	95.4	:	:	:	:	:	57.3	:
E	91.0	:	:	:	6.0	:	80.0	:
F	95.3	98.8	25.5	35.8	13.3	22.0	73.6	81.0
IRL	86.1	95.5	13.9	15.7	4.7	7.6	63.2	77.1
I	93.5	94.7	:	:	14.1	16.7	80.7	87.0
L	100.0	:	72.8	:	12.6	:	99.0	:
NL	97.8	98.5	37.2	40.8	8.0	7.3	86.8	89.8
P	72.0	:	:	:	:	:	30.0	:
UK	92.8	:	28.9	:	3.3	:	76.6	:

The family budget surveys conducted around 1980 and 1985 showed that a very high percentage (between 90 and 95%) of households throughout the Community were equipped with refrigerators, the exception being Portugal (72% in 1980). Although washing machines were less widespread, percentages increased substantially between 1980 and 1985 in France (from 73.6% to 81.0%) and in Ireland (from 63.2% to 77.1%). However, the percentage of households with freezers and dishwashers in 1985 was much lower.

The percentage of Community households with a telephone varies widely from one country to another. In 1985 the Federal Republic of Germany and France (88.1%) were well on the way to matching Denmark's already high percentage in 1980, while the Netherlands had already surpassed it with a rate of 94.9%.

10.12. Percentage of households with a telephone in 1980 and 1985

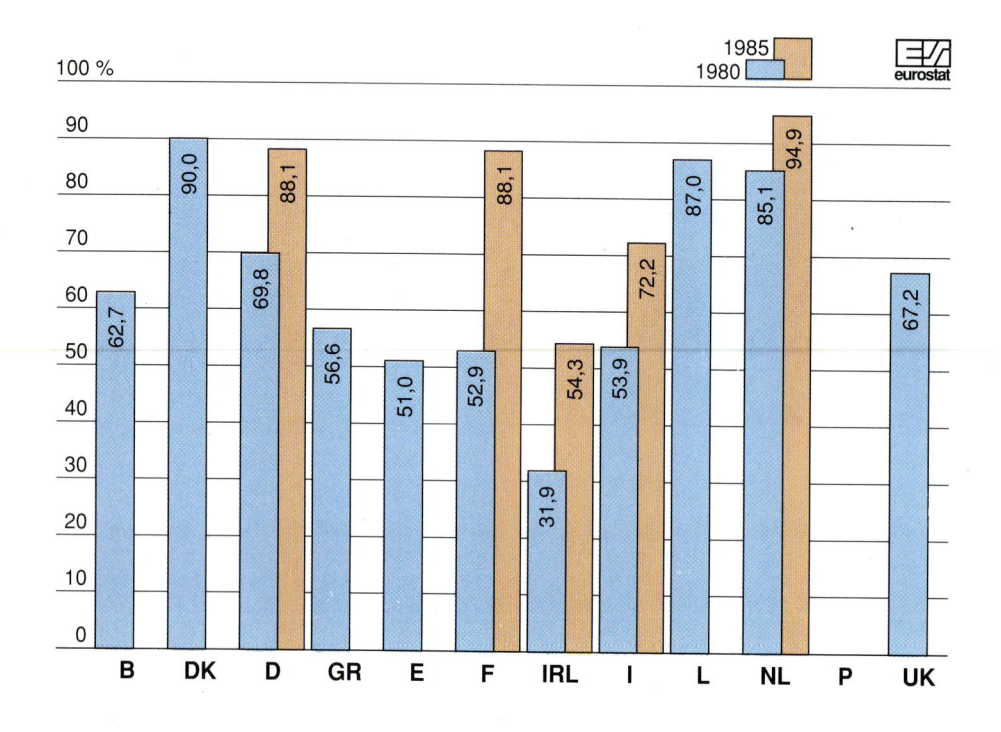

Country	1980	1985
B	62,7	
DK	90,0	
D	69,8	88,1
GR	56,6	
E	51,0	
F	52,9	88,1
IRL	31,9	54,3
I	53,9	72,2
L	87,0	
NL	85,1	94,9
P		
UK	67,2	

HOUSING
CONSUMPTION AND EXPENDITURE

Generally speaking, there was little variation between 1980 and 1987 in the share of housing, heating and lighting in the overall expenditure of households in the various Community countries. In 1987 this share was highest in Denmark (26.6% of final consumption), while in Portugal and Greece in 1985 it was a mere 5.0% and 10.9% respectively.

The period between 1980 and 1985 saw an overall downward trend in the share of furniture, household goods and household maintenance in the overall consumption of households, followed by a slight increase in certain countries between 1985 and 1987. The share is highest in Belgium (10.4% in 1987) and lowest in Denmark (6.6%).

The index of rents rose most significantly between 1980 and 1986 in Greece, Italy and the United Kingdom, increasing from base 100 to 281.5 in Greece, 226.1 in Italy and 202.3 in the United Kingdom. Rents rose least in the Federal Republic of Germany and the Netherlands, where in 1986 the index stood at 126.4 and 135.6 respectively.

10.13. Share of housing, heating and lighting (at current prices) in final consumption in 1980, 1985 and 1987

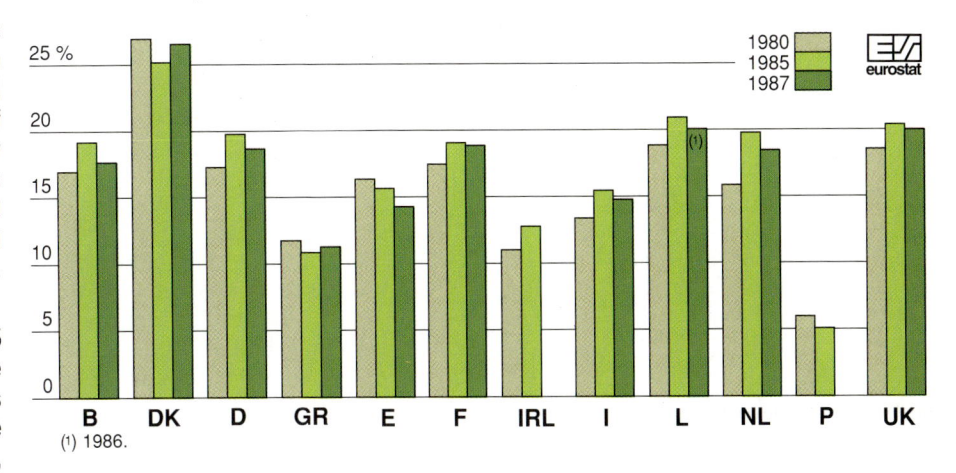

(1) 1986.

10.14. Share of furniture, household goods and general household maintenance (at current prices) in final consumption in 1980, 1985 and 1987

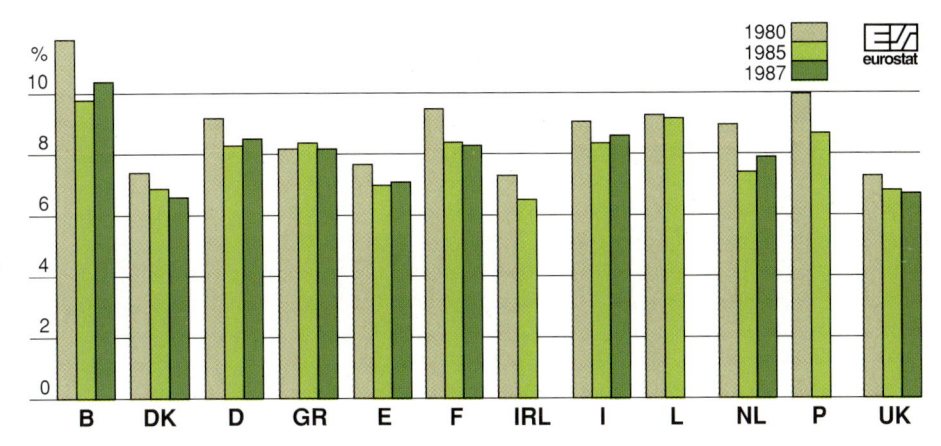

10.15. Index of rents from 1980 to 1986 (base 1980 = 100)

	1980	1981	1982	1983	1984	1985	1986
B	100,0	108,1	116,4	126,3	132,5	136,1	140,9
DK	100,0	107,8	118,3	129,5	139,7	147,0	153,2
D	100,0	104,4	109,7	115,6	120,0	123,9	126,4
GR	100,0	124,9	153,5	172,2	198,3	230,1	281,5
E	100,0	111,2	125,4	136,0	146,2	152,9	159,9
F	100,0	113,3	125,4	137,9	148,9	158,7	167,5
IRL	100,0	107,9	125,5	134,6	148,8	156,6	161,0
I	100,0	115,6	135,0	160,4	196,2	207,9	226,1
L	100,0	:	:	:	:	:	:
NL	100,0	107,0	114,6	122,4	127,9	131,9	135,6
P	100,0	:	:	:	:	:	:
UK	100,0	129,4	149,3	160,5	170,3	184,1	202,3

HOUSING
FOR FURTHER INFORMATION

Definitions

Dwelling: a dwelling is a room or suite of rooms and its accessories in a permanent building or structurally separated part thereof, which, by the way it has been built, rebuilt, converted, etc., is intended for private habitation. It should have a separate access to a street (direct or via garden or grounds) or to a common space within the building (staircase, passage, gallery, etc.). Detached rooms for habitation which are clearly built, rebuilt, converted, etc. to be used as a part of the dwelling should be counted as part of the dwelling. (A dwelling may thus be composed of separate buildings with the same enclosure provided they are clearly intended for habitation by the same private household, e.g. a room or rooms above a detached garage, occupied by servants or other members of the household.)

Dwelling stock: the dwelling stock includes only conventional (permanent) dwellings, whether occupied or not. The simple term 'dwelling' is generally used instead of 'conventional dwelling'. The dwelling stock does not include rustic (semi permanent) and improvised housing units (e.g. huts, cabins, shanties), mobile housing units (e.g. trailers, caravans, tents, wagons, boats) and housing units not intended for human habitation but in use for the purpose (e.g. stables, barns, mills, garages, warehouses).

References

Eurostat
- Censuses of population and housing
  1960-61, 1968-71, 1981-82
- Basic statistics 1971, 1980, 1990
- National accounts ESA, 1989
- Family budget survey

Eurostat databank
- Regio

LEISURE

More than half (56%) of the population of the European Community aged over 14 goes away on holiday, most (52%) to the seaside. The car is the preferred means of transport to the holiday destination (68%) (11.3) (11.4) (11.7).

In 1987, Europeans devoted between 6.4% (Belgium) and 9.7% (Ireland) of their expenditure to leisure, entertainment and cultural and educational pursuits (11.1) (11.8).

17.3% of Europeans claim membership of a sports club or association, particularly in the northern Member States: 33.6% in Ireland as compared with 5.4% in Spain. 31% are interested in sport, favouring football (36%), tennis (26%) and swimming (25%) (11.11) (11.12) (11.13).

Numbers of television sets have increased considerably in all Member States over the past two decades: from 267 to 386 per 1 000 residents in Denmark and from 217 to 333 per 1 000 residents in France between 1970 and 1987 (11.14).

Europeans visited the cinema on average once to three times in 1985 (11.15).

From 1970 to 1984, the number of titles of daily newspapers fell in almost all Member States (from 169 to 84 in the Netherlands and from 33 to 25 in Portugal). Circulation of daily newspapers per 1 000 inhabitants is highest in the United Kingdom (414) (11.16).

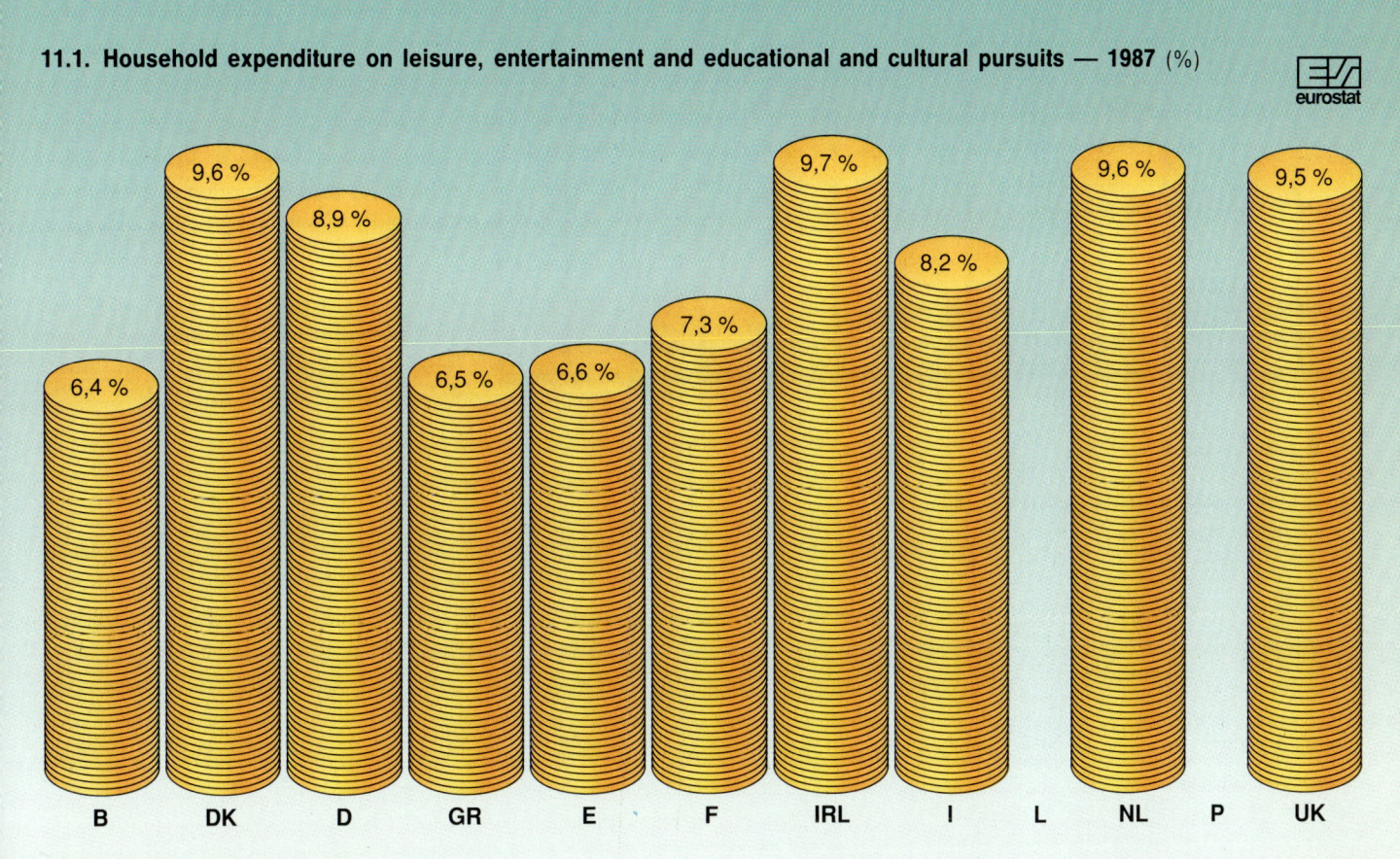

11.1. Household expenditure on leisure, entertainment and educational and cultural pursuits — 1987 (%)

B	DK	D	GR	E	F	IRL	I	L	NL	P	UK
6,4 %	9,6 %	8,9 %	6,5 %	6,6 %	7,3 %	9,7 %	8,2 %		9,6 %		9,5 %

LEISURE
HOLIDAYS

11.2. Countries visited during main holidays — 1985 (%)

	EUR 12	B	DK	D	GR	E	F	IRL	I	L	NL	P	UK
Holidays in the home country	68	44	56	40	93	92	84	49	87	6	36	92	65
Holidays abroad	32	56	44	60	7	8	16	51	13	94	64	8	35
Breakdown of destinations abroad													
Holidays within the European Community	20	47	25	34	4	7	11	38	8	69	46	7	21
Holidays in Europe outside the Community	10	6	20	24	3	1	2	:	5	18	17	1	10
Holidays outside Europe	3	3	3	3	2	1	4	5	1	9	3	1	5

Source: Eurobarometer.
[1] Total slightly higher than the proportion indicated in the 'holidays abroad' category because some visited both Community and other countries.

11.3. Percentage of persons who went away on holiday in 1985

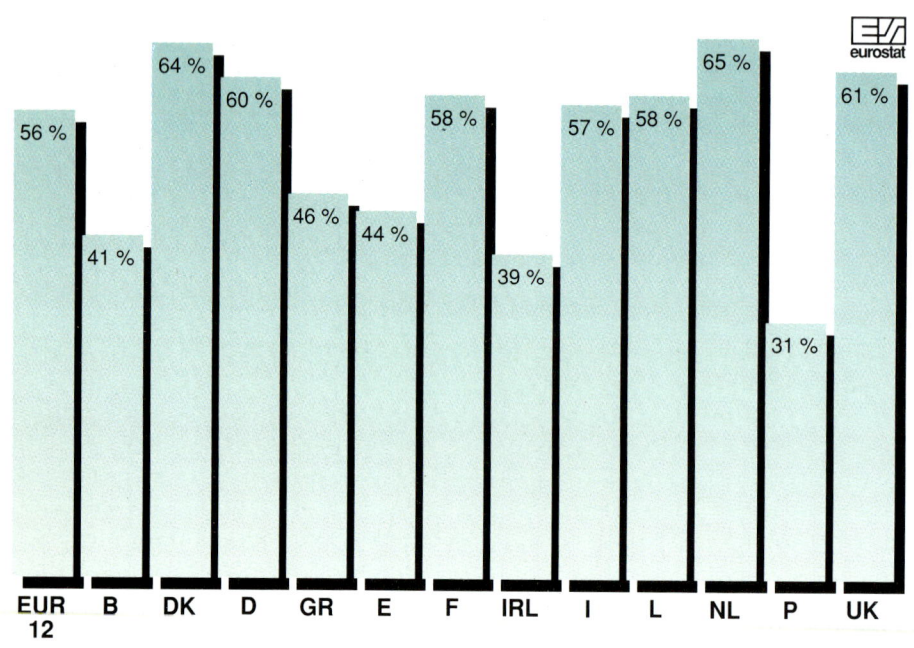

EUR 12	B	DK	D	GR	E	F	IRL	I	L	NL	P	UK
56%	41%	64%	60%	46%	44%	58%	39%	57%	58%	65%	31%	61%

Holidays are becoming a fact of Community society: in 1985, 56% of Europeans went away on holiday. This average percentage was not reached in a number of countries, such as Portugal (31%), Ireland (39%), Belgium (41%), Spain (44%) and Greece (46%). The Dutch (65%) and the Danes (64%) produced the highest proportions of holidaymakers.

More than two-thirds of Europeans spend their holidays in their own country, a proportion far exceeded in the south of the Community: Greece (93%), Spain, Portugal (92%) and Italy (87%). 20% of European holidaymakers travel and stay in Community countries other than their own (Luxembourgers: 69%, Belgians: 47%, Dutch: 46%).

Source: Eurobarometer.

11.4. Main holiday destinations — 1985 (%)

	EUR 12	B	DK	D	GR	E	F	IRL	I	L	NL	P	UK
Seaside	52	55	42	44	70	53	51	46	58	62	36	62	58
Countryside	25	25	35	34	8	27	29	27	11	19	39	29	29
Mountains	23	19	14	30	11	19	27	8	24	29	32	8	13
Towns or cities	19	5	40	15	20	27	18	37	19	17	21	24	19

Source: Eurobarometer.
Total over 100 owing to multiple replies.

LEISURE

HOLIDAYS

11.5. Number of days taken (main holidays) — EUR 12 — 1985

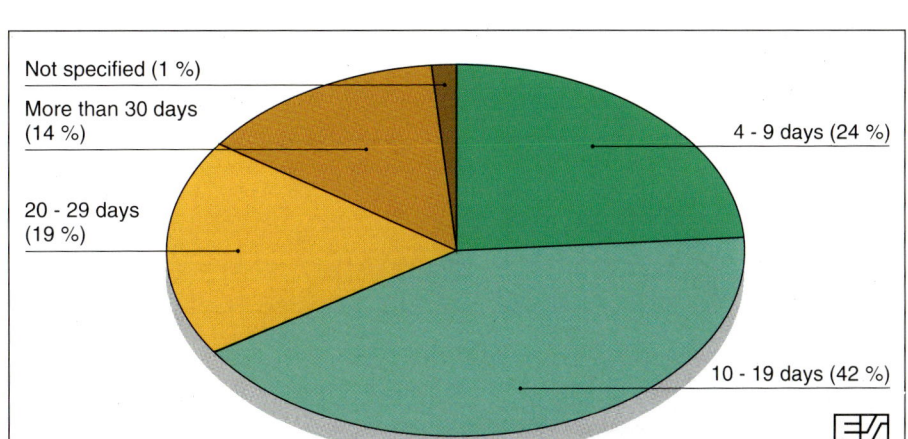

- Not specified (1 %)
- More than 30 days (14 %)
- 20 - 29 days (19 %)
- 10 - 19 days (42 %)
- 4 - 9 days (24 %)

Source: Eurobarometer.

3 % of the Community population spend their holidays outside Europe (9 % of Luxembourgers, 5 % of British and Irish, 4 % of French, 1 % of Spaniards, Italians and Portuguese).

The seaside attracts European holidaymakers approximately twice as often as the countryside and the mountains; towns and cities attract 19 % of tourists.

The length of the main holidays taken by Europeans varies widely, with the highest proportion, 42 % taking 10 to 19 consecutive days. Many go on holiday in July (28 %) and August (34 %). Over two-thirds go by car, the French being the most frequent car-users (81 %). Boats are most popular with the Greeks (25 %) and the Irish (18 %). 31 % of the Irish and 24 % of the British fly to their holiday destination.

11.6. Period of departure on main holiday — EUR 12 — 1985

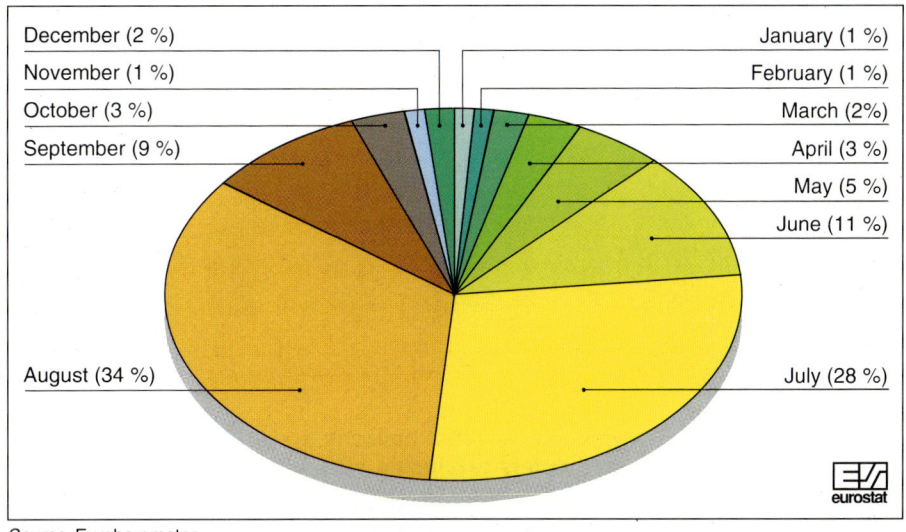

- December (2 %)
- November (1 %)
- October (3 %)
- September (9 %)
- August (34 %)
- July (28 %)
- June (11 %)
- May (5 %)
- April (3 %)
- March (2 %)
- February (1 %)
- January (1 %)

Source: Eurobarometer.

11.7. Means of transport to main holiday destination — EUR 12 — 1985 (%)

	EUR 12	B	DK	D	GR	E	F	IRL	I	L	NL	P	UK
Car	68	77	59	61	78	70	81	51	73	62	70	76	59
Train	14	6	14	16	4	16	15	11	15	10	8	17	11
Aeroplane	13	10	18	17	13	5	6	31	5	19	14	3	24
Boat	5	1	11	3	25	2	2	18	5	4	5	3	8
Motor cycle or bicycle	1	2	3	1	1	—	2	1	2	—	6	1	—
Other	10	7	4	7	—	12	7	6	11	15	14	16	14

Source: Eurobarometer.
Total over 100 owing to multiple replies.

LEISURE
EXPENDITURE

11.8. Trends in household expenditure on leisure, entertainment and educational and cultural pursuits as a proportion of total expenditure (%)

	B	DK	D	GR	E	F	IRL	I	L	NL	P	UK
1970	4,1	7,1	8,3	5,2	6,4	5,7	8,3	6,5	3,6	7,5	:	7,4
1975	4,9	8,4	9,7	4,8	7,0	6,3	8,2	6,4	3,6	8,7	:	8,7
1980	6,0	9,2	9,3	5,4	6,8	7,3	10,1	7,9	3,4	9,7	5,0	9,5
1985	6,0	9,7	8,8	5,9	6,6	7,1	9,6	8,1	3,4	9,3	5,8	9,4
1987	6,4	9,6	8,9	6,5	6,6	7,3	9,7	8,2	:	9,6	:	9,5

Source: Eurobarometer.
Total over 100 owing to multiple replies.

11.9. Trends in final household consumption of books, newspapers and periodicals as a proportion of total expenditure (%)

1980 / 1987

B: 1,0% / 1,1%
DK: 1,7% / 1,4%
D: (no data shown)
GR: 0,8% / 1,1%
E: 0,7% / (no data)
F: 1,5% / 1,6%
IRL: 2,0% / (no data)
I: 1,2% / 1,5%
NL: 2,2% / 2,1%
P: 0,7% / (no data)
UK: 1,3% / 1,4%

Europeans on average devote 6 to 10% of their expenditure to leisure, entertainment and educational and cultural pursuits. The proportion varies from country to country, but has increased since 1970 in all Member States except Luxembourg, where the percentage spent on these activities is lowest (3.4% in 1985). The highest values are recorded in Ireland (9.7%), Denmark (9.6%), the Netherlands (9.6%) and the United Kingdom (9.5%).

Household expenditure on reading (books, newspapers, periodicals) varies between 1% and 2% of total expenditure. This proportion remained fairly stable between 1980 and 1987, though with a slight increase in Belgium (+0.1%), France (+0.1%), the United Kingdom (+0.1%), Greece (+0.3%) and Italy (+0.3%) and a slight fall-off in Denmark (−0.3%) and the Netherlands (−0.1%).

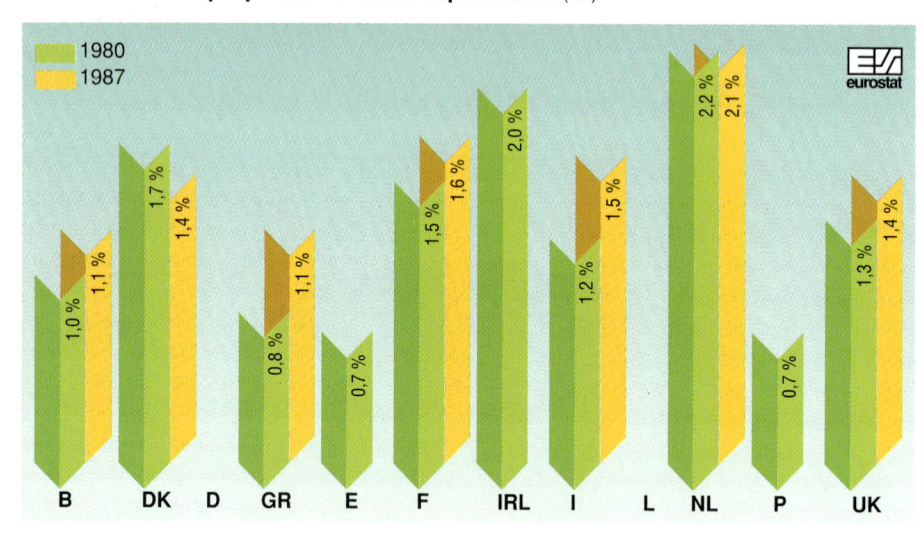

11.10. Trends in the proportion of total household expenditure devoted to restaurants, cafés and hotels (excluding alcoholic drinks) (%)

1980 / 1987

B: 7,5% / 7,9%
DK: 4,7% / 5,5%
D: 4,6% / 4,4%
GR: 5,3% / 6,3%
E: 11,2% / 14,0% (¹)
F: 6,4% / 6,6%
IRL*: 1,5% / 1,9% (²)
I: 8,1% / 9,8%
NL: 4,7% / 4,9%
P: 9,4% / 9,7% (²)
UK: 12,2% / 12,8%

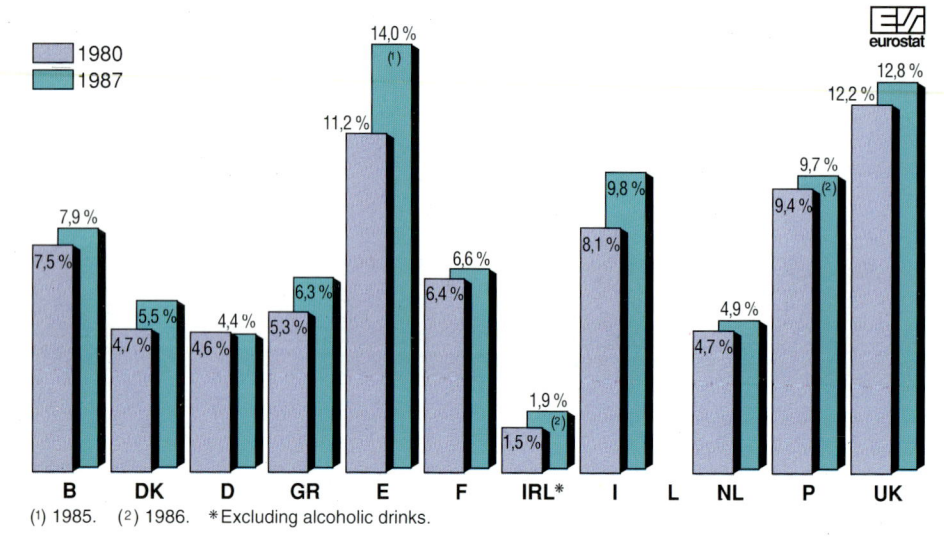

(¹) 1985. (²) 1986. *Excluding alcoholic drinks.

128

LEISURE
SPORT

11.11. Membership of a sports club or association, 1987 (%)

< 15 %
15 - 25 %
> 25 %

Map values: 33,6 — 31,9 — 22,1 — 31,8 — 20,6 — 21,6 — 32,1 — 17,5 — 13,8 — 5,4 — 10,9 — 6,4

About one European in five (17.3%) claims membership of a sports club or association, and nearly one in three professes an interest in sport. The desire to belong to sports associations is strongest in the north of the Community, which has the highest proportions of sports club members: around one-third of persons interviewed in Ireland (33.6%), Luxembourg (32.1%), Denmark (31.9%) and the Netherlands (31.8%). In the south of the Community, membership of sports associations is considerably lower: Spain (5.4%), Greece (6.4%), Italy (10.9%) and Portugal (13.8%).

Football attracts slightly more than one European in three, and tennis and swimming approximately one in four.

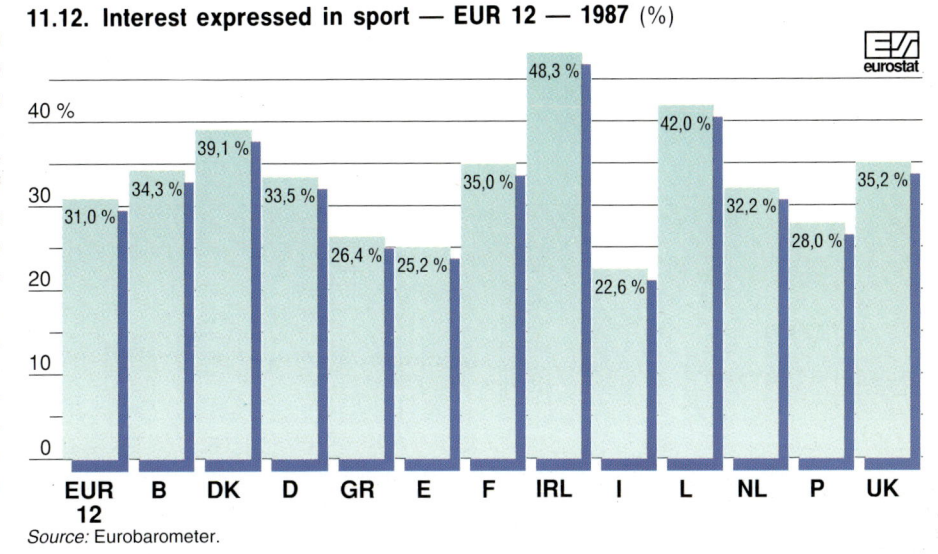

11.12. Interest expressed in sport — EUR 12 — 1987 (%)

EUR 12	B	DK	D	GR	E	F	IRL	I	L	NL	P	UK
31,0 %	34,3 %	39,1 %	33,5 %	26,4 %	25,2 %	35,0 %	48,3 %	22,6 %	42,0 %	32,2 %	28,0 %	35,2 %

Source: Eurobarometer.

11.13. Numbers of persons expressing an interest in a type of sport per 100 persons interviewed — EUR 12 — 1988 (%)

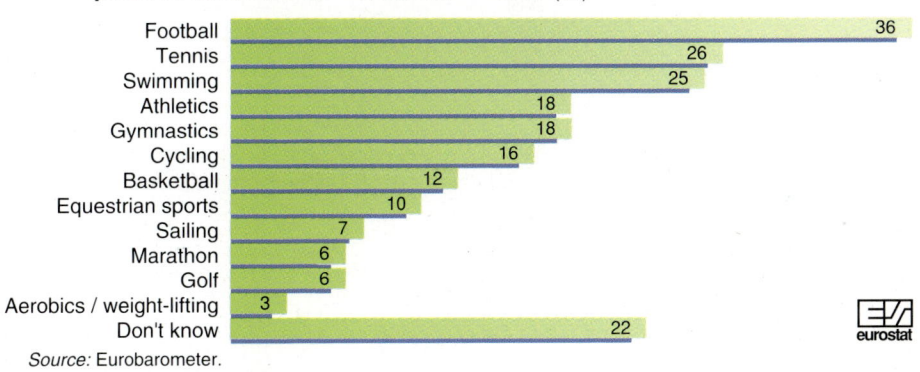

Sport	%
Football	36
Tennis	26
Swimming	25
Athletics	18
Gymnastics	18
Cycling	16
Basketball	12
Equestrian sports	10
Sailing	7
Marathon	6
Golf	6
Aerobics / weight-lifting	3
Don't know	22

Source: Eurobarometer.

LEISURE
MEDIA

11.14. Television sets (per 1 000 inhabitants)

	B[1]	DK[1]	D[1]	GR[1]	E[2]	F[1]	IRL[1]	I[1]	L[2]	NL[1]	P[1]	UK[1]
1970	218	267	276	114	:	217	152	181	210	:		294
1980	298	362	321	240	:	297	190	237	248	296	142	329
1985	301	:	345	272	:	.	213	:	:	316	158	331
1987	320	386	385	:	368	333	228	257	249	325	159	347

[1] Licences.
[2] Receivers.

11.15. Trends in the average annual number of cinema visits per head of population

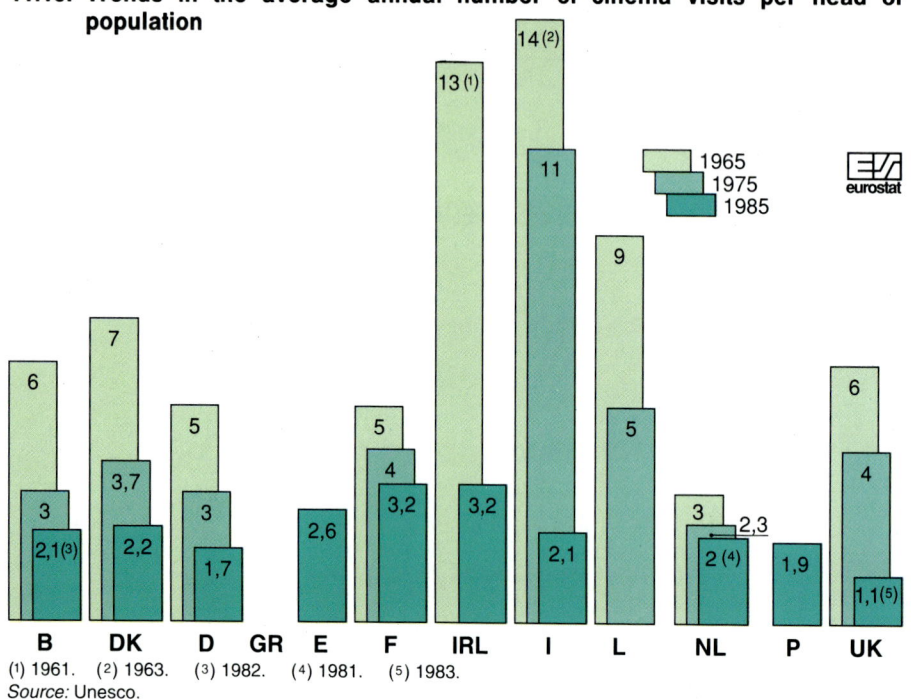

Legend: 1965, 1975, 1985 — eurostat

Country	1965	1975	1985
B	6	3	2,1[3]
DK	7	3,7	2,2
D	5	3	1,7
GR			2,6
E	5	4	3,2
F	13[1]		3,2
IRL	14[2]	11	2,1
I	9	5	
L		3	2 [4]
NL		2,3	1,9
P	6	4	1,1[5]
UK			

([1]) 1961. ([2]) 1963. ([3]) 1982. ([4]) 1981. ([5]) 1983.
Source: Unesco.

To judge by the number of sets in use between 1970 and 1987, television viewing in Europe is constantly on the increase. The number of television sets in Ireland rose from 152 per 1 000 inhabitants in 1970 to 228 in 1987; the latter figure is lower than that recorded in many countries, where it exceeds 300 per 1 000 inhabitants: for example, 386 in Denmark, 385 in the Federal Republic of Germany and 368 in Spain.

Cinema-going underwent a general decline in the Community between 1965 and 1985: the 14 visits per head of population per year recorded in Italy had fallen to 2.1 by 1985, while those in the United Kingdom dropped from six in 1965 to 1.1 in 1983. The average number of cinema visits in 1985 amounted to 3.2 per person per year in France and Ireland.

LEISURE
MEDIA

Where the press is concerned, the number of different daily newspapers has diminished since 1970 in virtually all Member States, sometimes very substantially (Federal Republic of Germany, Belgium, the Netherlands and Luxembourg).

Circulation per 1 000 inhabitants fell between 1970 and 1984, sometimes drastically as in Portugal (86 to 49), Ireland (232 to 186) and Italy (144 to 96), and sometimes slightly as in Denmark (363 to 359) and the Netherlands (315 to 310). Different countries show major disparities: in 1984, daily circulation was 414 per 1 000 inhabitants in the United Kingdom, 359 in Denmark, 350 in the Federal Republic of Germany and 310 in the Netherlands, but only 96 in Italy, 80 in Spain and 49 in Portugal.

11.16. Trends in the press

Trends in numbers of daily newspapers published

	B	DK	D	GR	E	F	IRL	I	L	NL	P	UK
1970	49	58	1 093	110	116	106	7	73	7	169	33	:
1979	26	49	380	116	105	90	7	75	5	80	22	120
1984	26	47	:	107	102	101	7	70	4	84	25	108

Trends in the circulation of daily newspapers (1 000)

	B	DK	D	GR	E	F	IRL	I	L	NL	P	UK
1970	:	1 790	19 701	705	3 450	12 067	686	7 700	130	4 100	743	:
1979	2 242	1 876	25 016	:	:	10 619	771	5 308	130	4 553	493	25 221
1984	2 209	1 837	21 362	981	3 053	11 598	663	5 477	:	4 474	495	23 206

Trends in the circulation of daily newspapers per 1 000 inhabitants

	B	DK	D	GR	E	F	IRL	I	L	NL	P	UK
1970	:	363	:	80	102	238	232	144	384	315	86	:
1979	228	367	408	:	:	199	229	94	358	323	50	:
1984	223	359	350	:	80	212	186	96	:	310	49	414

Source: Unesco.

LEISURE
FOR FURTHER INFORMATION

Definitions

Holidaymakers: all persons aged 15 or over leaving their homes to go on holiday for four days or more.

Main holidays: any period identified by a holidaymaker as his or her main holiday, regardless of the number of times holidays are taken during the year.

References

Eurostat
– National accounts ESA 1989
– Transport and communications 1970-86

Eurobarometer
– 'Holidays' survey, 1985
– Eurobarometer, June 1988
– Eurobarometer, November 1987

Unesco
– Statistical yearbook, 1988

Eurostat databank
– Cronos

EUROPARTICIPATION

In the 1989 elections 58.5% of the citizens of the 12 Member States of the European Community went to the polls to elect the 518 Members of the European Parliament (12.2).

In 1987, 31.0% of Europeans stated that they were members of an association and 5.0% that they were members of a political party or movement. 22.4% of those questioned were interested in their country's politics and 16.7% in international politics (12.4) (12.5) (12.6).

In 1982 almost 90% of Europeans stated that they were in favour of the efforts to unify western Europe; 70% regarded their country's membership of the European Community as a good thing; 72% considered that their country had benefited from EC membership; 53% stated that they would be very sorry if they were told tomorrow that the European Community was to be wound up (12.7).

In 1989 (12 Member States), 385 cases were brought before the Court of Justice of the European Communities compared with 79 in 1970 (six Member States). This increase reflects both the growing importance of Community matters and the legal guarantees and protection enjoyed by the citizens of the 12 EC countries (12.10) (12.11).

In 1988 the European Social Fund assisted nearly 2 700 000 people, of whom 71% were young people under 25 whom it helped to find jobs, 13.6% were unemployed persons and members of their families, and 8.9% were migrants and their families (12.16) (12.18).

12.1. Europeans and European integration

Your country's membership of the European Community is:

	EUR 12	B	DK	D	GR	E	F	IRL	I	L	NL	P	UK
A bad thing	9%	6%	29%	8%	6%	6%	7%	8%	5%	5%	3%	5%	18%
Neither a bad nor a good thing	21%	18%	27%	23%	14%	22%	24%	15%	14%	14%	10%	22%	27%
A good thing	70%	76%	44%	69%	80%	72%	69%	77%	81%	81%	87%	73%	55%

Source: Eurobarometer.

EUROPARTICIPATION
ELECTIONS

12.2. Turnout in the European elections (%)

	EUR 12	B	DK	D	GR	E	F	IRL	I	L	NL	P	UK
1979	62,5 (¹)	91,4	47,8	65,7	—	—	61,2	63,6	86,0	88,9	58,2	—	32,8
1984	59,4 (²)	92,1	54,0	56,8	78,4	—	57,4	47,6	83,4	88,8	50,9	—	32,5
1989	58,5	93,0	46,0	61,5	77,7	54,8	50,4	68,5	81,5	87,0	47,2	51,2	36,0

Source: European Parliament.
(¹) EUR 9.   (²) EUR 10.

12.3. Political composition of the European Parliament

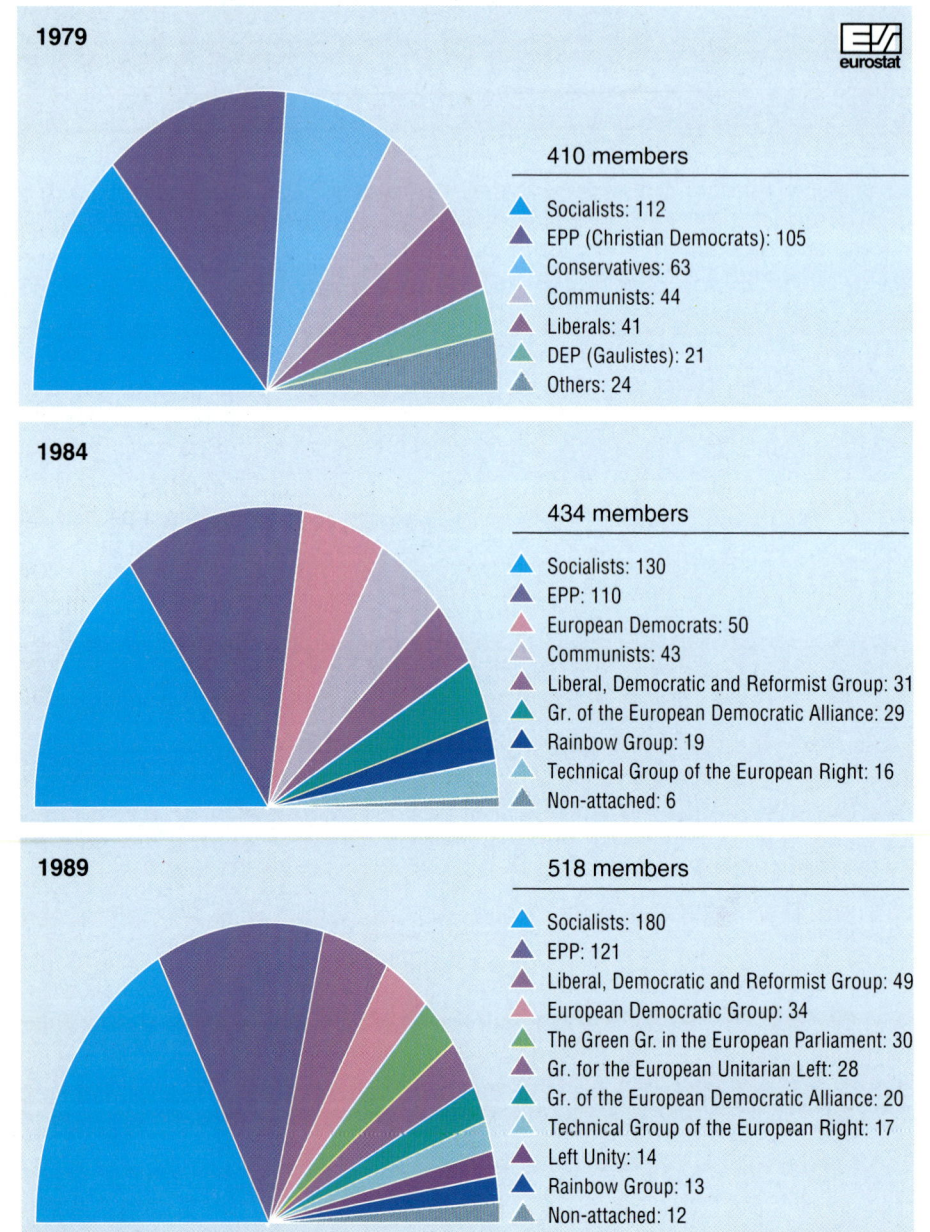

1979 — 410 members
- Socialists: 112
- EPP (Christian Democrats): 105
- Conservatives: 63
- Communists: 44
- Liberals: 41
- DEP (Gaulistes): 21
- Others: 24

1984 — 434 members
- Socialists: 130
- EPP: 110
- European Democrats: 50
- Communists: 43
- Liberal, Democratic and Reformist Group: 31
- Gr. of the European Democratic Alliance: 29
- Rainbow Group: 19
- Technical Group of the European Right: 16
- Non-attached: 6

1989 — 518 members
- Socialists: 180
- EPP: 121
- Liberal, Democratic and Reformist Group: 49
- European Democratic Group: 34
- The Green Gr. in the European Parliament: 30
- Gr. for the European Unitarian Left: 28
- Gr. of the European Democratic Alliance: 20
- Technical Group of the European Right: 17
- Left Unity: 14
- Rainbow Group: 13
- Non-attached: 12

Source: European Parliament.

Since June 1979, when the first European elections were held, the European Parliament has no longer been composed of members of the national parliaments but of members elected every five years by direct universal suffrage. There are 518 members: 81 for each of the largest countries (France, the Federal Republic of Germany, Italy and the United Kingdom), 60 for Spain, 25 for the Netherlands, 24 for Belgium, Greece and Portugal, 16 for Denmark, 15 for Ireland and 6 for Luxembourg.

The Members of the European Parliament form groups according to their political affiliation and not according to their nationality. At each of the three elections which have taken place since 1979, the Socialist Group and the Group of the European People's Party (EPP) obtained the largest number of members.

The turnout in the European elections, which was 62.5% in 1979 (for nine countries), is on the decrease, it being 58.5% in 1989 for the 12 Member States. In some countries voting is compulsory, and fines are imposed on those who fail to vote. This may partly explain the high turnout.

European voters elected 410 members in 1979, 434 in 1984 after the accession of Greece to the EC (1981) and 518 in 1989 after the accession of Spain and Portugal (1986).

EUROPARTICIPATION
PARTICIPATION

12.4. Membership of associations — EUR 12 — 1987 (%)

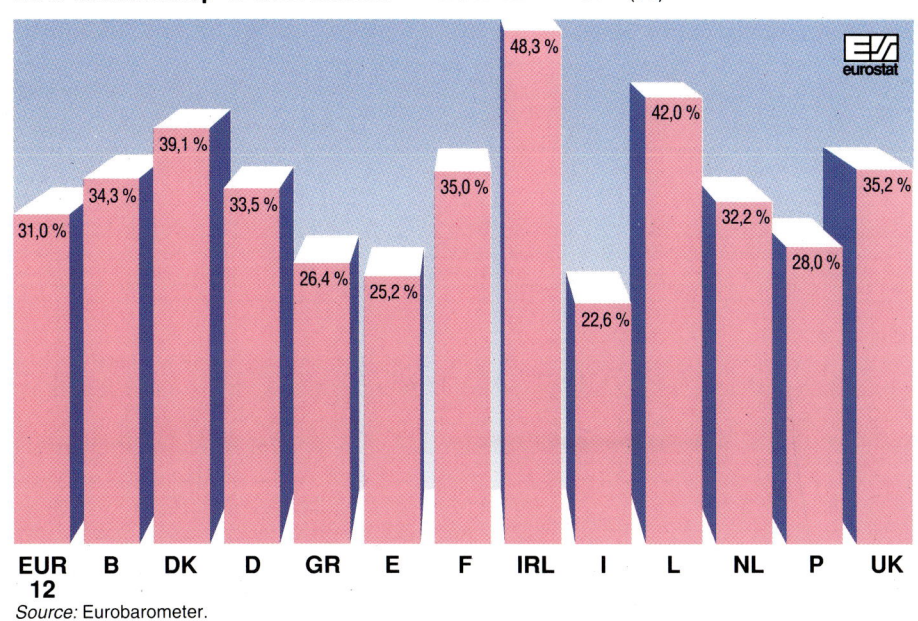

EUR 12	B	DK	D	GR	E	F	IRL	I	L	NL	P	UK
31,0%	34,3%	39,1%	33,5%	26,4%	25,2%	35,0%	48,3%	22,6%	42,0%	32,2%	28,0%	35,2%

Source: Eurobarometer.

12.5. Membership of a political party or movement — 1987 (%)

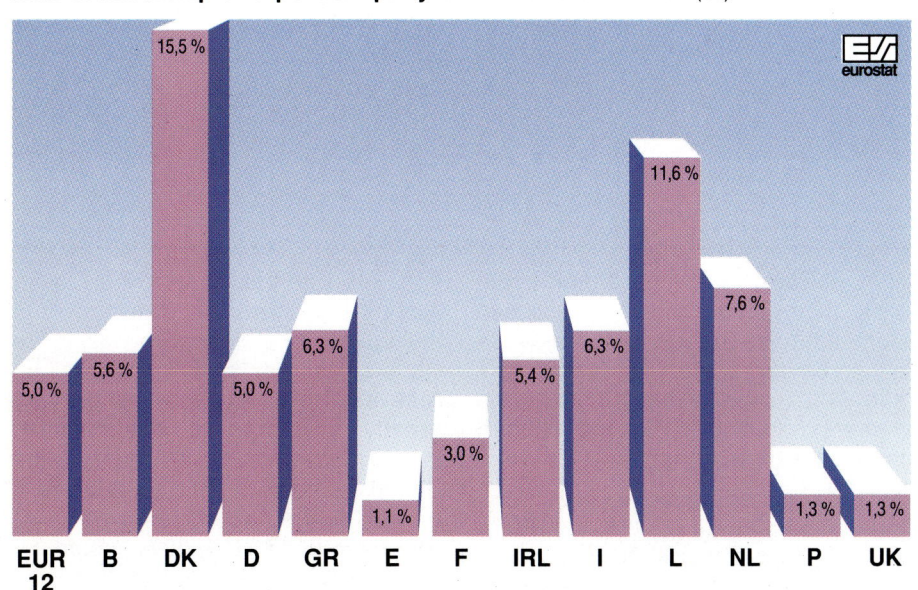

EUR 12	B	DK	D	GR	E	F	IRL	I	L	NL	P	UK
5,0%	5,6%	15,5%	5,0%	6,3%	1,1%	3,0%	5,4%	6,3%	11,6%	7,6%	1,3%	1,3%

Source: Eurobarometer.

31% of Europeans state that they are members of an association, although the percentage is higher for the Irish (48.3%) and lowest for the Italians (22.6%).

5% of Europeans state that they are members of a political party or movement; the figure is 15.5% in Denmark and only 1.1% in Spain.

22.4% of the inhabitants of the EC are interested in national politics and 16.7% in international politics. The percentages vary considerably from one country to another, with the figures reversed in France and the Netherlands, where there is more interest in international politics than in national politics.

12.6. Main interests — 1987 (%)

	EUR 12	B	DK	D	GR	E	F	IRL	I	L	NL	P	UK
National politics	22,4	20,8	36,5	30,2	33,0	14,2	18,4	22,1	17,0	40,8	22,4	17,9	25,1
International politics	16,7	17,5	24,7	19,7	21,7	9,8	19,6	12,9	13,2	35,1	24,4	5,8	16,4

Source: Eurobarometer.

135

EUROPARTICIPATION
EURO-OPINIONS

12.7. Opinions of Europeans on European integration — 1989 (%)

How do you feel on the whole about the efforts to unify western Europe?

	EUR 12	B	DK	D	GR	E	F	IRL	I	L	NL	P	UK
Strongly in favour	42	33	26	47	61	50	34	49	48	35	29	64	31
Fairly in favour	47	59	39	42	32	43	57	42	45	45	54	30	49
Fairly against	8	7	20	9	4	5	8	6	5	15	12	5	14
Strongly against	3	2	15	3	4	2	2	4	1	5	5	1	6

Your country's membership of the European Community is:

	EUR 12	B	DK	D	GR	E	F	IRL	I	L	NL	P	UK
A good thing	70	76	44	69	80	71	69	77	82	81	87	73	56
Neither a good nor a bad thing	21	18	27	23	14	22	24	15	14	14	10	22	27
A bad thing	9	6	29	8	6	6	7	8	5	5	3	5	18

Has your country benefited on the whole from its membership of the European Community?

	EUR 12	B	DK	D	GR	E	F	IRL	I	L	NL	P	UK
Yes	72	82	61	69	88	70	73	84	85	82	88	85	55
No	28	18	39	32	12	30	27	16	15	18	12	15	45

If you were told tomorrow that the European Community was to be wound up, would you be?

	EUR 12	B	DK	D	GR	E	F	IRL	I	L	NL	P	UK
Sorry	53	43	31	60	69	53	55	59	66	65	59	42	34
Indifferent	38	54	38	31	25	42	38	35	32	32	38	55	48
Very relieved	8	3	31	8	6	6	7	6	3	3	3	3	19

Source: Eurobarometer.

What do Europeans think of European integration? Almost 90% are in favour of the efforts to unify western Europe. The highest percentages are to be found in Portugal (94%), Italy (93%), Spain (93%) and Greece (93%), while the lowest are in Denmark (65%) and the United Kingdom (80%).

70% of Europeans regard their country's membership of the European Community as a good thing. The lowest percentages are 44% in Denmark and 56% in the United Kingdom, the highest being 87% in the Netherlands and 82% in Italy.

As regards the advantages of Community membership, 72% of Europeans consider that their country has benefited: only 55% hold this view in the United Kingdom compared with 88% in the Netherlands and Greece.

53% of Europeans would be very sorry if they were told tomorrow that the European Community was to be wound up; only 8% would be relieved. Here, too, the replies vary greatly according to the country: 31% in Denmark and 19% in the United Kingdom would be relieved if the EC were wound up; 69% in Greece and 66% in Italy would be sorry; 55% in Portugal and 54% in Belgium would not mind either way.

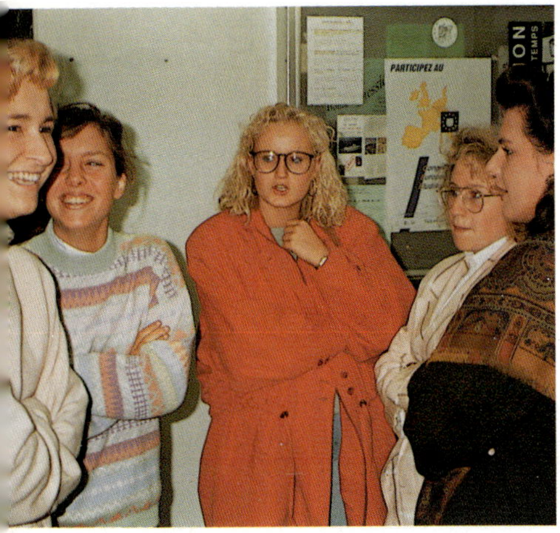

EUROPARTICIPATION
EURO-OPINIONS

12.8. Percentage of young people (15 to 24) who have been taught about the European Community during their education — 1987

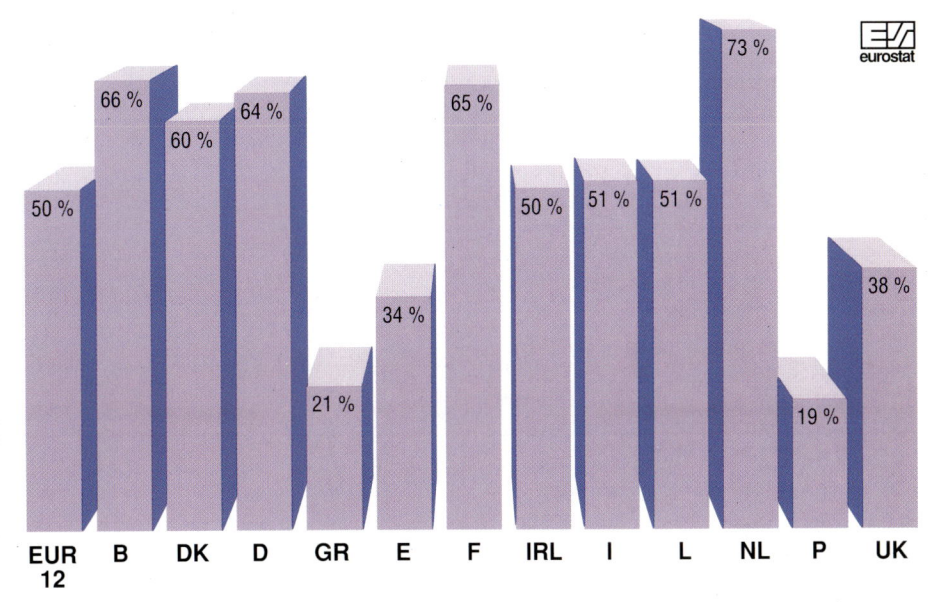

EUR 12	B	DK	D	GR	E	F	IRL	I	L	NL	P	UK
50%	66%	60%	64%	21%	34%	65%	50%	51%	51%	73%	19%	38%

12.9. General attitudes to the single European market of 1992 — 1988 (%)

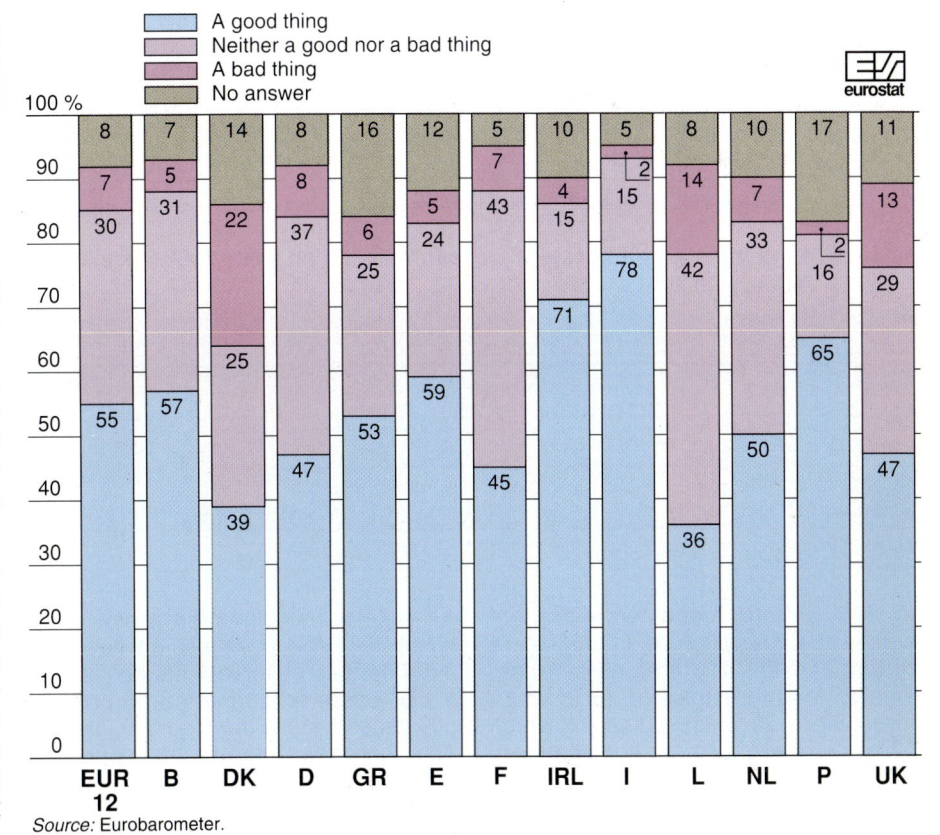

Legend:
- A good thing
- Neither a good nor a bad thing
- A bad thing
- No answer

	EUR 12	B	DK	D	GR	E	F	IRL	I	L	NL	P	UK
No answer	8	7	14	8	16	12	5	10	5	8	10	17	11
A bad thing	7	5	22	8	6	5	7	4	2	14	7	2	13
Neither	30	31	25	37	25	24	43	15	15	42	33	16	29
A good thing	55	57	39	47	53	59	45	71	78	36	50	65	47

Source: Eurobarometer.

The number of young people stating that they were taught about the European Community during their education is highest in the Netherlands, Belgium, France, the Federal Republic of Germany and Denmark. The figure for young people in other countries are 19% in Portugal, 21% in Greece and 34% in Spain.

With regard to 1992 and the creation of the single European market, 55% of Europeans are in favour, 7% are against and 30% have no opinion either way. Attitudes are most favourable in Italy (78%), Ireland (71%) and Portugal (65%), while the Danes (22%), the Luxembourgers (14%) and the British (13%) are the most pessimistic.

EUROPARTICIPATION
COURT OF JUSTICE

The Court of Justice of the European Communities is composed of 13 Judges assisted by six Advocates-General. Judges and Advocates-General are appointed for a six-year term by joint agreement between the Member States. The Court's main tasks are:

(a) at the request of a Community institution, a State or any directly concerned individual, to annul any acts of the Commission or the Council which are incompatible with the Treaties (direct action);

(b) at the request of a court of a Member State, to give a ruling on the interpretation and validity of the provisions of Community law (reference for a preliminary ruling).

By its rulings and interpretations, the Court of Justice helps to promote genuine Community law applicable to all: Community institutions, Member States, courts in the Member States, and private individuals.

12.10. Number of cases brought before the Court of Justice and references for a preliminary ruling

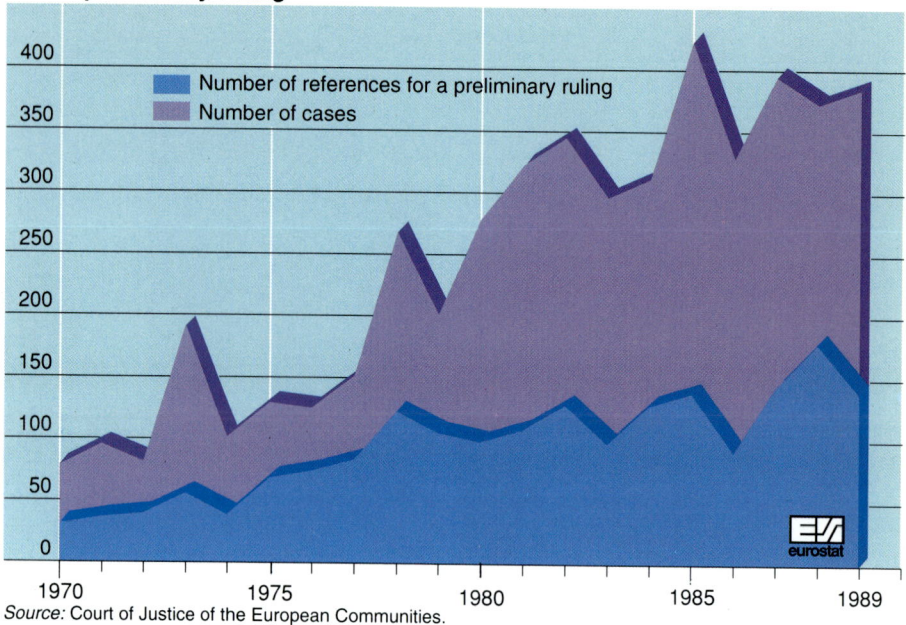

Source: Court of Justice of the European Communities.

12.11. Cases brought before the Court of Justice by category

Year	1965	1975	1980	1981	1982	1983	1984	1985	1986	1987	1988	1989
Direct actions	55	61	180	214	216	199	183	294	238	251	194	246
References for a preliminary ruling	7	69	99	109	129	98	129	139	91	144	179	139
Total	62	130	279	323	345	297	312	433	329	395	373	385

Source: Court of Justice of the European Communities.

12.12. Total number of infringement procedures initiated since 1981 classified by stage of procedure and Member State — 1 January 1990

	EUR 12	B	DK	D	GR	E	F	IRL	I	L	NL	P	UK
Letters of formal notice	3 514	376	189	292	410	85	540	271	577	241	253	31	249
Reasoned opinions	1 356	182	125	41	147	19	227	91	293	81	74	7	69
Cases brought before the Court of Justice	509	80	47	13	52	2	79	32	142	22	23	0	17

Source: Official Journal of the European Communities C 330/29, 30.12.1989.

In 1989, 385 such cases were brought before the Court, of which 139 were references for a preliminary ruling. This is far more than in 1970, when there were 79 such cases, of which 32 were references for a preliminary ruling.

As regards infringement procedures, since 1981 the Commission has sent 3 514 letters of formal notice, issued 1 356 reasoned opinions and brought 509 cases before the Court of Justice. This increase in the number of cases brought before the Court of Justice and of the resulting legal measures is an expression of the increasing legal protection enjoyed by the citizens of the EC Member States and the affirmation of a genuine European law.

EUROPARTICIPATION
STRUCTURAL FUNDS

12.13. Distribution of financial aid in 1987 (ECU per capita)

	EUR 12	B	DK	D	GR	E	F	IRL	I	L	NL	P	UK
ERDF	11.3	2.4	13.3	2.2	30.8	17.0	5.7	46.1	17.3	8.8	1.4	37.9	11.1
EAGGF	1.1	1.2	0.9	0.4	5.1	1.6	1.0	7.4	1.1	0.9	0.3	3.7	0.4
EIB	21.6	3.8	55.3	4.5	16.0	15.3	16.7	50.4	50.9	4.2	1.2	37.1	19.7
Euratom	1.0	—	—	0.4	—	—	1.3	—	1.9	—	—	—	1.9
ECSC	2.9	1.0	0.8	5.5	—	0.2	0.5	—	3.0	0.2	0.3	—	6.6
NCI	1.4	—	6.2	—	0.5	2.9	1.4	—	3.4	—	—	1.0	0.2

12.14. Regional distribution of ERDF operations — 1987
(ECU per capita)

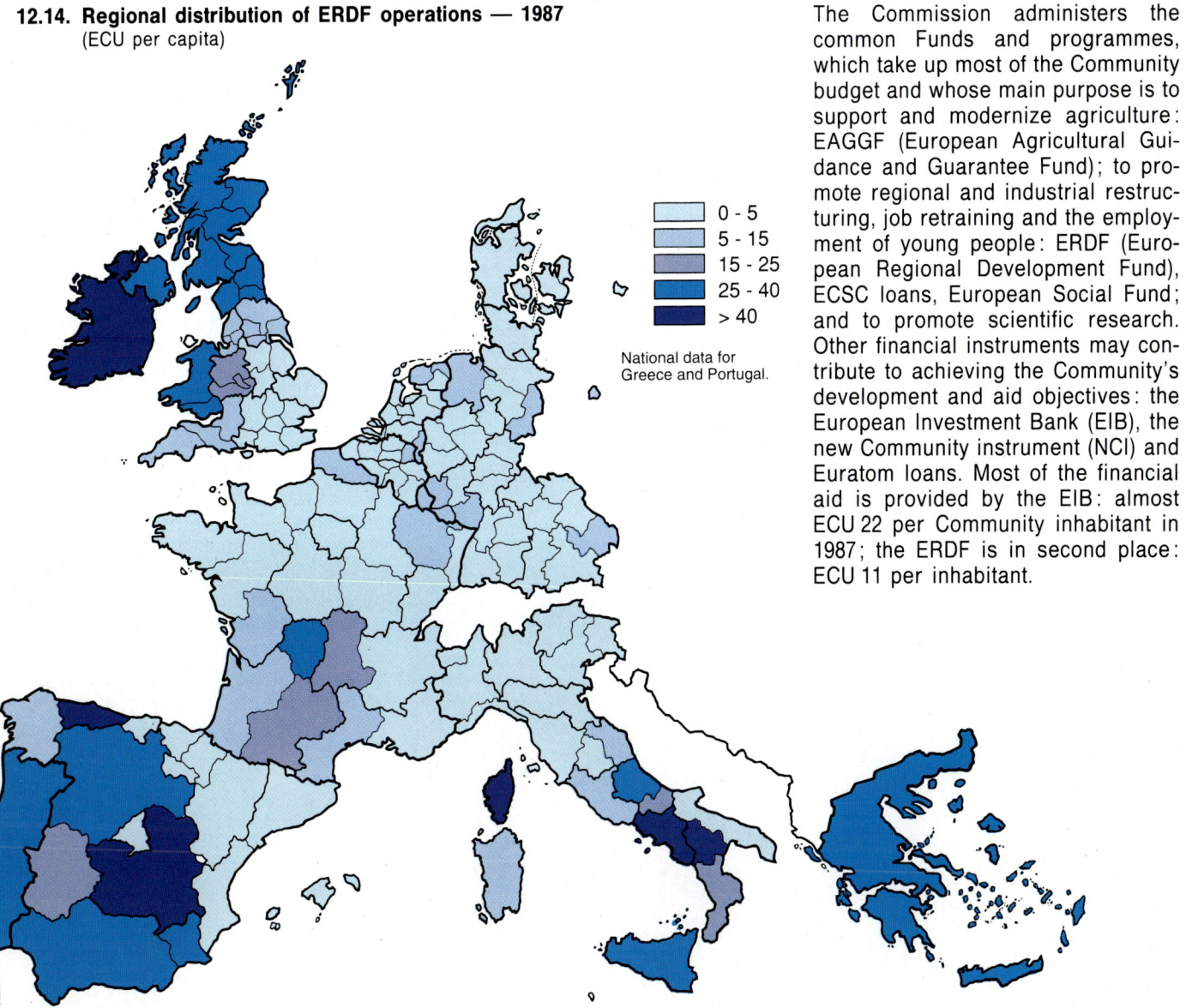

Legend:
- 0 - 5
- 5 - 15
- 15 - 25
- 25 - 40
- > 40

National data for Greece and Portugal.

The Commission administers the common Funds and programmes, which take up most of the Community budget and whose main purpose is to support and modernize agriculture: EAGGF (European Agricultural Guidance and Guarantee Fund); to promote regional and industrial restructuring, job retraining and the employment of young people: ERDF (European Regional Development Fund), ECSC loans, European Social Fund; and to promote scientific research. Other financial instruments may contribute to achieving the Community's development and aid objectives: the European Investment Bank (EIB), the new Community instrument (NCI) and Euratom loans. Most of the financial aid is provided by the EIB: almost ECU 22 per Community inhabitant in 1987; the ERDF is in second place: ECU 11 per inhabitant.

EUROPARTICIPATION
STRUCTURAL FUNDS

12.15. Social Fund budget (million ECU)

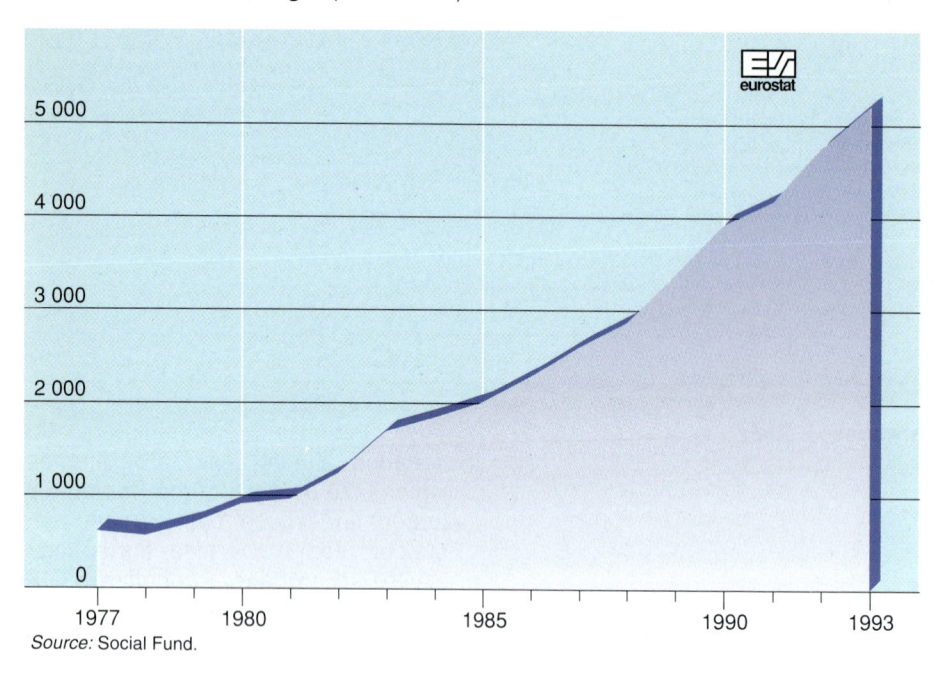

Source: Social Fund.

12.16. Number of persons assisted by the Social Fund, by sex — 1988

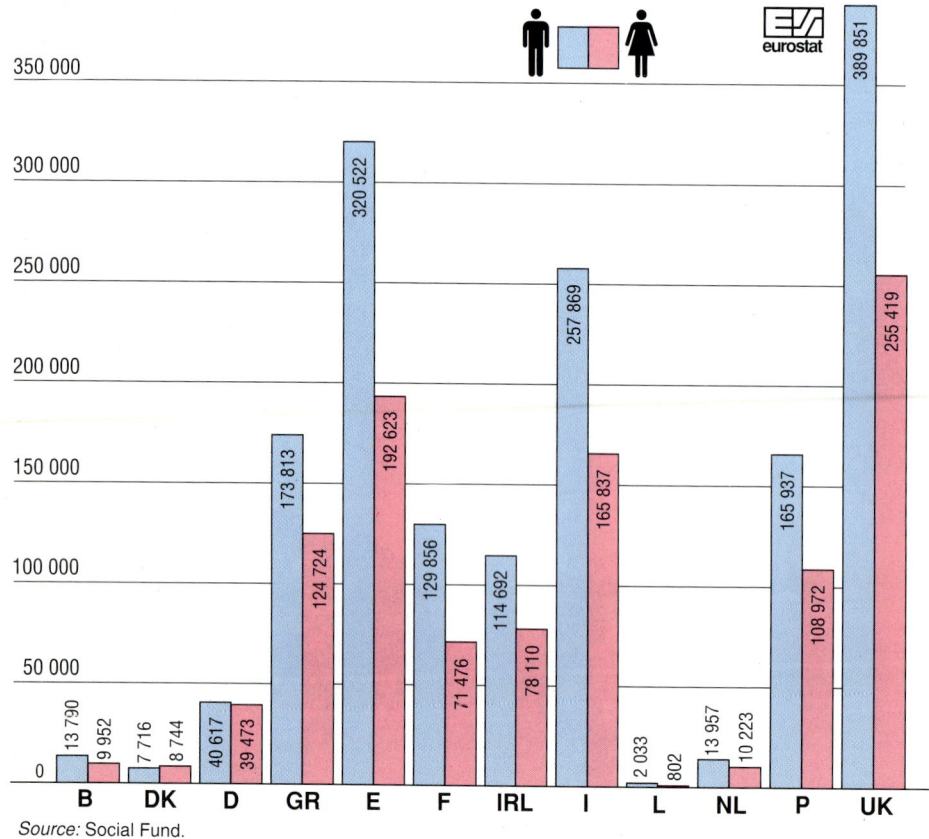

	B	DK	D	GR	E	F	IRL	I	L	NL	P	UK
Male	13 790	7 716	40 617	173 813	320 522	129 856	114 692	257 869	2 033	13 957	165 937	389 851
Female	9 952	8 744	39 473	124 724	192 623	71 476	78 110	165 837	802	10 223	108 972	255 419

Source: Social Fund.

In 1987, the Funds and financial instruments provided a total of ECU 40 per inhabitant throughout the EC.

The regional distribution of ERDF financial operations shows that more aid is granted to the regions which need it in the light of the priority objectives laid down by the ERDF. Thus, the south of Europe (Greece, Portugal and the southern halves of Spain and Italy) and the United Kingdom (except England) receive aid of between ECU 25 and more than ECU 40 per inhabitant.

The European Social Fund (ESF) has the overall task of helping to create jobs, supporting vocational training, providing recruitment premiums and assisting people to set up in business on their own.

Since the reform of the structural Funds, the ESF is deployed in the following ways:
(i) In the fight against long-term unemployment (Objective 3) and in assisting young people in the transition from education to work (Objective 5);
(ii) to back up the measures of the other Funds (ERDF or EAGGF) under the following objectives: 1 (promotion of backward regions), 2 (restructuring of regions in industrial decline) and 5b (development of rural zones);
(iii) in the funding of innovative measures in the field of vocational training and of measures intended to promote dialogue between the two sides of industry, to promote advisory activities and to provide guidance for the long-term unemployed.

EUROPARTICIPATION
STRUCTURAL FUNDS

ESF action is targeted either geographically or at certain categories of persons: the long-term unemployed or young people under 25 who have completed their full-time education, and zones selected by the Commission for Objectives 1, 2 and 5b.

12.17. Number of persons assisted by the Social Fund by sex as % of the labour force — 1988

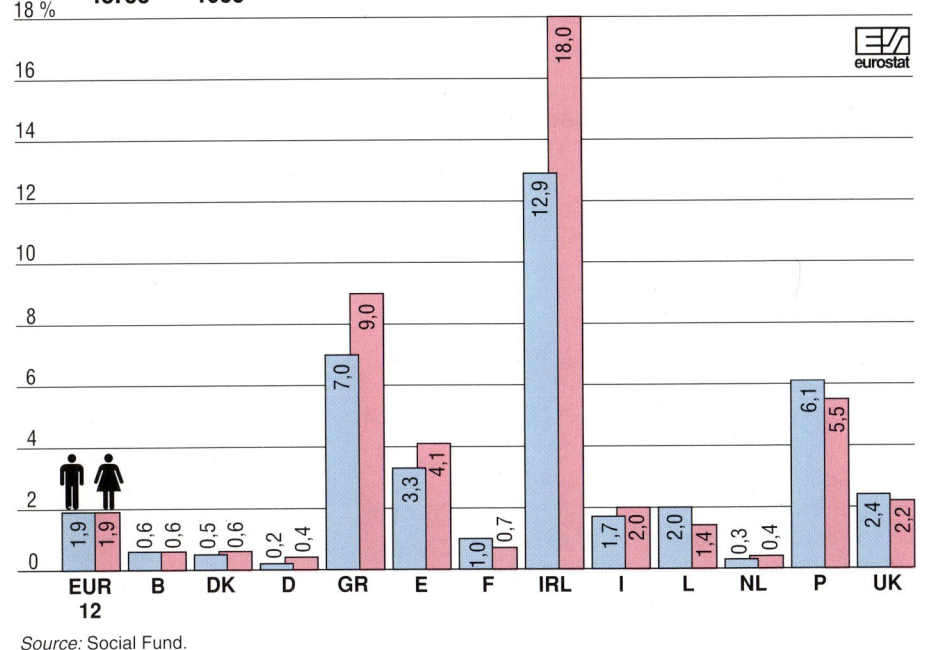

	EUR 12	B	DK	D	GR	E	F	IRL	I	L	NL	P	UK
Men	1,9	0,6	0,5	0,2	7,0	3,3	1,0	12,9	1,7	2,0	0,3	6,1	2,4
Women	1,9	0,6	0,6	0,4	9,0	4,1	0,7	18,0	2,0	1,4	0,4	5,5	2,2

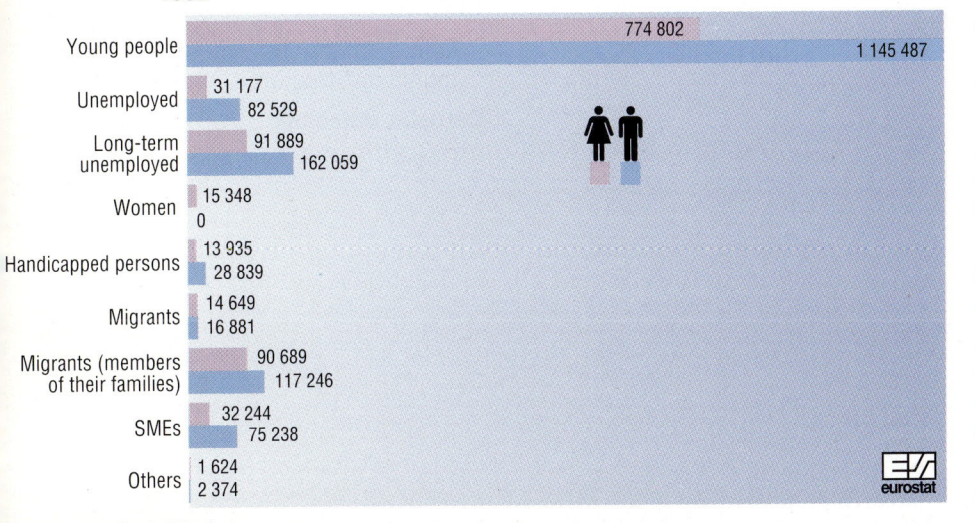

Source: Social Fund.

Between 1989 and 1993, ECU 20 000 million are being made available to the ESF: ECU 10 000 million for Objective 1 (backward regions); ECU 7 000 million for Objectives 3 and 4 (long-term unemployment and young people starting work); ECU 2 000 million for zones covered by Objective 5b (development of rural zones).

Action to achieve these objectives is the reason for the spectacular increase in the annual ESF budget, which has risen from ECU 617 million in 1977 to ECU 5 200 million in 1993.

With the reform of the structural Funds which came into effect in 1989, Community aid will increase progressively until it doubles in real terms in 1993 with respect to 1987.

In 1988 the ESF assisted almost 2 700 000 people, of whom 1 631 000 were men, which represents 1.9 % of the EC labour force (men and women); the percentages range from 12.9 % (men) and 18.0 % (women) in Ireland to 0.2 % and 0.4 % in Federal Republic of Germany.

Of those assisted by the ESF, most were young people: 1 920 000 (71.2 % of the total); next in line are the unemployed: 368 000 (13.6 %) and migrants and their families: 239 000 (8.9 %).

12.18. Number of persons assisted by sex and Social Fund objective — EUR 12 — 1988

Category	Women	Men
Young people	774 802	1 145 487
Unemployed	31 177	82 529
Long-term unemployed	91 889	162 059
Women	15 348	0
Handicapped persons	13 935	28 839
Migrants	14 649	16 881
Migrants (members of their families)	90 689	117 246
SMEs	32 244	75 238
Others	1 624	2 374

Source: Social Fund.

141

EUROPARTICIPATION
FOR FURTHER INFORMATION

Definitions

Preliminary rulings: in accordance with Article 177 of the EEC Treaty, the Court of Justice has jurisdiction to give preliminary rulings on the interpretation of the Treaty and on the validity and interpretation of acts of the EC institutions. However, requests for preliminary rulings may only be submitted by national courts or tribunals.

Direct action: this procedure is instituted by written unilateral request of the Member States, the Community institutions or private individuals.

Financial aid: funding granted by the EC under its economic policies aimed at improving the development of the regions by promoting investment in production and infrastructure.

European Social Fund (ESF): the purpose of the European Social Fund is to assist job creation and vocational training. ESF financial aid is governed by certain priority objectives. ESF action is targeted either geographically or at certain categories of persons.

ERDF: provides investment aid in the form of non-returnable payments to fund gross fixed capital formation. Its purpose is to help to correct the main regional imbalances in the EC by participating in the development and structural adjustment of backward regions and in the restructuring of industrial regions in decline.

EAGGF: through its Guidance Section, contributes to the funding of expenditure incurred through the structural changes made necessary by the development of the common market or necessary for its proper operation as regards agriculture. The data published here refer only to direct measures for which subsidies have been granted for EC-approved projects in the Member States.

EIB: by granting loans, can help to fund projects put forward by any institution, public or private, in all sectors of the economy. It has the task of supporting, by means of loans, private, public, industrial and infrastructure investments which help to achieve the Community's priority objectives: regional development (approximately 60% of loans in 1985), reduction of energy dependence, modernization of communications and industry, development of advanced technology, and environmental protection. To do this, the EIB borrows funds on capital markets and onlends them on a non-profit basis.

Euratom: the EC Commission is authorized to issue Euratom loans to fund investment projects connected with the industrial production of nuclear power and with industrial fuel-cycle installations.

ECSC: the EC Commission is authorized not only to assist in the implementation of the programme of investment in coal and steel companies by granting loans or by guaranteeing borrowings but also to grant loans (at reduced interest rates) to coal and steel industries or any other industry in order to create new activities or to convert existing companies.

NCI: NCI financial loans are granted for projects which must meet the EC priority objectives in the sectors of energy, industry and infrastructure works in the light of, among other things, the regional impact of the projects and of the need to combat unemployment.

References

Eurostat
- Review 1977-86
- Regions — The Community's financial participation in investments, 1987

Eurobarometer
- Eurobarometer, November 1987
- Eurobarometer, November 1989

CEC
- Guide to the reform of the Community's Structural Funds

Eurostat databank
- Regio